Literature in Late Monolingualism

Literature in Late Monolingualism

Literacies for the Linguacene

David Gramling

BLOOMSBURY ACADEMIC
NEW YORK • LONDON • OXFORD • NEW DELHI • SYDNEY

BLOOMSBURY ACADEMIC
Bloomsbury Publishing Inc
1385 Broadway, New York, NY 10018, USA
50 Bedford Square, London, WC1B 3DP, UK
29 Earlsfort Terrace, Dublin 2, Ireland

BLOOMSBURY, BLOOMSBURY ACADEMIC and the Diana logo are trademarks of Bloomsbury Publishing Plc

First published in the United States of America 2025

Copyright © David Gramling, 2025

For legal purposes the Acknowledgments on p. viii constitute an extension of this copyright page.

Cover design by Eleanor Rose
Cover image © NOEL CELIS / AFP / Getty Images

All rights reserved. No part of this publication may be reproduced or transmitted in any form or by any means, electronic or mechanical, including photocopying, recording, or any information storage or retrieval system, without prior permission in writing from the publishers.

Bloomsbury Publishing Inc does not have any control over, or responsibility for, any third-party websites referred to or in this book. All internet addresses given in this book were correct at the time of going to press. The author and publisher regret any inconvenience caused if addresses have changed or sites have ceased to exist, but can accept no responsibility for any such changes.

Whilst every effort has been made to locate copyright holders the publishers would be grateful to hear from any person(s) not here acknowledged.

Library of Congress Cataloguing-in-Publication Data

Names: Gramling, David, 1976- author.
Title: Literature in late monolingualism: literacies for the Linguacene/ David Gramling.
Description: New York : Bloomsbury Academic, 2025. | Includes bibliographical references and index.
Identifiers: LCCN 2024016588 (print) | LCCN 2024016589 (ebook) | ISBN 9798765113912 (paperback) | ISBN 9798765113929 (hardback) | ISBN 9798765113936 (ebook) | ISBN 9798765113943 (pdf)
Subjects: LCSH: Fiction–21st century–History and criticism. | Fiction–Translations–History and criticism. | LCGFT: Literary criticism.
Classification: LCC PN3347 .G68 2025 (print) | LCC PN3347 (ebook) | DDC 809.3/05–dc23/eng/20240629
LC record available at https://lccn.loc.gov/2024016588
LC ebook record available at https://lccn.loc.gov/2024016589

ISBN: HB: 979-8-7651-1392-9
PB: 979-8-7651-1391-2
ePDF: 979-8-7651-1394-3
eBook: 979-8-7651-1393-6

Typeset by Deanta Global Publishing Services, Chennai, India
Print and bound in Great Britain

To find out more about our authors and books visit www.bloomsbury.com and sign up for our newsletters.

for
the students and teachers
of the Islamic University of Gaza
لا يفصلنا حصار
and especially for
Prof. Nazmi's newest,
Nishan,
as from darkness comes light

Contents

Acknowledgments	viii
Preface	xi
Introduction: Monolingualism's Ages	1
1 A Citizen's Compromise	45
2 A Translator's Vertigo	87
3 An Engineer's Contempt	127
4 An Immerser's Ecstasy	167
Afterword: Literacies for the Linguacene	191
Works Cited	205
Index	223

Acknowledgments

I wrote this book as an uninvited settler on the sovereign lands of the Tohono O'odham, the Coast Salish, the Muwekma Ohlone, the Nipmuc, the Haida, and particularly the Musqueam, the Duwamish, and the Nauset peoples. The book's efforts to unmask the ever-innovative coloniality of monolingualism yield a mere flicker, amid the ongoing and powerfully multilingual work alive in today's Indigenous communities around the world, where futures are forged on presently occupied lands. Indigenous colleagues like Bernard Perley, Nadia Joe, Piki Diamond, Mathilda Magga, and Tim Frandy have helped me in recent years to begin the work of rematriating critical multilingualism studies, broadly conceived (Tuck 2011; Gramling and Warner 2012), back into the Indigenous lands and communities that have always hosted me, my home, my kin, and my writing life. I intend to follow their guidance wherever it may need to lead.

Literature in Late Monolingualism was written in two adjacent yet estranged times—one south of, then one north of the 49th parallel. A first, pre-pandemic period of discovery began during a 2018 sabbatical from the University of Arizona Department of German Studies. I took a year away from the beloved saguaros, mesquites, palos verdes, and my many friends in the desert to be a visiting scholar in the Department of German Studies at the University of Washington in Seattle, and it was there that I found my way to the range of novels that are taken up in this book.

The second writing push took place mid-pandemic, after jumping a closed international border the week of the 2020 US Presidential election to start work as Head of the Department of Central, Eastern and Northern European Studies (CENES) at the University of British Columbia (Vancouver campus). This was a position I truly loved every day I held it—but one I arrived utterly underprepared for, even in non-pandemic conditions. Thanks to everyone in Tucson, Seattle, Denver, Vancouver, and Cape Cod for bearing with me through this time, whenever I wasn't as good a companion as I could have been.

I will not write another book about mono/multilingualism, at least not in English. But I do hope many other scholars and activists will, and I'll keep learning from those people who've been working so vividly on this problem in recent years, including among many others Chris Chang-Bacon, Li Wei, Alison Phipps, Jerry Won Lee, Sara Ganassin, Sarah Hopkyns, Zhu Hua, Khaled Al Masaeed, Ana Deumert, Joseph Lo Bianco, Anne-Marie Fortier, Kamran Khan, Angelica Galante, Luke Holmes, Josh Prada, Joseph Sung-Yul

Park, Anjali Pandey, Rachel Gilmour, Adriana Díaz, Andrea Ciribuco, Till Dembeck, Başak Çandar, Rey Chow, Mélanie Jouitteau, David Martyn, and Sandro Barros. I ask those people to please keep writing in many languages about all the ways monolingualism remains an acutely critical matter socially, materially, emotionally, politically, and aesthetically for different communities today, and about the ways it will likely continue to do so for the quite unforeseeable future.

An author is truly lucky when at least a few of their more eager critics make their views known once the first draft is written, and not just after the final publication. Such was certainly the case with this book. One powerful scholar in the field of Anglophone literary comparatism skimmed a first full draft, panned it half-heartedly, and told my former press editor *It's not for me*—after which that press lost interest entirely. This dismissal was hard to recover from.

New breath came into the project thanks to the good company and thoughtfulness of scholar–friends like Ann-Kathrine Havemose, Elebetel Assefa, ganyamatopé dzapasi tawona t. sitholé, Geoffrey Winthrop-Young, Ervin Malakaj, Caroline Rieger, Aron Aji, Barbara Schmenk, Steven Wakefield, Ashley Samsone, Hillary Hurst, Roberto Rey Agudo, Besmir Fidahic, Uma Kumar, Colin Gregory, Barbara Kosta, Thornton Hatter, Mike Brin, Lorna Chepkwony, Meike Werner, Thomas Kemple, Patrick Kilbane, Carolyn Doherty, Yuliya Komska, Hussain Laghabi, Agnes He, Shikaripur Sridhar, Alberto Bruzos, Loredana Polezzi, Chantelle Warner, Claire Kramsch, Olena Morozova, Jennifer Miller, Eriko Sato, Katie Bernstein, Patrick Ploschnitzki, Julia Ruck, Lena Karlström, Mo Pareles, Kyle Frackman, Erik Kwakkel, Alison Phipps, Martin Kagel, William Donahue, Karin Graf, and Mirto Stone. Without their care and wisdom, I would have probably just given up the ghost on this book entirely.

Bloomsbury's willingness to try out a new gambit with me has been solid, unflinching, and nothing less than miraculous. I'm still grateful to Michelle Woods for nudging me, at a hotel bar at the 2013 American Literary Translators Association conference, to get in touch with a Bloomsbury editor named Haaris Naqvi. I keep following that advice, now a decade later.

Very short portions of this manuscript appeared in altered form in Chapter 4 of my 2021 Cambridge University Press book, *The Invention of Multilingualism,* and in the *Journal of Literary Multilingualism.* Short talk versions of some of these arguments, for better or worse, were presented at Dartmouth College, the University of Washington-Seattle, Simon Fraser University, Tokyo College, Princeton University, the German Literary Archive at Marbach, the Dahlem Humanities Center, and the University of British Columbia Department of Linguistics.

If the arguments before you hold up, much of the credit for this should go to the inimitable early career literary critic Dante Prado, whose own future books I am so eager to read. If they don't, it's in part because Dante's editorial interventions were, in the end, too gentle. Two additional anonymous peer reviewers of the improved second draft turned out to be kind, inspiring, and detailed in their suggestions for additional change. My scholarly sister and best friend ever, the anthropologist Sarah Richardson of Pitch Pine Editorial, made sure these sentences before you don't dangle or muffle too much, lest they trouble earnest readers. If they still do, know that Dr. Richardson tried her best to teach this prose to sing in a short amount of time. The wondrous Barbara Schmenk also read a draft, and she ok'd what she gently calls its "Gramlingish" style. Other folks who worked on the manuscript, and whom I'll likely never meet, include Hali Han, Arun Rajakumar, Kavitha Kalaimani, Karthik Jeyachandran, and Magendra Varman. To each of them, I owe that special gratitude I owe to any as-yet-unknown friend who has taken patient care, in my absence, of something cherished and delicate.

My Mom, the emeritus nurse-educator Dr. Kathryn Louise McEnelly Gramling, always wants to read everything I write. I love her for that, and for everything else she's ever done for me, and for our family. Happy 80th, You Hot Ticket!

—DJG
Marbach, Germany,
June 2024

Preface

> Late style is what happens if art does not abdicate its rights in favor of reality.
> —Edward Said, "The Rage of the Old" (2004)

Thinking about what "lateness" means in art, music, philosophy, theater, and literature, Edward Said suggested a number of contradictory possibilities. From Ibsen, he'd seen what happens when an artist careens into their own late period "angry and disturbed"—having become someone for whom art-making provides just another "occasion to stir up more anxiety, tamper irrevocably with the possibility of closure, and leave the audience more perplexed and unsettled than before" (2004). Said saw still other literary artists draw toward their mortal end serenely, embracing a resigned formalism or a summative mood of retrospection.

Authors hospice their late work in different ways, though few fail to do so vividly (Andreotti et al. 2015, 27). In his own late years, Said witnessed these variants of literary lateness, from the sober to the fitful, expressing a strained relation between aesthetic style and bodily condition—conciliatory or defiant as this relation might turn out to be. The late art-making body—its days in this one long-familiar skin vaguely numbered—etches into the late work some vexed signals about its own spectacular and alarming limitedness. Assessing its own fast-approaching finitude, a literary artist's body is dragged into timeliness in its acts of composing—alongside, or despite, the work's other commitments of format, style, cultural politics, and theme.

Such late work may pulse with an array of irritating signals, strewn across it, which illuminate for readers what it's really like to be in an active struggle with time. Without any particular intent to do so, late work discloses a reckoning about the indignity of writing in the nick of time, in the wrong time, or out of time. Often a "late style" ends up refusing to submit in any way to such an alleged Real—whistling past that graveyard, storming brusquely away from that mundane nightmare. The resulting style crouches, or soars, into a cascade of fantasy entitlements, expanses, glories, and vetoes; it encases and aggrandizes itself in them, come hell or high water. Such a late style's swoon may be egged on and redoubled by the authorial subject's ever-mounting and dazzling tantrums of rebuke, remorse, panic, denial, purification, fear, anguish, and nostalgia.

But why should Said's characterizations of late style apply only to individual artists and authors, diverse as they are? Might such a conception of lateness account, potentially, for whole moments and movements of literary productivity in ages like ours? What could Said's proposition about lateness help us to understand about literature's—and specifically the novel's—general bodily conditions and life-limited circumstances in sociohistorical time, particularly in the emerging time of so-called Artificial General Intelligence? And what if one of the enduring signature compulsions at the authorial helm of such late novels is the disowned specter of political monolingualism itself?

If so, can we glimpse a kind of late style—or styles—loosely typifying some of Eurocentric literary monolingualism today, in an age when the very primacy of embodied human language is itself being doubted in the face of Large Language Models (LLMs) for Machine Translation (MT) and of AI-generated "original" compositions? Is novelistic literature today sensing, lately and moodily, the limitations of its own conventionally single-language formats and aesthetic rationales? Beyond literature, are today's single-language ideologies—now variously at large in the political sphere—themselves feeling a lateness too, and are they therefore more poised than ever to crash the party of literature in an intense, insistent fashion? And is this perhaps why (literary) monolingualism has grown grandly exhibitionist (Pandey 2016) in recent decades, such that the ample and loud social demand for alternatives to monolingual literary storytelling and knowledge-sharing has been as yet unable to defray the Global North's ceaseless supply of monolingual literary products?

If what we sense when sorting out such questions is intriguing enough to follow further, what evidence in published literary novels from this era (since 2000) will help us spot signs of the kind of bodily reckoning that gets a monolingual "late style" swooning and soaring in the ways it will? What unrealistic, delirious, and unrighteous rights will these late monolingual literary modes muster for themselves, when they find they are staring down a new AI-driven global language–industrial age? And how can we readers talk in honest detail about the ways such a late mode deals, or cannot deal, with a worldly multilingual reality that clamors against (national) literatures' presumptive prerogative to foreclose us readers into one language at a time? Can we still love literature that finds itself in such a disputed, defiant predicament? Or must we find it wanting?

Breaking Up with "Multilingual Literature"

It took me decades to name the hunch that led me to write this book. Obvious enough as it was all along, it was also elusive, even embarrassing.

Meir Sternberg (1981) had spotted the awkward problem well enough some forty years ago, in his article on "Polylingualism as Reality and Translation as Mimesis," but he'd been a bit too polite to name it squarely. My own belated stance now reflects a kind of bless-and-release admission, after decades of insisting otherwise. Namely, I've found that the contemporary published novel in a European mold may just not be all that well suited to worldly multilingualism after all—at least, significantly less so than are film, video, music, theater, audiobooks, radio plays, podcasts, and other bi-graphic creative formats.

Such is not the mere argument of this book. But it is surely this vein of recognition that first jarred, and then burnished, much of the thinking and feeling about literature (the sentipensamiento about it, Fals Borda 2009) that comes across in the novels (by Tidbeck, Nors, Miéville, and Stephenson) to which the forthcoming chapters are devoted. As for my own delay in facing up to this disappointing unmutuality between "the novel" and multilingualism—two domains of study that I truly love, and love to think about—blame may have lain all along in a gross category error of my own.

Maybe I'd just spent too much time listening to applied linguists talk eagerly about translanguaging (Williams 1994; Zhu Hua and Li Wei 2019; Lewis et al. 2012; García 2019), which led me to over- or misapply that concept in and around literary studies generally. Or maybe the problem lay in my less-than-precise reading of Bakhtin (in Emerson's translation, 1981), or in some other willful matchmaking fantasy between literary heteroglossia and social multilingualism (see Holquist 2014).[1] But beyond these apparent analytical missteps of my own over the years, I do think there's been some kind of tacit collusion in literary studies keeping the outsized wishful thinking about literary multilingualism going longer than it might should have done.

Throughout my early training, many luminous people in the research fields I aimed to join seemed assured that the relation between literature and multilingualism had to enjoy a kind of Most Favored Nation status, treasured if sometimes complicated. In 2020, no less than the Modern Language Association—most of whose assembled attendees are contracted to teach monolingual literatures and languages in (mono)lingually named academic departments like "Spanish and Portuguese" or "English Languages and Literatures"—announced multilingualism as the umbrella theme for its massive annual convention. After all, one might think, with all the vivid

---

[1] I thank Dante Prado for pointing out the apparent irony that, while Mikhail Bakhtin theorized the polyvocal and dialogic voices within the single-language works of Dostoevsky and Rabelais, it was the more "conservative" elite modernists like Thomas Mann who tended to confidently include extended multilingual voices and passages in their works.

linguistic experimentation going on in the works of Zora Neal Hurston, Jamaica Kincaid, Aleksandar Hemon, Nicholasa Mohr, and Chimamanda Ngozi Adichie, even Anglophone novels must be inclined toward multilingualism on some essential level, mustn't they? Or, at least, always verging upon a deep and granular engagement with it?

Conferences, seminars, journals, and calls for papers heralded this relation as a kind of epic win on the horizon, presuming multilingual literature to be both an epitome and a belated birthright of the humanities—in academia and in the trade publishing industry alike. That shimmering, assonant relation "multilingual literature" felt like a magical just-in-time key—poised to open for us literary scholars a menacing lock, at just the historical, geopolitical, disciplinary, and post-Theory moment when we'd begun rummaging around for its like amid the bludgeoning fuzz of neoliberal globalization's "monolingual international" (Anderson and Donato 2015).

The aspirational design of that key–lock relationship was persuasive enough. It went something like this: literary novels are vitalizing and vindicating caretakers of languages, of idiomatic styles, of divergent voices, and of polysemous meanings—while other sorts of instrumental and institutional texts (sometimes themselves also referred to as "the literature," even when they're boilerplate institutional PDFs) tend rather to diminish languages, fear them, coerce them, attenuate them, anaesthetize them, or otherwise hollow them out. A twin presumption held that multilingual persons are the loving, inclusive, and creative champions of languages—while monolingual people and institutions most often mistrust languages, or begrudgingly tolerate the one language they do design to require.

Many powerful pretexts about "multilingual literature" simply married the valiant exceptionalism of these two energetic affirmations about multilingual persons and literary novels. It's easy enough to see why these two visions about care for language have rhymed emotionally, and in such a charismatic way. The relation between literature and multilingualism did feel for many of us like a match made in heaven—particularly since the hybridity-minded, customs-deregulated, and downsizing-and-amalgamation-zealous 1990s.

The presumed pairing opened up a new vein of purposefulness for literary scholarship in a complicated, doubtful, and violent moment. It amplified a fresh social mandate and innovated a new horizon, to which few scholars could find ready reason to object: if literature was ultimately, imminently, and immanently multilingual, a certain floodgate could open under this new aegis for queries and curiosities about texts and their hypotextual cultural politics. Multilingual inquiry would just supersize for the humanities an already vivid enthusiasm across the interpretive social sciences for heteroglossia, inclusiveness, universal access, refuge and migration, and dialogicality.

On such a tide of linguistic multiplicity, literary critique could then enjoy a new leasehold for a good long while. It could pivot away from elite traditions and toward highlighting all the world's exquisite textual examples of the relation literature=multilingualism: the techniques used in such exemplary literary texts, the practical genius of those who've honed those techniques in local meaning-making contexts, and the insights about inclusive social life these techniques could uncover for us. In a historical moment wracked with so many impending aporias and dreadworthy things, "multilingual literature" seemed a wide, fecund, welcoming, and egalitarian path of inquiry and promise—all of which could defensibly be housed in an English Department, if that's what the budget forecasting required. To live up to the challenge, all literary scholarship would have to do was cast off its canon wars and look around for multilingual authors to read and appreciate.

Since the 1990s, the virtue of interdisciplinarity has cajoled academic literary scholars to suit up and spell out exactly what relevant things the study of literature has to offer for ongoing conversations elsewhere—in sociology, anthropology, economics, linguistics, data sciences, computational engineering, philosophy, history, business, human rights, medicine, ethnic studies, gender studies, geology, and more (see, for instance, in the natural sciences Gordin 2015; in business Hogan-Brun 2017; in anthropology Hanks 2010; and in computational engineering, well, almost anything published daily by the Institute of Electrical and Electronics Engineers). With discourses of "real-world interdisciplinary applicability" flooding the rhetorical space at universities with unquestioned zeal, multilingualism seemed a flexibly generic and unimpeachable hook to hang the hat of literature on when such discourses took their listening tours.

But—I found myself thinking in the midst of this all—what if there was just something about the modern and contemporary novel, in the major publishing houses' Eurogenic mold, that would routinely betray this promise of inclusivity, applicability, and ecumenical convergence, precisely when it came to the matter of linguistic multiplicity? Put bluntly, what if published literature (and the Eurocentric novel in particular) was, on the evidence, just too ideologically and formally monolingual to champion the multilingual world in any kind of credible way?

Worse, what if "the novel," as a conventionalized format, was acutely more monolingual in its idioms, timbres, discourses, disseminations, and orthographies than was everyday social life in the vast majority of the world? And if, gods forbid, the hunt for multilingualism-in-literature had therefore to be set aside pending an investigation, what sort of role would be left for literary criticism, and for literature, amid all the talk of multilingualism across the disciplines?[2]

In retrospect, it's not clear whether those of us who'd tacitly promoted a kind of transitive formula "literature is good for multilingualism/multilingualism is good for literature" were indeed sure of it all this time, so much as that the pretext seemed a very important one to make work somehow for the big picture of our vocations and their contemporary exigencies. Perhaps we scholars suspected, on some level, that the proposed amorous embrace of novels and multilingualism was a relation whose failure to be persuasive would cause a lot of downstream consequences we were unwilling to think much about—especially when the humanities were already fighting an endless war of attrition and self-justification.

The potential downstream consequences of a messy public separation between multilingualism and literature might be—among other things— curricular, disciplinary, political, ethical, institutional, commercial, translational, budgetary, and personal. Like any breakup, it would show us a few things we probably couldn't afford to know right now about our disciplines, their vestigial investments, and their current interest convergences (Bell 1980), at least not in a bearish budget season like this one.

These are not my anxieties anymore, nor those of this book. But they amount to what has been an interestingly indicative problem over the last thirty years in the humanities, since literary publishing really went transnational. And yet, the proposition that multilingualism and literature are not now on the same team (and likely haven't been for several centuries at least) still tends to prompt more irritation than insight.

Routinely culpable of this myself, I remember for instance coleading a seminar on German Turkish Studies in 2014 during which a participating labor historian, sotto voce, indicted the seminar's predominant focus on literature as "elitist." From her view, the group seemed unwilling to see the ways its outsized spotlight on published literary texts would structurally diminish the multilingual, and sociolectally rich, lifeworlds of Turkish Germany and Turkish Germans' meaning-making repertoires. The seminar, with its reliance on relatively high-profile literary publications, foisted an inappropriate probative burden on standardized monolingual (German or, more rarely, Turkish or Kurdish) works, one which did not correspond

---

[2] Amid the many problems John Guillory (2022, 45–6) and Rita Felski (2015, 15) note around the contemporary credibility of literary criticism as a professional activity, dilemmas around methodological or textual monolingualism haven't yet surfaced for discussion.

in a linguistically responsible way to the human communities we'd said we intended to highlight.

Of course, that labor historian was right in so many obvious ways, and I felt it. But I couldn't admit this to myself or to her at the time, because I still wanted the premise suggested above (literature is ethically and politically multilingual, isn't it?) to be right somehow. *Literature in Late Monolingualism* is about what I came to know and love again in literature, and in the multilingual world, when I gave up on that idealized marriage altogether—when I became willing to see literature and multilingualism not so much as an obvious match, but as a dicey relationship between relatively independent, still-potential friends who likely don't know each other as well as they thought they do. Since then, I've been trying to make a workable peace with the notion that "it's complicated" between them—as have, more importantly, the novels explored in this book.

By the end of my doctoral training, I'd made it far enough in this line of thinking to suspect that we'd better regard the modern Eurocentric novel as a prohibitively, though never essentially, monolingual metaform (Gramling 2008, 28). But somehow, despite that concession, I still both yearned and searched for examples to the contrary, whenever I actually wrote about novels. Then, in February 2012, I was sitting in a bar in Philadelphia, where my new friend Bethany Wiggin asked me, over a second beer, whether I'd yet read Tim Parks's essay about "the dull new global novel" (2010). I hadn't, and the furtive conversation that ensued between us then reminded me how taboo it was at the time for academics to call any kind of world literature dull, let alone "monolingual."

Tim Parks was, as I read him now, unleashing contempt not exactly for contemporary world literature itself, but rather for an ascendant mode of literary *acquisitions*, one that favored foolproof translatability over endogamous aesthetic particularity as the gold standard for literary scouts, executive editors, supply chains, and prize juries to trade on. This alleged dullness worked, I began thinking, somewhat like the literary version of a Special Economic Zone—utterly reliant on (while dismissive of) concentrated multilingual life and labor, and, nonetheless, unwilling to divest just yet from the nation-state order altogether (Slobodian 2023).

For me, mounting reservations on this matter of "multilingual literature" began to creep in soon after that bar conversation in Philadelphia, and I quickly started to discover work that helped me understand why. Writings by Paul Kae Matsuda on "linguistic tourism" (2014), Anjali Pandey on "linguistic exhibitionism" (2016), and Yuliya Komska on "conspicuous multilingualism" (2018) in literature would come to sharpen some of those initial hunches toward writing this book. And—with the good guidance of applied linguists like Nelson Flores (2016), Robert Moore (2015), and Noah Katznelson and Katie Bernstein (2017)—I began to trace some of these rumbling troubles in the discourse of multilingualism (beyond literary studies) back to earlier cautionary accounts.

For instance, already in 1997, the educational linguist Guadalupe Valdes had been concerned about neoliberal trends in bilingual education that tended to reprivilege white Anglophone monolinguals who aimed to *acquire* Spanish for competitive purposes, while actual bilingual Latinx speakers of Spanish and English lost ground and were disincluded from curricular decision-making (Freire et al. 2017). In all the ways it could easily hijack the discourse of multilingualism when we weren't looking, monolingual supremacy in the late 2010s seemed a newly perfect and anthropogenic storm.

Monolingualism—Isn't It Personal?

I should spell out a few things honestly about myself as a reader, writer, translator, teacher, and critic early on, lest my stances on the matters forthcoming in this book appear hypocritical. There might seem to be, already in this Preface so far, a line of thinking that promotes multilingual literature as essentially and politically *better* literature. The truth is that I love monolingual novels. I chase them with deep and needful appreciation. I translate them passionately, and even try to write them. I do not wish for monolingual novels to disappear summarily in a pyrrhic moment of critical renunciation.

Rather, I want monolingual novels to be better able and ready to share the road—the literary traffic-in-meaning (i.e., the infrastructures of meaningful uptake and dissemination, Pratt 2002; Yeager 2007)—with texts that translanguage boldly and resile linguistically in many of the everyday, unbridled, and virtuosic ways that the peopled world already capably does and desires to do (Li Wei 2017). I am worried about why it is that multilingual literature has not yet garnered a sturdy lane in which to emerge enduringly in commerce as "better literature" too, crowded out as I see it being by certain economies of monolingual overproduction, translational austerity regimes (see Chapter 2 on Dorthe Nors), and publishers' low expectations about readerly pleasure and comprehension. The ongoing suppression of multilingual literariness, and of multilingual aesthetics generally, has never been the result of absent or lagging public demand, just of insufficiently *effective* demand—this difference being one of late capitalism's lasting tragedies.

For novels are always, among other things, powerful idealizations about human communication and human being. Whatever one's critical orientation may be, we cannot sidestep the fact that novels project a durably immersive world of meaning and meaningfulness, of sense and senselessness, which in each case intends to solicit our desire, our ambivalence, and our eventual amplification through conversations with our friends. Like good conversations, novels are, at their best, "visions of sanity" for us (Tannen 1981). Overproducing monolingual projections of the world, through novels, will reliably constrain and skew what count as plausible and desirable forms of meaning-making socially. The monolingual metaform of the Eurocentric novel can socialize us into harsh and unnecessary foreclosures about what kinds and combinations of language(s) are and are not eligible for meaningfulness and credibility, even in nonliterary arenas of social practice.

In the end, this book is the result of a humbling process of mid-career unlearning for me as a literary scholar, literary translator, applied linguist, mid-level academic administrator, and language(s) teacher. It is about what happened when I stopped trying so hard to set up ill-advised blind dates between literary novels and social multilingualism, between literary studies and multilingualism studies, or even between translation and multilingualism—each being a venerable pair of things whose profiles never suggested an easy date in the first place. The result, as we shall see in the novels taken up in the following chapters, turns out to be a pretty racy and hopeful story.

Introduction

Monolingualism's Ages

It was late evening when K. arrived. [. . .] There was no sign of the Castle hill, fog and darkness surrounded it, not even the faintest gleam of light suggested the large Castle. K. stood a long time on the wooden bridge that leads from the main road to the village, gazing upward into the seeming emptiness.[1]
—Franz Kafka, *The Castle* (1924, translated by Mark Harman [1998, 1])

This is a book about the fretful lateness of monolingualism in the literary era this side of 2000. It strives to understand the moody, foreboding hunch in the air about a linguistically belated state of things in the age of Artificial Intelligence, which expresses itself in the novels of some globally marketed, Eurocentric authors. It is not a work in the sociology of literature, nor a comprehensive data-driven study of diverse global literary industries and their supply-chain infrastructures. It is a book of textual incitements and conceptual inquiry, whose focus will be that oddly alluring, jagged castle of single-language immersiveness we would rather not have to call "monolingualism"—this being one of literature's own, and least cherished, nightmares-of-the-self.[2]

The book considers an emerging kind of literary novel I call *literature in late monolingualism*. What such works share is a willingness to observe and critique the industrial commercialization of (their own) translatability from one monolanguage to the next—launching this critique from their variously situated cultural vantage points in Danish, Swedish, US American, and

---

[1] "Es war spätabends, als K. ankam. . . . Vom Schloßberg war nichts zu sehen, Nebel und Finsternis umgaben ihn, auch nicht der schwächste Lichtschein deutete das große Schloß an. Lange stand K. auf der Holzbrücke, die von der Landstraße zum Dorf führte, und blickte in die scheinbare Leere empor." (1982, 2)

[2] Since 1994, Marie-Laure Ryan has been alerting literary scholars to criteria of immersion, immersiveness, "vividness of display," and "depth of information" (Steuer 1992, 81) in readers' experiences of both literary and virtual-reality worlds. To what extent does monolingualism effectively provide an immersive experience for readers, rather than simply monopolizing their attention and suppressing alternatives? Thanks to Dante Prado for raising the matter of immersion to me in this context.

British letters. These works problematize the controlled traffic-in-meaning today between global languages (Pratt 2002; Cronin 2013)—seeing in detail what infrastructure this sort of literary traffic uses, whom and what it accelerates, whom and what it denies, and what aesthetic and semiotic sacrifices it makes along the way to preserve for itself a passably monolingual form, and to thereby avoid ending up stranded somewhere indefinitely on "world literature's outsides" (Çandar 2019).

In this, *Literature in Late Monolingualism* pulls up alongside many books before it that have scrutinized a powerfully unmarked norm—like whiteness, masculinity, cisgender, coloniality, Anglocentricity, or heteronormativity—each of which cohabitates along with monolingualism as one of literature's many stolid objects of partial disavowal. This book is fueled by my own personal conviction that a near-future world free of the structuring powers of monolingualism is in fact ever possible. Though not inevitable, nor even probable under current conditions, such a world beyond monolingualisms is always quite practically near at hand, and tantalizingly so. This is likely why monolingualism must innovate ever more aggressively from age to age in a bid to capture our imaginations and affections, often through literary and aesthetic products. Understanding monolingualism's affective workings through and with literary novels may help us envision that possibility, in the century to come, of a world uncaptured by an economistic fiat system of monolanguages.

We begin in Chapter 1 with Karin Tidbeck's self-translated science-fiction dystopia, *Amatka*. Hypervigilant about the prospect of its own self-translation and translatability from Swedish into English, the novel exudes a stoic crisis mood around translingual compromise and the performative commensuration of language(s), which I grasp through Rachel Greenwald Smith's (2014) conception of "compromise aesthetics." In Chapter 2, we turn to Dorthe Nors's Danish-language novel, *Mirror, Shoulder, Signal*, which foregrounds one literary translator's challenges with vertigo and dizziness in the lived ruins of the managed "global language system" (de Swaan 2002)—and of its ordoliberal, anti-protectionist modes of translatability in service of cheap, mobile meaning.

Neal Stephenson's virtually endless 1999 techno-thriller *Cryptonomicon* follows in Chapter 3, epitomizing an antielitist, tech-bro mood of rebuke toward university-educated humanistic multilingualism's pretensions, but mixed with an equally potent elitist contempt toward us mere finite lay human speakers in the age of early AI. These are contradictory aggressions in the novel that cancel out any triumphal celebration of multilingual subjectivity (Kramsch 2009) we might hope to encounter over its one thousand pages. Lastly, in Chapter 4, China Miéville's space odyssey

Embassytown unfurls a mood of ecstasy and disinhibition around the transformative experience of language learning, while portraying a future in which our many current methodological hangups—the alleged nameability and countability of languages, the notion of the self-sufficient individual speaker, and the conceptual binary "mono- vs. multilingualism"—have become moot.

Each of these four novels, these auto-theorizations about literature in the age of late monolingualism, conjures to differing intensities four linguistic moods—of 1) compromise and commensuration, of 2) dizziness, disorientation, and disorder, of 3) contempt and rebuke, or of 4) ecstasy and disinhibition—often with explosive combined effects. (There are, furthermore, strong overtones of each of these four core moods in each of the respective other novels.) These language-moods drive or detour the narratives, the characters, the action, the inaction, the poesis, the worldliness, and the theoretical expansiveness of the novels. In Stephenson's case, the defiant mood around monolingualism's lateness in *Cryptonomicon* seems to compel the novel's very lengthy length itself; its chipper, almost filibuster-like devotion to incessant enunciation in English over a thousand pages drives home the anxious point, almost as if it fears being the last monolingual novel ever written. Taken together, these novels present a forensics around the specter of monolingualism's lateness and its insistent unworldliness in our time, profiling the aggressive sociopolitical refortifications that such a specter prompts and engenders around us.

Is Monolingualism in Decline?

Now, a decade since writing *The Invention of Monolingualism* (2016b), I must concede how uncomplicated it was then to indict monolingualism in public. After all, no one seemed the least bit interested in standing in monolingualism's defense back then. When seen through a sociopolitical lens alone—unredeemed by literature's immersive enchantments and aesthetic intensifications—monolingualism-at-large was obviously an unlikeable thing. Though I tried in that book not to make monolingualism out to be a mere beast, or a farce, or a curable ailment (Peel 2001; Oller 1997), I did want to take it seriously as a worthy and genius adversary, one structured into colonial modernity in ongoing ways that are minutely banal, often lucrative, and hard to articulate honestly—especially when monolingualism itself is still generally left in charge of managing the very means of honest articulation (Solan 2017, 335).

"There has always been that divergence," wrote Joan Didion in 1967, "between what we say we want and what we do want, between what we say we admire and what we secretly desire, between, in the largest sense, the people we marry and the people we love" (59). *Literature in Late Monolingualism* is a study about literature's ongoing, sometimes remorse-filled love affair with the monolingual, in an age otherwise awash with performative goodwill toward multilingualism and translation.

I did push a strong analytic distinction in *The Invention of Monolingualism* between the historically well-honed epistemic–affective grooves of monolingual regimes (what they sanction for us to know, do, convey, and feel through a given singularized language) and, on the other hand, the actual people who might seek to operationalize these (self-)impositions in their practical lives. An obvious example of this distinction is any literary author of novels, who may or may not "be monolingual" in any personal way, but who may find reason—when in a pinch, or perhaps their whole life long—to *use* monolingualism for strategic, situational, aesthetic, or formal ends.

My insistence on distinguishing structure from subject—and on holding apart what Bourdieusians might call the "field of monolingualism" from its lived habitus (Gogolin [1994] 2008)—stems from a belief that human language will always be both more, and less, than "mono-" lingual. Each of our languaging lives, talkative or entirely nonverbal as those lives may turn out to be, is replenished in an ongoing way from a splashy and abundant imaginary number of language sources—never just from an orderly integer like "English," never neatly countable, always a bit, or a lot, "extra." Monolingualism has always been too NARPy an idealization to last on this planet, but it's going to hold on exactly as long as we allow it to.[3]

Shortly after that 2016 book came out, my friends and I saw newly vengeful forms of authoritarian (linguistic) nationalism—and anti-Asian, anti-Black, anti-Latinx, anti-Muslim, anti-Jewish, anti-trans, and anti-Indigenous racist violence—angling to recolonize Europe and the United States. Our fierce critical rebellions against ethnic subjugation, white supremacy, and nationalism that had been gaining political ground since the 1990s seemed to have roused large swaths of the Anglophone white-identifying US population not to disavow and deplatform those pernicious structures, but rather—in a kind of "late style" of their own—to grotesquely reelect and refortify racialized political monolingualism (Gramling 2019), sensing well enough all the while how decrepit and irreal such structures had become on

---

[3] The word *NARPy* comes from the HBO television show *Industry* (dir. Mickey Down and Konrad Kay), whose leading character Yas (Marisa Abela) uses it to describe people whose style and language suggest they might be *Not A Real Person*.

their tongues. The Trumpist era's intersectionally transphobic, xenophobic, racist, and opportunistically disdainful animus toward language(s) was best expressed by Florida governor Ron DeSantis, at the July 2023 Family Leadership Summit, where he and Tucker Carlson frothed together about a terrifying future in which "our kids or grandkids are memorizing thirty-seven different pronouns in Mandarin" (Dáte 2023; see also Komska et al. 2019, 6ff.).

In the twin domains of political monolingualism and linguistic nationalism since 2000, a surprising late reinvestment in these apparatuses in Great Britain, the United States, Turkey, Germany, and elsewhere seemed less a proof of people's true belief or enthusiasm for them than of half-heartedly making do with a handy and comparably unimpeachable administrative instrument—that is, of retaining monolingualism as at least reliably operational for civic projects of exploitation and exclusion, when ethnicized rationales of supremacy were no longer so easy to leverage in the public eye. There's a gulf, surely, between the utilitarian approach of insisting that everyone needs to speak a certain shared civic language to get into a country and live there for a while and, on the other hand, claiming that such a national language must be acquired *because* that language is superior to others in its elegance, precision, and cultural expressiveness. These are two very different strategic enactments of political monolingualism, and novelistic literature is a lush (because overdetermined) scene for spotting when and whether the latter supremacist mode, or rather the former pragmatist mode, is being activated most intensively in its outreach to readers.

Faced with the twenty-first century's resurgent political reinvestments in monolingualism, literary authors have been implicated in this violent, ambivalent picture in new ways too. Subject as they are to such transformations like everyone else, novelists are increasingly alert to the thickening political instrumentalizations of linguistic citizenship lawfare around the planet (Khan 2019; Gramling 2009; Cameron 2013; Dowling 2018; Craig and Gramling 2017), and curious about what it would consequentially mean for literature to give up its own monolingual privilege at all stages of literary production.

For centuries before them, the novel had served as a complex katechon: a testing ground for calibrating an appropriate interface between cultural cosmopolitanism and formal monolingualism, between multilingual world and national–linguistic self-expression, and between social multilingualism and (often translated) monolingual heteroglossia. Today's trade novels inherit this high-wire act and its katechontic function, still tending in the main to desirously court, and then ultimately stave off, the Real of planetary (multi-)linguistic life. Some novels do so ruefully, others do so in tacit defense of, emulation of, or nostalgia for Eurogenic universalist orders and the preferred forms of soft linguistic nationalism they've invented (Khan 2019).[4]

Monolingualism in the Age of Artificial Intelligence (or Vice Versa)

The historical term *late* monolingualism is designed, in part, to shift the punitive scrutiny of the word "monolingual" away from individual meaning-making persons and onto political economy.[5] Much as Werner Sombart used the term "late capitalism" in 1902–27 (König 1979: 358), and later Ernest Mandel in 1972, the purpose of the term late monolingualism is to show that monolingualism is a changing, surprising, and historically adaptive—though not necessarily declining—system.

Its "lateness" refers not to an eventual demise, but to the unanticipated and resurgent intensity and innovativeness with which its defenders seek to uphold it—often through discourses of so-called "multilingualism" (Moore 2015) or rebranded "bilingualism" (Katznelson and Bernstein 2017)—even when those innovators are not ideological nationalists in any conspicuous sense. My provisional dating of the end of high monolingualism at 1948, with the drafting of the Universal Declaration of Human Rights (Kellman 2016), intends to suggest that the period between 1950 and 1980, also the

---

[4] At times throughout the book, I use "Eurogenic" instead of Eurocentric—and Anglogenic instead of Anglocentric—to emphasize the performative, reproductive nature of discourses and utterances that solicit or require more and more of their own kind from a respondent, i.e., a homogenesis of monolanguages. The UK Home Office asylum process, and most citizenship/residency processes, require extensive reproduction of monolanguages from a claimant in the course of a high-stakes, repetitive, and opaque adjudicative process. The "-genic" conception suggests something more compulsorily productive than "-centricity" does—namely, a material–ideological force, or supply- and value-chain, that wishes to see and reproduce more and more European forms and Anglophone meanings for global uptake, particularly among non-European, non-Anglophone-dominant speakers. This is also a primary pathway for generating and securing xenos rights (Slobodian 2018) for Euro-American discourses in the lifeworlds of others, i.e., to ensure the ongoing colonial supremacy of such discourses throughout sovereign spaces, communities, and subjectivities beyond Europe and North America, where they otherwise hold no actual jurisdiction.

[5] Over the course of this book, my approach to defining "late monolingualism" will be recursive and ongoing, rather than dispositive. If computational engineers can beta-test, prototype, and iteratively soft launch their models to figure out what works best, perhaps readers will find the humanities monograph a suitable space to responsibly do the same with complex concepts too.

early heyday of Machine Translation, was a volatile gestation period for what would soon become a truly "late" monolingualism in the 1990s.

A key feature distinguishing *late* monolingualism from *high* monolingualism is that, to the extent its mundane operations are now wrapped up in the mystified realm we call Artificial Intelligence, late monolingualism is accelerated by the financialized infrastructure that governs computational technology today (see Chapter 3 on Stephenson's 1999 *Cryptonomicon*). Monolingualism's "robust, unsupervised" automated instruments today rely heavily, for instance, on iteration-without-validation (Iwata and Ishiguro 2016)—that is, the tendency among language-tech engineers to deploy unfinished models and products for public use, on the assurance that the public's end users will edit out the (linguistic) bugs from these platforms for free, instead of taking pains on the supply-side to identify and remove problems before initial market deployment (Dourish et al. 2020).

This iterative supply-side paradigm has unique consequences globally in the realm of everyday linguistic practice, where vernacular LLMs that are launched and socialized among users as allegedly benign beta tests can cause acute extractivist drains and misprisions, or other ongoing hardships, for communities whose practices do not align easily with the dominant settler monolanguage(s) upon whose cosmological pretexts the models have been developed. More broadly, these hidden social costs of iteration were one of the concerns that led thirty thousand tech leaders in 2023 to call for a Pause on Giant AI Projects, after the debut of OpenAI in December 2022 (Future of Life Institute 2023).

During the era since 1990, a profound change has taken hold in the way major planetary languages are made to coordinate with one another through supply-side algorithmic Cross-Language Information Retrieval (CLIR) platforms and Machine Translation innovations. The industry's "good-enough" operational horizon for quality, which I call "ordolingual" translatability (2020), has become the key measure and target for a certain dominant stratum of global commerce—including, often indeed, literary commerce.[6] In talking about "supply side" horizons, I intend to emphasize the ways in which institutional designs, premises, and products for language management are being promoted so as to comply and align with what technology innovators (suppliers) foresee as imminently possible and

---

[6] In *The Invention of Multilingualism* (2021), I defined *ordolingualism* as "the ongoing practice and principle of adjusting languages to one another into a global order that minimizes protectionism, opacity, decolonial resistance, and other barriers to the free flow of capital. Key to ordoliberalism, and ordolingualism, is that they appear to generously promote cultural expression and particularity, but do so only to a degree that does not hamper 'free trade.'" (13)

deliverable, rather than with what we users (i.e., "demand") actually are saying we want and need to suit a just and abundant world.

Though the two rough explanatory poles of supply and demand are always in an intricate, desirous dance with one another, language technology engineers today (on the supply side) have amassed unprecedented public license and funding to build hierarchies of linguistic infrastructure and multilingual management platforms that not even a sincerely interested layperson (on the demand side) can understand. The language of language technology today (for instance in the research annals of the Institute of Electrical and Electronic Engineers [IEEE]) reads a bit like the Ottoman court language of the eighteenth century which, though authoritative and hegemonic in its vast imperial jurisdictions, sounded like gibberish even to the astute and critical Anatolian villager who was subject to its everyday practical impacts.

How though, we shall ask in the chapters that follow, have these linguistic transformations over the last thirty years structurally impacted literary texts and the subjectivity of literature-makers? How also, over this period, has monolingualism (under color of ordolingual modes of translation; see Chapter 2 on Dorthe Nors) reorganized arenas of human life often presumed to be nonlinguistic or linguistically indifferent (Pipestone Group 2023)—including environmental justice, climate emergency, citizenship technologies, resource management, well-being and spirituality, supply-side industrial manufacture, jurisprudence, asylum administration, national security, corporate war-profiteering, nuclear proliferation, primary education, overfishing, and electoral politics?

What *Is* an Author—in the Age of Monolingualist Artificial Intelligence?

If new discursive expressions of monolingualism are indeed on the rise globally, we will of course want to know who is producing these structures, and who benefits from them the most. Put another way: which version of the current story of global linguistic order and innovation is helping to fortify, rather than to dismantle, monolingualism? And how is this fortification, paradoxically enough, achieved most effectively by some ascendant models of neoliberal *multi*lingualism and translation/translatability (Worley 2017; Moore 2015; Katznelson and Bernstein 2017; Freire et al. 2017)? Jacques Lezra has written in this spirit about how "translatability" has become

> [t]he conceptual basis of the global credit–debt market-system, an analogy tying the sorts of equivalences and convertibilities required by

the importing and exporting of goods across markets to the phenomenon of linguistic translation. A universal principle of exchangeability moves the market of markets that abstractly holds together the circuits of global capitalism; a universal principle of translatability obtains between particular languages or, even more atomically, between idioms or idiolects and languages, and then among languages. [. . .] This untranslatability in no way troubles the analogy between the principle of global exchangeability under credit–debt capital and the principle of universal translatability. [. . .] [T]his untranslatability which is one, we might say, is translatability's determinate negation. (2015, 177–8)

From this view, literary (un)translatability can easily become a proxy sphere for a much wider and overdetermined set of political-economic anxieties about policy, revenue, planning, technology, markets, and uptake on a global scale—none of which can be laid back at the doorstep of literary and professional translators in their capacity as individual practitioners. Indeed, the majority of translingual information traffic today fueling the globalized political economies we've built occurs by way of corpus-based Cross-Language Information Retrieval (CLIR) and Machine Translation platforms, and not under the careful eye and craft of individual translators or translation teams.

Untranslatability—or what is sometimes called *semodiversity* (Halliday 2007, 13–14)—is a menacing barrier and gadfly in the flow of these commercial supply chains, except when a particular token "untranslatable" gets successfully distilled as a boutique sector item to be commoditized in its own right, like champagne. But, in the main, platforms for *inducing* translatability prevail, aiming to commensurate disparate languages to one another and aggressively minimize their differentness, so as to produce "soft multilingualisms" (Noorani 2013) made up of increasingly securitized translatabilities.[7] Late monolingualism, as I understand it, is an age where a certain set of about 100 major global languages—what de Swaan (2002) calls "central" languages—becomes technologically fortified to facilitate such unobjectionable and efficient content distribution across language barriers.

As wary philologists and responsible literary translators, we may behold this industrial management of (un)translatability through Jacques-Alain Miller's caution that "every science is structured like a psychosis: the foreclosed returns under the form of the impossible" (Miller 1968, 103)—the "science"

---

[7] Here and elsewhere in the book, "securitized" will have a dual meaning both as 1) the effort to protect a commodity from tampering, hacking, hijacking, and unauthorized use, and as 2) the stabilization of a future commodity-valued financial instrument that can be traded easily and instantaneously between unacquainted parties, i.e., a "security."

here being the global logistical management of meaning by economistic means. As a reader of literature, I do want to understand how recent supply-side transformations in the newly managed world-language system play out—unevenly or surprisingly—in the literary craft of multilingual novelists, a domain that is sometimes held up as more impervious to free-market manipulations than other forms of cultural production (see Bourdieu 1993), due to literature's aura of slowness; its aesthetic particularity; its presumed cultural specificity; and its linguistic, poetic precision.

Even armed with such a presumptive mystique, though, transnational novels have had a bumpy go of it in early twenty-first-century criticism. With his short 2010 essay in *The New York Review of Books*, Tim Parks set a foreboding tone for criticism about literature written under conditions of globalization and late capitalism, warning that the advent of "The Dull New Global Novel" was upon us. Concerned that true literary genius had little chance at global recognition these days, Parks summarized that "what seems doomed to disappear, or at least to risk neglect, is the kind of work that revels in the subtle nuances of its own language and literary culture, the sort of writing that can savage or celebrate the way this or that linguistic group really lives." This worry about the irrevocable dissolution of particularity in language seemed to rebuke the general excitement about transnational hybridity that had boomed in the literary 1990s.

It is however a key premise of this book that literary authors in this era since 2000 are not blissfully naive about, nor immunized from, the systemic transformations and pressures that language-intensive industrial developments have been posing to their aesthetic craft. Nor are authors unconcerned, whether on principle or by disposition, about the complications these industrial changes create for their own emergence on the global stage—through either de facto or de jure literary translatability, through prize circuits, and in promotional stratagems.

Far from being aloof, these authors' literary work increasingly recognizes "the assumptions nexus" (Ramanathan 2005, 37) around ascendant linguistic ideologies in the publishing industry, and, in view of that nexus, critically textualizes "how much of our knowledge and imagination is a priori preselected" (Pandey 2016, 25). If, as Sarah Dowling contends, "translingual poetry responds to the coercive clarity of settler governance with critical dissonance" (2018, 169), *Literature in Late Monolingualism* seeks to find out just how much critical power and consciousness there may be in this late era among authors of monolingual novels, as they endeavor to dismantle the very nexus of linguistic assumptions that have accompanied their success.

The exploratory chapters that follow elaborate on this question, identifying evidence of four varying moods within the Eurocentric literature of late monolingualism since the beginning of the twenty-first century. Each of these moods could at first glance be regarded (uncharitably, I think) as an expression of what Anjali Pandey calls "linguistic exhibitionism" (2016) in monolingual literature. But I believe the novels under consideration here go far beyond mere commercial opportunism by linguistic means. Like any anxiously foreclosed system, like any repertoire that has identified its constitutive outsides, late literary monolingualism industriously cultivates a new and interesting future for itself, and a new set of epistemological horizons that may not be accessible through self-consciously "multilingual literature."

One specific literary presumption underlying the analyses that follow, though, is that monolingualism and literary novels are deeply and somewhat furtively joined at the hip, in historical intensities that do not pertain elsewhere in cultural life. Novelistic literature, in the Western European mold especially, has routinely upheld a conservative, romantic interest in national languages even when it swears it is doing nothing of the sort. The boom in interest over the last twenty-five years in literary translingualism has made an awkward and sometimes disingenuous go of accounting for this mutually conservative relation, leading to what Boyden and Kelbert call a "Theory Deficit in Translingual Studies" (2018).

The Title of This Book

Literature in Late Monolingualism's title was never meant to be particularly provocative. But its stodgy ring does hide some controversial claims. Who's to say that literature is "in" anything, let alone in something called "monolingualism"? And haven't the recent decades of postmodern stylistics, comparative literary studies of language play, and aesthetic cultures of code-meshing suggested that literature is actually a paragon of rebellion against monolingualism (see, for instance, Bhattacharya 2018)? Even when a novel is written "in Russian," let's say, don't its enduring designs promise something well beyond the confines of existing nationalized Russian language, even if the text itself does not engage in overt linguistic iconoclasm? How dare someone call such a thing merely "monolingual"? The literary works by Tidbeck, Nors, Stephenson, and Miéville explored here take a less defensive and incensed view about such charges of literary monolingualism; these novels are gracious, curious, and (self-)critical at once about the ways in which single-language constraint indeed enables their authorial emergence and aesthetic figurations. These authors do us the kindness of heeding what jurists call the "ostrich instruction": the duty during a proceeding not to feign ignorance about any elephants, or ostriches, who may be plainly in the room for all to see.

In choosing these works, I did want to distinguish the novels of late monolingualism from novels that wrestle with other historically related structures of constraint and subjugation through language. There are ample and riveting novels, for instance, written "in" and certainly against linguistic imperialism (Sharon Dodua Otoo's *Ada's Realm*), in or against linguistic nihilism (James Kelman's *Translated Accounts*), in or against linguistic extractivism (Chigozie Obioma's *An Orchestra of Minorities*), against linguistic standardization (Chetan Bhagat's *One Night at the Call Center*, see also Szurek 2015), against linguistic globalization (Terézia Mora's *The Only Man on the Continent*), against linguistic greenwashing (Kim Stanley Robinson's *The Ministry for the* Future), against linguistic racism (Abbas Khider's *A Slap in the Face*, see also Tankosić and Dovchin 2021), against linguistic opportunism (Robert Menasse's *The Capital*), and against linguistic authoritarianism (Orhan Pamuk's *Kars*). Though the concerns of those novels are my personal concerns too, and are kindred and overlapping with the arguments in the following chapters, their varying techniques and critical premises often surpass the category of late monolingualism itself.

For instance, Robert Menasse's 2017 novel *Die Hauptstadt* (*The Capital*, as translated by the historian Jamie Bulloch) is indeed "literature in late monolingualism" not merely because it concerns itself with multilingual social landscapes while doing so primarily in one narrative language (here German). Such could be said about any number of works, from Goethe's *Wilhelm Meister* novels to Brossard's *Mauve Desert*. The world of Menasse's novel isn't merely one in which many languages interact consequentially; it is one in which the political economy of monolanguages is recognized as organizing the liveability and tellability of the stories it relates, and where such organization is the object of intense and intricate critical devotion throughout it. And yet, it is not a novel ostentatiously *about* language. Thematically speaking, it is about Brussels as the administrative capital of Europe and, specifically, the workings, feelings, work cultures, and political misgivings of European Commission personnel—Austrian, Greek Cypriot, English, Czech, or Polish as they may be by language, citizenship, or ancestry.

And yet, Menasse's novel is not, as one might have good reason to anticipate, a scathing portrayal of hollowed-out bureaucratic double-speak, essentialist national pageantry, power-jockeying over minutiae, or of institutional rudderlessness. Nor is it a study in ironized hybridity, prepackaged transnational culture, or mystified planetary interconnectedness, as it may have been had it been written in the late 1990s. *The Capital* is a much more sober, rueful, and portentious affair. It is concerned with truly vexing logistical problems around how to convey historically multilayered meanings and sensibilities across a communicative space involving twenty-three official monolanguages, and doing so through official public channels maintained by real people working together or working against one another.

People in the novel not only realize routinely that they themselves cannot be precise enough in one shared monolanguage to convey an aspect of their own meaning-making repertoire that feels utterly essential to them; they are also themselves the people shaping and governing the infrastructure of such meaning-making conveyance across monolanguages. Melancholy ensues, more often than does cynicism. Ultimately an instance of late literary monolingualism, Menasse's novel is about frustrations seriously felt and handled across such a socio-communicative landscape of controlled monolanguages (Cronin 2013), despite and amid an institutional infrastructure constructed to promote and manage mobility between languages, cultures, jurisdictions, and nations in a progressive though securitarian way.

One critical feature of literature in late monolingualism, in both senses of the word critical, is thus its consciousness that divesting from monolingualism in literary or social activity is not a simple act of will, creativity, or translanguaging. Novels that work consciously within the conditions of late monolingualism express a particular stamina to stay with the trouble it has caused (them), to contemplate its very form and historical implicatedness, and to uncover the internal structures that tend to preempt speakers' voluntary divestiture from monolingualism in our various social and institutional spaces.

And yet, it has been a common and uncontroversial default in academic and broader social discourses alike to sacralize multilingual authorship symbolically as a font of creative plenitude that reliably enriches and innovates literary culture. This affirmative stance occludes the arguably more salient fact that multilingual authorship is also often a predicament of diminishment and attenuation, in which a multilingual subject (Kramsch 2009) compels themselves to attempt to do business with and through a prohibitively monolingual literary form or institution.

Even if they have no political interest in multilingualism as such—either as a cosmopolitan horizon for social life or as a creative aesthetic ideal—multilingual authors must continuously contend with monolingualist constraints and prescriptions nonetheless, housing within themselves all the while dynamic multilingual ranges of meaning that will sometimes rush intensely forth, like a hostile witness, in the otherwise monolingual scene of their novels. The chapters that follow detail how such a pugnacious linguistic subjectivity reveals itself in these antagonisms of the compositional process, not by brazenly breaking monolingualism's rules, but through what I've called the four moods of late literary monolingualism: compromise, disorientation, contempt, and ecstasy.

Before we turn to the novels themselves, it may help to first imagine and enumerate some of the least controversial reasons a literary author—like Neal Stephenson, Dorthe Nors, Karin Tidbeck, or China Miéville, among thousands more—might find fault with monolingual constraint, and might strain moodily against it, involuntarily or otherwise. They may do so

- because the social world of the text they are composing is already overtly bi- and multilingual in its meaning-making interactions;
- because the psychical or emotional range necessarily explored in the text cannot be accommodated in any one language;
- because experiences of language learning, language loss, translation, or other translingual processes strongly condition the world of the text;
- because the world of the text is conditioned strongly by a language or languages that are not the language of composition;
- because an author's (monolingually construed and constrained) language of composition is at an objective disadvantage to other potential languages of composition, given among other things the expense and delay associated with translation and with achieving attention internationally;
- because an author's idiolectal variant of a monolingually constructed language is currently dispreferred for purposes of composing, publishing, marketing, and translating;
- because the presumptive language-of-composition is itself an antagonist-with-impunity in the social world of the text (say, Russian in a Ukrainian social setting);
- because the presumptive language-of-composition evades interactional, typological, or semantic climes needed for one or another figural project within the text—for instance, the need for a rogative, reportative, or optative tense, which the compositional language may lack or disprefer when conveying reported speech, rumors, or dubious information (see Filipović [2007] on "language as witness");
- because the author or characters dwell in a place where monolingualism is patently uncredible, whether because their social relations know no such structure, or because their epistemic horizons do not comport with it.

The list could go on, and these reasons are only the least fussy among the many possible. But, when we move into the focused textual studies that make up the core of this book, such reasons will prime us to think about the predicament of making monolingual literary art in the vastly multilingual twenty-first century. Already a century ago, Kafka felt the lateness of monolingual figuration in his own time, when his late novel *The Castle*'s main character K. stood down below the long-promised castle of Count Westwest, looking up to find only emptiness above him.

What the authors brought together in this book have in common is a not particularly rare problem, but one we might call logistical, infrastructural, or ergonomic. Their problem, like Kafka's always was, is how to get certain kinds of worlds into certain kinds of texts—without breaking those worlds, or their own commitment to them. Late literary monolingualism is a sustained gauntlet-run in this predicament, and we shall turn to specific cases in that endeavor in the pages to come.

In the end, "being in" monolingualism—being subject to it in a somewhat compulsory way—is neither a necessary diminishment of a novel's aesthetic quality overall, nor a mark against its potentially revelatory cultural politics around language and linguistic diversity. It simply means that most novels that succeed in publication and dissemination today are still routinely implicated somehow in the refortification process that contemporary supply-side monolingualism demands. A novel's participating role in (rather than aloofness about) monolingualism isn't happenstance, nor necessarily hardship. Nor do all novels always yearn, dismayed, to get out of monolingualism, even when they very well apprehend the social and epistemological harm the structure does, and will tend to do, to the world.

The second provocation in the main title of this book is this proposal of a "late" form of monolingualism, to which most of the analyses will be dedicated. Surely, not all literary creation today is "in late monolingualism," nor is most of it. Historically, planetarily, the majority of literary creation (broadly conceived) would barely be able to imagine something like monolingualism, let alone its recently fortified and intensified late forms in a Eurogenic, financialized, AI-driven mold. But I do believe that much contemporary published literature is compelled in some ways to emerge through and "in" late monolingualism, in the sense that it is subjected to publishers' and distributors' heightened anxieties about how to effectively service the global supply-chain infrastructure's just-in-time demands on the manufacture of meaning for multiple end-user monolanguages.

This foreclosive demand is afoot, for instance, when acquisitions departments look for texts that will be immanently accessible in scores of translated target languages, a procedure that most midsize and large presses' business models now overwhelmingly heed. Here, "overwhelmingly" suggests not only that the vast majority of presses who can afford it will speculate on a future of unproblematic translated access—that is, what we could call, with Quinn Slobodian (2018, 123), linguistic "xenos rights"—for the texts and authors they contract with.[8] It also means that such omnilingual supply-side aspirations (Kellman 2016) are frequently experienced as overwhelmingly prerequisite for any successful project, author, or translator—throughout the conception, composition, marketing, and touring process, as we'll see in Chapter 2 on Dorthe Nors's novel *Mirror, Shoulder, Signal.*

Periodizing Untimeliness

But being "in" late monolingualism doesn't mean merely that a novel or novelist will assent to surveilling and preempting untranslatability in their work. That is a kind of attentiveness which can very well be achieved without the bracing and pious foreclosures of late monolingualism. And being "in" late monolingualism also doesn't mean that a text is docile, flat, defenseless, servile, or compromising. Rather, often enough, late monolingualism activates and stimulates texts to do things differently, to forge critical and aesthetic routes that would not occur to authors unwary of monolingualism's active, practical demands on them.

Such literary works are often, importantly, not "about" language at all—but about another layer of social life—politics, morality, science, vocation, community, sensation, desire, or imaginative worldliness—that is itself threatened by monolingualism's fetishistic distortions. For a remedy to the threat, such novels don't necessarily take immediate topical recourse to a corrective linguistic sensibility—that is, to the ostensive go-to talismans of "multilingualism" or "translation"—but rather stay with and intensify the trouble of monolingualism's figural repertoires and constraints.

It is routine for intellectual traditions around politics, culture, and literature to designate periods, however imprecise or revisionist they might end up being: Romanticism, the Third Reich, the Great Society, Decadence, Reconstruction, the Cold War, the Great Depression, Neoliberalism, the End of History, the War on Terror, and various other apples-and-fruits categories. Drastically less common is to see a periodization of, in, or about *language(s)*, a fact that suggests an enduring indifference about the relation between

---

[8] Slobodian's use of this term derives from Hayek, and is not—as we use it here—intended for linguistic purposes, but rather for the rights of capital and property owned by foreigners/xenos, "guest-friends," so that they can expect, as Hayek foresaw as essential for global market equilibrium, to be "assured individual admission and protection within an alien territory" (cited in Slobodian 2018, 123).

history and language in interdisciplinary knowledge production, global manufacture, and political economy.⁹

What is the peculiar nature of the contemporary *linguistic* age around us? Is this linguistic age—since 1990, say—driven by popular language ideologies, by extralinguistic or language-indifferent technological shifts, and/or by technological shifts in the very nature of languages and symbolic regimes? What have been the precursors and preparatory discourses for this age?

The novels discussed in *Literature in Late Monolingualism* think about how the thirty-odd years since 1990—a window spanning the rollout and refinement of algorithmic Cross-Language Information Retrieval and Machine Translation technological capacities—have enabled a new age in matters of language and meaning. Endemic to this age is the supply-side management of global multilingualism through pathways that primarily serve commercial clients, security agendas, and borderless market stratagems by reducing the time and expense necessary for translation and for other forms of cross-language conviviality.

Of course, it's true that not all novels and novelists today are telling this kind of intense story about paradigm changes around language and meaning and monolingualism. True, too, many courageous multilingual writers surpass the trappings of national monolanguages altogether, fending off the downstream consequences for them personally of such a divestment, and rebelling against publishing industries' insistence on presuming certain kinds of monolingual end users for their books. But novelists who do tell this kind of implicated late monolingual story, which is implicitly often about their own linguistic compromises and work-arounds in monolingualism, are sharing with us some interesting and difficult lessons about what it feels like to be multilingually imaginative in a social world conditioned by ubiquitous and surprising late monolingual constraints. It is to those stories, and to what they tell us about such a repertoire, that this one book seeks to listen.

---

⁹ While the convention of periodizing politics and literature is as standard as it is imperfect, attempts to periodize language are more tentative and infrequent. Michael Cronin, in a 2013 book on translation, invoked the Digital Age for languages. Yasemin Yildiz, around the same time in *Beyond the Mother Tongue*, developed a temporal conception of the "postmonolingual condition." While Lyotard put forth the condition of postmodernity as an incredulity toward metanarratives, Yildiz foresaw a growing contemporary uneasiness in literary and civic stances toward the monolingualisms that had been erected for Europe since pre-Enlightenment days through various traditions of organicism, nativism, and nationalism. Ignacio Infante, in *After Translation*, took up a broad movement of literature-making issuing from Afro-Latinx Transatlantic histories of translation (2013), evoking the temporal framing "after" to characterize it. Rebecca Walkowitz offers the implicitly temporal and periodizing figure "born translated" (2017) to a range of literary footings that express the circumstance of having been thrown into an unevenly multilingual world hamstrung by Anglocentrism.

As Edward Said intended it to be understood, "late style" is neither a unified phenomenon nor a set of stable characteristics so much as a predicament in the relation between aesthetics and a vulnerable bodily condition. In the arguments to come, "bodily condition" in late monolingualism means two things concretely, though these diverge a bit from Said's idea about late finitude. Literature in late monolingualism, I'll suggest, strains awkwardly in its attempts to dignify the linguistic capacities of the human body—the always comparably modest linguistic repertoire of any human writer, editor, translator, or publishing scout—when set against an AI-equipped globalized political economy that now cannot countenance being managed in only one, or even in a mere handful of, language(s) at once.

What often results in such a moment of confrontation, as we shall see in the novels ahead, is less a constrained and circumspect humility of style than a grand overreach and a hallucinatory affectation, like the exhaustion of a red giant star. Edward Said had seen how late work tends to bring forth alienated masterpieces that, as Adorno has it, express "the outer reaches of art, in the vicinity of document" (Adorno 1993, 564). What is documented there, he thought, is the collapse of art back onto the body that keeps on making the art despite its own accelerated corporeal disappearance. A rationalist might expect that, when "confronted by the dignity of human death, the theory of art [would] divest itself of its rights and abdicate in favor of reality" (ibid.). But in the novels of late monolingualism (like Stephenson's spectacularly defiant *Cryptonomicon*), the prompt to divest and abdicate from monolingualism is often dramatically deferred, despite and amid the mounting indices of its lateness.

For, as Said suggested, late style often scoffs at the idea of abdicating from its long-beloved *illusio*[10]—here, the modern "game" of aesthetic monolingualism, and its subtle but deeply consequential rules of play. Having looked hard at the prompt to step aside in favor of the socially multilingual world before it, the contemporary novel finds such an option ultimately preposterous, annoying, or undignified—like the prospect of playing several sports at once on a field meant for cricket alone.

Meanwhile, literary trade presses, agents, scouts, editors, marketers, and literary translators (like myself) tend most routinely to delay and defer this divestment from monolingualism in our practices and products as well, while promoting multilingualism politically and rhetorically. Faced with the multilingual, translingual world (lived and known in all the ways it is),

---

[10] A Bourdieusian term related to "game" (i.e., the "ludic"), where one's own investment in a particular game and its potential stakes must be strategically misrecognized as such (Heidegren and Lundberg 2010).

literature in late monolingualism doubles down. It fortifies into an aesthetic style that forges a new life of forms sovereign (i.e., out of touch) from the multilingual Real, which has since midcentury thrown itself urgently at literature and at scenes of literature-making. Literature that vigorously reenlists in monolingualism, despite having been amply scolded for doing so, is prone to be composed in such a *late style*. Such novels are often—among other good things and despite their best ambitions—products of, and matrices for, what Sarah Dowling calls settler monolingualism (2018, 167).

The Global Literary Supply Chain's Imagined Monolingual End User

The novels and novelists foregrounded in *Literature in Late Monolingualism* devote significant attention to the changing norms and instruments of the trade publishing industry, which has been transnationalized since the mid-1980s (Thompson 2010; Kong 2004; Rectanus 1987). It is not too much to wager that most literary artists since that corporate-transnational turn, particularly those who write in a language other than English, have experienced (to differing intensities and in different constellations) the profound impacts of the automatization and coordination of multilingualism, and not just the more general effects of late capitalism on literature. They glimpse this looming managerial apparatus sometimes in the conception, acquisition, and composition process, but also later (or simultaneously) in the translation, copyrighting, contracting, and marketing of their works. They have also witnessed the ways in which such coordination of multilingualisms abets Anglogenic processes—that is, the making of more and more English.

True, published literature has always found itself adhering to new and overwhelming demands, which can issue abruptly from the technological relations that surround and consume it. Though rebellion is often a central motif of literary stories themselves, the linguistic demeanor of novelistic literature tends to acquiesce to standard-language constraint—whether that constraint be a subtle linguistic doxa (sociolinguistic, monolingual, modal, paratextual, orthographic, typographic, etc.) or a more overt linguistic orthodoxy (political, ideological, nationalist, accentist [Ramjattan 2019; Orelus 2017], raciolinguistic [Flores and Rosa 2015], etc.). A text can adhere to subtle linguistic doxa while professing linguistic or cultural iconoclasm, just as a text can narrate or valorize orthodox linguistic conformism while profoundly undermining linguistic doxa. Put another way, and in the terms of this book, a novel can be monolingual while praising and prizing multilingual subjectivity, just as it can be multilingual in practice while championing monolingualism on an overt ideological level.

Attempting to understand the diverging potential energies between narrative rebellion and formal acquiescence in this way can be important, especially when doing so helps us spot intersections within texts that seem designed to conflate the two planes—that is, to hide linguistic iconoclasm under ideological conservatism, as Tidbeck does in Chapter 1. I believe it is important to resist the temptation to see such discrepancy between overt linguistic ideology and covert linguistic doxa as some kind of weakness, hypocrisy, inconsistency, or unplanned irony in a work of literature—which, after all, never promised anyone to be consistent, let alone "lingual" in any specific way (Stockhammer 2017). There is no "gotcha moment" in the current study; it is never out to catch literature in some kind of bad, as in monolingualist, behavior we may imagine it claimed to have risen above, or sworn off, in previous ages.

In *Postprint: Books and Becoming Computational*, N. Katherine Hayles is interested in how "a literary work [. . .] reflects within itself the technological conditions of its composition and production" (2021, 27). Hayles notes how Jonathan Safran Foer and Mark Danielewski's literary works, for instance, overtly reference the technological media of their own production. Likewise, the literature of late monolingualism tends to signpost its own productive embeddedness in a particular, contingent global infrastructure of controlled languages (Cronin 2013). Its novels cannot help but foreground authors' exquisite awareness about how the ordolingual infrastructure they are expected to uphold and reproduce indeed becomes part of what Hayles calls their "technotext."

As Hayles suggests, metamedial or technotextual awareness can be more, or less, overtly interested in technology itself. Authors can be relatively indifferent to (language-) technological innovation (Tidbeck in Chapter 1, Nors in Chapter 2), or their work can focus topically on contemporary technologies themselves (Stephenson in Chapter 3, Miéville in Chapter 4). Some works of literary late monolingualism may focus more intensively on the political economies, statecraft, and social–material relations these technologies helped to engender (Tidbeck, for instance), and develop whole new philosophies to account for them. In each case, we are led to ask to what extent "'techno-epistemological configurations' [. . .] and software architectures generate the output that humans see" (Hayles 2021, 29). At what point do translation, translatedness, and translatability begin to count as part of the techno-epistemological scene configured into the text we read itself, rather than as pre- or postproduction epiphenomena to be considered sociologically? When is the supply chain of translational monolingualism acknowledged as present and consequent enough to critique as a first-order evidentiary matter, in the course of what we call "close reading"?

Further to this question, Intan Suwandi points out the ways global commodity chains are often construed and analyzed without regard for laborers and labor exploitation. In her corrective model for value chains in global capitalism, Suwandi offers an approach that "can address both issues: the macro workings of the labor-value chains and the way these mechanisms affect production processes in specific firms, in particular how they ultimately affect the workers who make the commodities" (2019, 19). Suwandi continues to explain how her framework, called labor-value commodity chains, "takes into account the questions of power, class, and control—questions that must be addressed if we want to bring the exploitation/expropriation that occurs in global commodity chains out into the open [. . .] [by] incorporate[ing] a calculation of cross-national variation in unit labor costs in manufacturing" (17).

In the spirit that Suwandi proposes, I view the production of literature in late monolingualism as a matter of densely populated supply-chain infrastructures, rather than just of technotextuality or metamediality. That is, books in late monolingualism (including this one) are performances of a certain layered and laminated (translingual) infrastructure that has desired and produced them—a supply chain of human relationships requiring a logistically sophisticated manufacture for the least expensive conveyance of meaning to allegedly monolingual end users. Here we see emerging a corollary to sociologist Jason Moore's (2016) conception of "cheap nature"— in the literary provision of *cheap meaning* across language frontiers. How is cheap meaning actually manufactured, translingually?

Consider, for a moment, what a reader is to make of Randy Waterhouse from Neal Stephenson's 1999 novel *Cryptonomicon* (Chapter 3)—and of Randy's code-crunching machine Ordo, a late-capitalist digital descendant of the Typex and the Lovelace Analytical Engine:

> [Randy] is not bothering to look at the screen; he is staring out the window at the lights on the trucks and the jeepneys. He is only using one hand, just flailing away loosely at the keyboard. [. . .]
>
> Ordo wants randomness. It only wants the least significant digits. [. . .] It wants a whole lot of random numbers, and it wants them to be very, very random. (1999, 54)

Having moved to the (multilingual) Philippines from a (monolingualist) Silicon Valley (Shankar 2008), *Cryptonomicon*'s Randy is having a kind of pastoral moment here, melancholic for a previous age's simpler, higher modernisms. He has come to the Philippines to launch a tax-sheltered tech company whose proprietary data-encryption system, Ordo, demands the most random and casuistic authentication codes possible from his body, so as to enable the global flow of information, revenue, and capital. The best, most "authentic" way for Randy to provide Ordo with what it requires from him is to ignore his own input keyboard entirely, to withhold consciousness from it.

In a bid to make acceptable meanings for his coding platform Ordo, Randy must position his body so as to produce senseless, near-involuntary movements that translate into stochastic but standardized digital alphanumeric monolingualism. Meanwhile, and almost as a palliative remedy, he averts his gaze onto the urban landscape out his window, and onto the classic, comprehensible inventions of modernism: gas-powered motorcars and electric lights. Distracting his eyes from "code" in this way isn't just a coping strategy; it's a material precondition for code's manufacture and function. Such is the kind of split "creative" subjectivity that both informs Randy's expertise and alienates his articulacy.

It's one thing to think about what Randy is doing here—"just flailing away loosely at the keyboard" (54)—as an interesting glitch of the end-user (human) condition at millennium's end. It's another thing to think of Randy doing this *in*, *amid*, and *for a monolingual novel*—a literary form that has for centuries fended off the aspersion that it is, or ever could be, composed by "just flailing away loosely at the keyboard."

Someone has indeed written this very novel, *Cryptonomicon*, quite carefully—some human with a name, a body, and a vividly specific linguistic subjectivity, one that likely does not take kindly to subjugating itself to something called "monolingualism." And then, someone edited it, over and over, provided feedback on it, typeset it, proofed it, adorned it, marketed it, and also translated it into more than ten other monolanguages. Every one of those persons' and agents' specific (multi)linguistic subjectivities gets indexed practically in the product through various stages of its manufacture.

And yet, what we all are ultimately compelled to read (whether in the English, or in Wojciech Próchniewicz's Polish or Pedro Jorge Romero's Spanish) is a monolingual text: a text that is, however, no less obsessively "about" this world's essential, impending, alarming multilinguality—in all senses of the word *about*. In Didion's metaphor from above, *Cryptonomicon* is a melancholic novel about deciding it's probably still the smart call to marry multilingualism for its good reputation and its promising financial prospects, while secretly and passionately *loving* Anglophone monolingualism. The text itself is, knowingly, the loquacious and condemned expression of that passion.

Randy's code Ordo, the enabling and secret crypto-language at the heart of Stephenson's novel, brings these two antihumanistic specters of randomness (unintentionality) and orderliness (lifelessness) into a strained dramatic contest—one central, I will argue, to the various moods of literary late monolingualism. Throughout *Cryptonomicon*, Randy's bodily subjectivity is pressed into producing and reproducing Ordo's dynamically orderly, random code. His body can only avail itself of conventional humanistic, lyrical, and novelistic consciousness when he is *not* working away tending code's future. Therein lies the novel's desirous, and bitter, pastoral sensibility.

As Andy Hageman notes, though, infrastructure (systems of transport and communication, as well as their maintenance, engineering, and decommissioning) has never been much of a hot concern for literary criticism, and so he encourages us to start to "examine infrastructure as a focal point, beyond the more conventional emphases on character and emplotment" (2019, 3; see also Rubenstein 2010). Linguistic and translational infrastructure were, however, not foremost on Hageman's mind, nor on Jason Moore's. On the one hand, language has long been left behind in most material–practical theories of political economy and industrialization, and thus also of their ecological consequences.

But—as *Cryptonomicon* painstakingly and painfully spells out, very much against its own will—language has become newly central to the relations of production at large in twenty-first-century manufacture, not only because of service and information economies' communicative needs, but because of the globalized management of supply-chain logistics, from extraction to end user, which requires interoperability (and therefore socialization) among a broad and opaque array of translingual subjects and laborers/managers, when global English is simply never enough.

The collusion between these two contemporary macro-phenomena—the erasure of language(s) from theories of political economy, and languages' suddenly pivotal logistical role as a new capital frontier in globalized commerce—is both striking and ominous. Indeed, we can try imagining an alternative intellectual history of modernity and its institutional designs in which materialists and political economists took language and translation seriously as central to the processes that mattered to industrial processes and their analysis—and that, therefore, made matter itself—rather than diminishing or sidelining language and translation in favor of other kinds of (linguistically indifferent) analytics of production. We could simply try imagining what would have happened if neoclassical economics in the twentieth century—and then at business schools, in supply-side manufacture, and in logistics design alongside it—had developed a high analytical regard for language(s) and their implications for trade, industrial, and social relations. Neither of these scenarios is in evidence, alas, and yet language(s) as a financialized, productive, and extractable frontier for capitalization is only now beginning to come into sight.

Mostly headquartered in Global North cities, the globalized trade literature industry has responded to this sudden and unexpected new search for revenue-generating multilingual affordances in quizzical and reactionary ways. Here is how Pandey describes its gold-rush mood around linguistic diversity:

> What we encounter in twenty-first-century prize-winning fiction [. . .] is a privileging of parallelism over complementarity—textual uses of multilingual content used for cosmetic augmentation and designed to spotlight familiarizing rather than foreignizing urges. "Foreignizing" effects are deliberately designed to create an aesthetic estrangement on readers (Gibeau 2013). For multilingual-averse readers, such strategies can have the effect of unease, and a hyper-enhanced pluringuaphobic effect. The ultimate effect could potentially render a writer so unfamiliar as to gain neither recognition nor notoriety in the market of literary exchange. In contrast, on the opposite end of the cline, we have the possibility of an adoption of shallow appropriation strategies in which multilingual inclusions aim to accomplish a "familiarizing" effect. (2016, 103)

It would be both ungenerous and analytically narrow to dismiss prized and prize-winning literary–linguistic exhibitionists—like, for example, Sonja or Gösta in Chapter 2, or Franz Kafka, for that matter—as somehow pernicious agents in the history of multilingual subjectivity. Like them, our authors Stephenson, Tidbeck, Nors, and Miéville are commendable for, among other things, grasping the mechanism of late monolingualism in an exquisite literary way—rather than racing away from it, as one races away from any nightmare of the self. These authors have stayed with the trouble of monolingualism, worked to hospice it (Machado de Oliveira 2021). As a student of monolingualism as a historical structure, I find their insights anything but dull. Stephenson's contemptuous excess, Nors's sometimes ecstatic vertigo, Tidbeck's compromising asperity, and Miéville's heroic immersiveness all exude a certain kind of aesthetic pleasure in the baffling confines of late monolingualism, much as a Victorian clothier might dilate in the pleasures of a muted and constrained sartorial repertoire.

And yet, since the late eighteenth century, prestige literature has most often been measured by its distinctive stylistic untranslatability, relatively sovereign from the machinations of transnational marketing. While they enjoy this presumptively market-agnostic aura, modern novels of various kinds have nonetheless harbored an uncanny ideological intimacy with *monolingualism*, rather than with the more readily admired virtue of multilingualism. Now as then, great novel(ist)s of national traditions in a single language—from Henry James to Gabriel García Márquez to Toni Morrison and Thomas Mann—are elevated as the distinctive, mystique-bearing gold standard for younger generations of speakers to aspire to, even conversationally. They serve this wider function, as symbolic bastions for retroactive communitarian myths about national and ethnic style in a single, though multicultural, language.

This relationship changes profoundly in the age of late monolingualism, when the imperative to translate and market novels globally begins to require that that novel itself be written in a way that does not impede multiple-language distribution and uptake on the global prize circuit. In their style formation, what is prized in late monolingual novels is the kind of finesse that ensures egress, rather than the genius that mystifies access. It is an often rued, but less often questioned, truism of the literary industry in this age that Nobel-caliber novels need to be just *cultural enough* to convey an aura of uniqueness, and be just translatable enough to sell very well in 20–30 allolingual markets—without thereby entailing any "delta" or delay in distribution.

When rising stars like Junot Díaz and Feridun Zaimoglu—who wrote iconoclastic breakout novels that were intractably multilingual and difficult to translate—discovered how much difficulty their early creative stances caused them and their translators, marketers, and editors in international reception, they often opted in their later work for a more translatably monolingual palette (Gramling 2014). Aphasia about these dynamics is not the fault of literary studies alone, but is part of a broader disinterest in meaning-making subjectivity in economic reasoning, including but not limited to disinterest in linguistic or aesthetic subjectivity.

What Pandey describes is an industry intent on rushing to the rescue of imagined monolingual readers, despite a new global landscape that ascribes surplus value to the flexible multilingual dimensions of commodities. It is this presumed and projected telos of a monolingual end-user reader, waiting for monolingual books, that allows the overall multilingual infrastructure of dissemination to work in an orderly way for global value chains (Suwandi 2019). This setup alleges to protect and insulate prospectively monolingual readers (and reading communities, at universities and in neighborhood book clubs [Tekgül 2019], for instance) from multilingual practice, while enlisting them nonetheless into multilingualism's symbolic valorization.

I propose *late* monolingualism to mean this historical era, from the late 1980s to (presumably) the mid-twenty-first century, when modern colonial and nationalist (i.e., high) monolingualism has been suspected of general ineffectuality, irrelevance, and operational exhaustion in global commerce, but which has yielded oddly fortified new supply-side forms and infrastructures that correspond to fewer and fewer people's lived realities. Rather than hastening high monolingualism's end, so as perhaps to move into a newly multilingual planetary era, what has taken hold in a cluster of powerful sectors (including administrative states, universities, and private industries) is a collusion between anti-protectionist political economies, transnational manufacturers, and policy actors who rally, often unwittingly, to make monolingualism great again—to refortify monolingualism with new technologies, policies, affects, comforts, accessories, curricula, and citizenship protocols so as to protect so-called "monolinguals" from globalization and the destabilizing effects of other languages and their meanings. Monolingualism is a prophylactic structure that idealizes a certain kind of irreal speaker, primarily so as to commoditize all of the revenue-rich routes of symbolic access to that idealized person's artificially constrained attentions.

The Animus of Monolingualism

I view monolingualism as a true "-ism" because it is a tireless ideology, an energetic idealization—one with a zealous and practical ambition in mind for any potential domain of work, conviviality, or expression. It is designed to make any respective "other language" unnecessary in a given context—frequently by nearshoring or friendshoring language expertise (El-Erian 2023) in ways that ensure that the needfully adjacent, though assiduously ignored, other language(s) will remain readily serviceable as needed.

Because of this hungry ideological efficiency, typical and clever of monolingualism, I will sometimes ascribe a vivid subjectivity to it, saying things like "monolingualism does x" or "monolingualism wants y." When I do so in this book from now on, I'll be careful to flag the figural metonymy and anthropomorphism afoot in my own expressions, and then will endeavor to reroute the claim back to actual subjects and agents: people, writers, publishers, government agencies, jurists, schools, funders, supply-chain managers, and other decision-making collectivities.

But just as one might say, with some acceptable imprecision, that "Artificial Intelligence wants to . . ." or "white supremacy aims to . . ." the purpose of such a formulation is to acknowledge the animus that humans (those with governing authority) have willingly ceded to a given construction over time, and to suggest that this construction can now often run very well on its own, reproducing a set of effects in a range of settings without any effortful human prompting and intention. Activating monolingual stricture in any domain is monstrously easy in much of the ordered world now; monolingualism has advanced through colonial history to become its own kind of Cooperative Principle (Grice 1975, 45) overseeing good and transparent communication: something we feel we need to apologize for having violated before, after, and while doing so.

Every time, for instance, someone apologizes nervously to another person in a public forum for having "butchered their name," monolingualism hovers knowingly in the background—admonishing those present that such a mess could have been avoided if only the name and its exhausting pronounceability hadn't insisted on being there in the first place. This always avoidable, and yet gruesomely repeated, phrase "sorry for butchering your name" calls to collective consciousness a scene of physical violence in which this name in question bears its natural portion of shame for the indignity of having turned an otherwise conscientious host/speaker into a butcher, and for necessitating from them an otherwise uncharacteristic act of violence. The literature of late monolingualism offers much practical, "dirty theory" (Connell 2007) about such everyday discursive moments of monolingual consolidation, much as feminist and queer movements have always helped us to see how the everyday (dys)affordances of gender are ever in need of our untiring, collective, hard-won critical interventions.

Who Regards Monolingualism?

Throughout this book, it will always be the case that "monolingualism" means any approach foreseeing that a single, named language's repertoire of signs will be the best and only necessary linguistic means for getting a whole job done. "A whole job" can be any of the following: telling a story, providing a credible account, offering evidence, being in community, constituting a state, loving another, articulating an identity, doing justice, knowing the land, cooking a meal, enacting policy, making amends, publishing a book (even in translation), bearing witness, assuring "universal access," being "on the same page," averting a disaster, adjudicating a claim, teaching an idea, trading securities, writing code, finding the truth, colonizing Mars, decolonizing Turtle Island, or staffing a school. Monolingualism wants to prove that one single language's meaning-making resources are plenty for pulling off any of these things supremely. In this way, monolingualism is a powerful tutor in language socialization (Schieffelin and Ochs 1986) and in preserving the tyranny of existing concepts (Bull 1977).

When it sleeps, monolingualism dreams of a meaning-making world made up only of individualistic, panfunctional, isomorphic, can-do languages that fend for themselves, clear their debts daily (but avoid on-the-books debt entirely, when they can), trade predictably with their neighbors, and police their own rough-and-tumble borders in a homeostatic way. I attribute this potent and pious dream of the monolingual ideal to late seventeenth-century colonial metropoles, with for example the work of Royal Society members like Thomas Sprat, who sought to specify what would in future characterize the minimum criteria for a well-formed language. These powerful templates of empire-building and high-modern national expansionism are what I call monolanguages.

Accordingly, monolingualism's unconscious doesn't like being reminded that some languages have particular grammars that can do things that other languages' particular grammars cannot, because this fact conjures images of sovereignty, protectionism, tariff wars, and an eventual failure of the perfectibility (Butler 2004, 11) of universal grammar. Flexible and capacious in its work, monolingualism is a triage system that disposes of such dreaded imputations of unevenness and furnishes reputational security for those languages that have already gained—through nationalization, colonization, and literary supremacy—the credible distinction of being named "a language." At the same time, monolingualism will rebuke and exploit as so-called deficiencies the meaning-making differences of modality, orthography, genre, idiom, taxonomy, typology, aspect, and prosody at work in languages whose status claim as "a language" is doubted or pending.

Amid an emerging critique of monolingualism, the overall elaboration in the humanities of a counterpart definition for "multilingualism" is still rather loose, as is the case likewise for translinguality, translanguaging, plurilingualism, and other adjacent concepts, which neighboring fields have now spent some decades sorting out (Boyden and Kelbert 2018; Li Wei 2017; May 2013). One interdisciplinary discrepancy between literary studies and applied linguistics at present, for instance, is the outspoken readiness in applied linguistics to normalize and center people's "translanguaging" practices of all sorts, across the field's various domains and objects of inquiry. Li Wei describes translanguaging as

> using one's idiolect, that is one's linguistic repertoire, without regard for socially and politically defined language names and labels. [. . .] This is not to say that the speakers are not aware of the existence of the idealized boundaries between languages and between language

varieties. As part of the language socialization process, we become very much aware of the association between race, nation, and community on the one hand, and a named language on the other, and of the discrepancies between the boundaries in linguistic structural terms versus those in sociocultural and ideological terms. (2017, 12; my emphasis)

In Li Wei's gloss of translanguaging here, intended mostly for applied linguists, the word I find most consequential is "regard." Etymologically, regarding is a practice that is not just about seeing and respecting, but also about "re-guarding" something valued by the collective, and indeed about decisively intensifying the ways we guard it. For better or worse, academic literary scholarship has played a proud role in the ongoing history of guarding and re-guarding "language names and labels"—through our department names, our professional titles, our syllabi, the names of our fields, our press series labels, and even through the grooves of "comparatism" itself.

In a moment when engineers explicitly pursue LLMs for Artificial Intelligence through so-called language-agnostic strategies and designs (e.g., Ojo et al. 2023), we literary scholars might consider what it would require of us also to "disregard" the language-as-named-entity frame for analysis, and to do so while not sliding into mere "linguistic indifference" (Pipestone Group 2023)—and, specifically, not into indifference about the historical, cultural, and material effects of monolingualization (ibid.). The linguist Robin Sabino (2018)—a clear-eyed proponent of such an empirical methodology, ready to relinquish any analytical "re-guard" for languages as named entities—models her own data-rich research program upon the premise of "languaging without languages." What, in turn, might a literary studies without monolanguages eventually be and do?

A History of the World in Eight Cheap Things

While applied linguistics as an international interdiscipline has its own troubles around monolingualism, including its ongoing investment in English as the presumptive language of scholarly concept-making, it has nonetheless taken a big step toward abdicating methodological re-guard for historically named languages and language borders. It has declared this methodological commitment in ways that Anglophone literary criticism, even in a comparative mode, struggles to sustain—though venues like the *Journal of Literary Multilingualism* are taking strides to close this gap (see also Stockhammer 2017 on "langagification des langues"; see also Taylor-Batty 2013).

But more influentially perhaps, and far beyond the sphere of literary studies discourse, there are strong forces at work politically and institutionally making sure that we continue to "re-guard" monolingualism and its structural integer of monolanguage(s). The definition above for monolingualism is, after all, written in deceptively guileless and confident terms. Who determines what a "single" language is, and what makes "one" language passably countable as a single entity, much like an ocean or a sea gets deemed separately countable? The designation is never a mere semantic sleight or a naturalistic approximation, but rather in each instance of monolingualization the result of a momentous campaign of cultural capital and institutional investment over centuries.

But these monolingualization campaigns have not been forged on the national(ist) level alone—that is, in the proud name of the nation—but also, in parallel, in service of transnational economic infrastructures. In the definition of monolingualism above, I suggested that monolingualism was an ideological structure most interested in getting the "whole job" done in one language, whatever the job is. This is a telic metaphor cut from the discourse of labor productivity, and I choose it not for its terminological crudeness but for its economic rationalism.

Since Hayek in the 1940s, microeconomics has suspected that information-sharing is likely the "chief efficiency of competitive markets" (Farrell and Rabin 1996), in the sense that ordinary, informal talk plays an ill-recognized but profoundly material role for the near- and middle-term structuration of global economic activity. Since at latest the eighteenth century, workforce strategists and workplace designers have aimed to refine forms of "cheap talk" across local languages (Farrell and Rabin 1996; see also Dudley 2017) that will yield optimal economic results across markets—what economists sometimes call Pareto-optimal Nash equilibria (Farrell and Rabin 1996).

Today's late monolingualism—for all of its ultimate disinterest in the kind of cultural specificity and national sovereignty that an earlier, nineteenth-century-style high monolingualism often sought to exalt—fulfills these market aims of "cheap talk" miraculously well—by deploying Machine Translation, Large Language Models (LLMs), and Cross-Language Information Retrieval technologies that are good enough to "get the whole job done" for well-paying client corporations, and to jam through whatever fuzzy imperfections of meaning crop up along the way. For the moment, monolingualism-by-automated-multilateral-translation is the simplest and most alluring way to model global cheap talk for the cascading multiplicity of markets that suppliers and clients wish to saturate.

Eager to oblige, a current gold-rush generation of research on "language-agnostic" and "language-configurable" LLMs, published under the aegis of the Institute of Electrical and Electronic Engineers, naturalizes language borders precisely so as to manage and accelerate effective commerce across them, while alleging all the while to be dismantling inequities for "low-resourced languages." Monolingualism's resulting product, *cheap meaning*, is likely thus the eighth "thing" to add—alongside *nature, money, work, care, food, energy*, and *lives*—to Raj Patel and Jason Moore's *History of the World in Seven Cheap Things* (2018).

Monolingualism, High vs. Late

What, though, distinguishes late monolingualism (1990–present) from high monolingualism (1789–1948)—in and beyond literature? How different are literary enactments of late monolingualism from civic, industrial, political, and communicative ones more broadly? If the premise of high monolingualism—which I periodize from 1789 (Paris) to 1948 (Paris)—was the alternatingly essentialist and pragmatist centralization of language use around the available nation-state form (often through violently oppressive re-educational and military means; see also Boyer 2012 on "unilinguisme"), *late* monolingualism reflects a reluctant but unequivocal truce with the interests of global capitalism and economic anti-protectionism which, it acknowledges, have won out over nationalist attempts at cultural sovereignty as potentially expressed through language.[11]

For the critical purposes of this book, monolingualism is not however a unified phenomenon that comes to blows with another unified phenomenon called literature. Neither of these two domains is an entity, nor an essence, nor a steadily coherent discourse across all or even most languages and cultures. There are many forms, indeed traditions, of monolingualism—from the Turkish, to the te reo Māori and Bangla, to the Rooseveltian Anglo-American. And *litteratura, Dichtung,* ادب, and *edebiyat*, for their part, have always evoked different though overlapping domains, genres, formats,

---

[11] The postcolonial republic of Iceland and its language represent a valiant and deliberate twenty-first-century attempt to buck this trend, often with the consequence of being faulted for allegedly undermining internationally coordinated social justice movements in so doing (Josephson and Einarsdóttir 2016). Such attempts at protecting cultural sovereignty have been under fire since the early decolonization period of the 1940s; in 1955, the German economist and social critic Wilhelm Röpke gave a lecture at the Hague in which he insisted that "to diminish national sovereignty is most emphatically one of the urgent needs of our time" (cited in Slobodian 2018, 11).

occasions, social orders, and themes (see, for instance, El Shakry 2024). But what I will call high monolingualism is rather more generalizable because it is a model reproduced by modern nation-builders' confident and effortful pursuits of a single-language repertoire for their national communities to the exclusion of others—in the globally competitive and time-sensitive interest of national becoming (see Cerny 1997), under threat or recent memory of industrialized empire.

But beyond its brutal longue-durée employment by empire builders, extractivist colonizers, and supremacist civilizers, high monolingualism had, and has, its clear and often righteous critical purposes in various Indigenous and autochthonous settings around the world: chief among these justifications being anticolonialism, anti-Anglophone protectionism (Josephson and Einarsdóttir 2016), cultural sovereignty (Domokos 2016), and national self-determination. Consider the Dominican critic Pedro Henríquez Ureña, writing in his 1928 *Seis ensayos en busca de nuestra expresión*:

> We have not renounced writing in Spanish, and the problem of an original expression of our own begins there. Each language is a crystallization of modes of thinking and feeling, and everything written in it is bathed in the color of its crystal. Our expression will need redoubled vigor to impose its tones over the red and the golden yellow. ([1928], English translation from Sánchez Prado 2023, 58)[12]

As Henríquez Ureña saw it, not only did his Latin American comrades' literary Spanish need to excel aesthetically, it had to do so in ways that vividly superseded Iberian Spanish so as to undo the Spanish crown's presumptive claim upon it. High monolingualism in this nationalizing and anticolonial mode was (and remains) an urgent and arduous means to equalize a chosen single language to its elite philological competitors in Europe, and to deepen its independent aesthetic commitment to local affairs and communities.

Dominican or Mexican monolingualism in literary Spanish wasn't meant to be an inheritor and extender of Europe's high literary cultures, but rather to exhibit in every sentence a free agency that overcomes such an inheritance, by flaunting its own depth of panfunctional specificity. Effectiveness in such overcoming would enable any curious reading "user" of that monolanguage to immerse themselves—in Marie-Laure Ryan's contemporary terms—in the

---

[12] "No hemos renunciado a escribir en español, y nuestro problema de la expresión original y propia comienza ahí. Cada idioma es una cristalización de modos de pensar y de sentir, y cuanto en él se escribe se baña en el color de su cristal. Nuestra expresión necesitará doble vigor para imponer su tonalidad sobre el rojo y el gualda." (Henríquez Ureña [1928] 2020, 13)

representational idiom of Dominican life, "to move around the virtual space and [...] apprehend it under various points of view" (1994, 11).

Unevenly but prohibitively, key literary genres throughout the modern era of nationalizing imagined communities prided themselves around a humanistic drive to plump and emboss authoritative named languages (American English, Russian, Czech, Brazilian Portuguese, Mexican Spanish, Egyptian Arabic, post-Ottoman "pure" Turkish) for a mix of regional, civilizatory, national, educative, and globalist objectives (Anderson [1983] 2006). In turn, those proud novelistic languages became mystified as ballasts against industrial dehumanization, economic internationalism, and mere instrumentality. The novel became a main vitalizing shrine to such emerging monolanguages' sacred and enduring credibility; it became the modern monolanguage's vivid global "communicator" for the uniquely historical spirit of the nation, as potently attested in most Nobel Prize for Literature conferral announcements over the past century.

Noorani (2013), however, shows how campaigns to mystify a charismatic literary monolanguage in this way didn't necessarily promote linguistic sovereignty, nor did the efforts mean crystallizing for a certain language repertoire more emic national specificity than it may have evidenced in previous ages. Pan-Arab and Arab nationalist poetry in the 1910s onward tended rather, as Noorani demonstrates, to adopt a panoramic mode of address (Saktanber 2002, 269) that intended to be stylistically legible to other sibling nationalist movements the world over, whereas its lush courtly predecessor languages had neither attempted nor succeeded at being externally compelling in this way to anyone, besides perhaps to philologists.

This new soft literary nationalism could function as a kind of embossed exogamous signaling register, where the hierarchy of intended readers (i.e., intralingual primary readers versus crosslingual secondary readers in translation), was flipped—or at least rendered into parallel and complementary interpellations. In part as a result of this kind of gradual reorganization of intended addressees, Jaroslav Stetkevych could claim in 1970 that "the contemporary Arabic literary language has crossed its genealogical linguistic borders and has entered into cultural linguistic affinity with the broad supragenealogical family of modern Western languages" (115). Orhan Pamuk's 2002 Turkish-language novel *Snow* is, I have argued, a vivid critical diagram portraying how ostensibly nationalist literature can get repurposed into a "transmission belt" for international attentions (Cox 1992; Gramling 2007).

A strategic intension within high monolingualism was thus often not to intensify languages typologically in their own contexts and climes, but rather to cast off the cherished rhetorical conventions that might frustrate outsiders' grasp, to smooth and soften the way for the kind of transparent competitive mutuality and panoramic etic address that would serve as ante for a sensible global race for national self-distinction. Amid this mystified linguistic resplendence of the modern novel, any enduring worries about looming language standardization or economistic monolingualism had to be swept under the rug as, at worst, an awkward externality.

Today's late monolingualism is, I believe, one of the many sociopolitical domains where intense practical investment in an ideology does not necessarily reflect actual credence or substantive conviction among its adherents and engineers (Riley [1979] 1983). Late monolingualism is a facilitative structure for economic optimization, rather than the trusty artifact of a belief system. It is a paradigm that has expediently opted to inherit what was prepared and bequeathed to it by its zealous high-monolingual predecessors—namely, the accrued cultural, conceptual, and institutional capital put in service of the unquestioned pretext of a world made up of well-bordered, panfunctional, named languages as the required vehicles for global commerce, communication, and political emergence. But, at newly global scales and financialized ends, late monolingualism strives harder than high monolingualism did to ensure through technological means "that structural incompatibilities between languages have been and continue to be eliminated" (Noorani 2013, 9).

In both cases, high and late, monolingualism comprises dual and mutually quickening ideologies that are relatively independent of speakers' actual beliefs and practices. It is devoted to the premise of lingualism (i.e., that bounded and totalizing languages exist and are the natural basis for planetary linguistic ecology; Stockhammer 2017) as well as to the premise of monolingualism itself (that one language is enough, and that exhibiting more or less than one language-in-use for a particular task indicates an alarming deficiency, methodological inefficiency, circumstantial exception, or symbolic excess). I will occasionally place a slash in mono/lingualism to suggest that there is a mutually reinforcing relation between monolingualism and lingualism. In 1991, the historian Jonathan Dollimore used the slash, rather than hyphen, in a similar way in "post/modernism" to indicate that "post" was not a temporal distinction from a preexisting modernism so much as an ongoing recursive relation between modernism and its critical rejection.

Late Monolingualism as an Antielitist Expert Discourse of Capillary Power

I suggested above that neither monolingualism nor the novel genre is a unified entity, essence, or tradition—or at least they haven't had a shot at being so until the last few decades of effective institutional, corporate, and infrastructural globalization. Indeed, the once messy and hyperlocal phenomena of multilingualism, monolingualism, and translation in literary publishing have each been innovated into something new and increasingly coordinated over the past forty years, as the first algorithmic, corpus-based Machine Translation platforms began their rollout.

No longer is monolingualism presumably a nationalist rallying cry for linguistic purism, multilingualism a sheer liberatory or cosmopolitan vision, or literary translation a slow artisanal craft. Amid profound technological and economic reorderings of planetary markets and institutions since the 1970s, each of these realms (monolingualism, multilingualism, and translation) has been fused infrastructurally with the others to become part of a globally interlocking delivery platform for commercial products—linguistic, literary, and material alike.

As much as many of us would love to have a say in the matter, this transformation has stormed social life with the same unrelenting, intense convergence of interests and resources as has neoliberalism, making potential rebellion (as is explored in Nors's *Mirror, Shoulder, Signal* and Tidbeck's *Amatka*, for instance) feel like more of a private reverie than a powerful social movement. But while these sociopolitical transformations are momentous and intriguing processes on their own, this book is primarily concerned with how these changes register in literary fictions, particularly in novels.

There are many ways to chart out such a momentous change in how the functions and potentials of language have been literarily seen, aesthetically apprehended, and technologically harnessed in the commodity form of the novel. We could begin tracing late literary monolingualism in the 1980s, starting with literary publishers' awareness about customs deregulation and the transnationalization of corporate holdings, when international (literary) trade could no longer be plausibly designed as a sequence of one-by-one bilateral (and bilingual) market relationships (Rectanus 1987; Thompson 2010; Mazzucato 2018; Kelly-Holmes 2010).

By the 1990s, mere bilateral relationships for distribution were simply too clunky, costly, and specific to promise the kind of future revenue that literary trade corporations were preparing for (Hall and Soskice 2001). To future-proof their operations, corporate clients needed a securitized wall-to-wall multilingual outlay, assured through low- or no-delay translation services (Kelly-Holmes 2010, 196). This newly intensive orientation toward languages quickly came to form the revenue baseline for any commercial enterprise that sought to compete on a global field. Languages were no longer a pesky externality of doing regular business, delegated as needed to local language experts; now they required stabilized valuation as a systematic and financialized precondition for industrial revenue "at scale." A newly antielitist class of computational engineers foresaw the need to replace the once indispensable local translator with the kind of "capillary power [. . .] [that] act[s] without the trappings of authority or public status" and that "exists outside of any norms of discourse or conduct" (Davies 2017, 229).

In the hands of this new antielitist expert class of engineers, who are keyed into the computational needs of financial technology, language(s) have effectively crossed what economists call the "production boundary" (Mazzucato 2018), in similar ways as financial products and services got recategorized as "value creating" in the 1970s. Languages and meanings now are expected to be active participants in securitized, free-marketized trade—that is, to be valuated, even if they are not valued. The recent boom in celebratory thinking about multilingualism, in and outside of academia, has much more to do with this new financialized value-creating matrix for multilingual commodities than it might with shifting political horizons, post-migration social diversity, and the announced decline of the ethnonational state.

(Authors) Theorizing Late Literary Monolingualism

Any number of important theoretical studies could be made of late monolingualism in a range of fields and phenomena—from sociology to finance to law to engineering, advertising, gaming, and theater. But this one book intends to address, in a modest but persistent way, a theory deficit in the relationship between monolingualism, global political economy, literature, and literary translation.

Traditions of Eurocentric literary theory—emanating from France, the United Kingdom, Germany, and the United States over the course of the twentieth century—have not had enough to say about multilingual authorship. The resulting default assumption of a "near-native" monolingual creative author in philosophy and literary theory has left multilingual authorship underthought and marked as a sociological phenomenon rather than a form of critical subjectivity. Texts written by conspicuously multilingual authors (Komska 2018) tend to garner among researchers a kind of forensic attention to so-called interlanguage phenomena, which are evaluated negatively or positively depending on the institutional setting (Matsuda 2014). Or, they are celebrated biographically as an expression of a multilingual life the author has lived.

Though these kinds of research queries (the biographical and interlingual) are not unreasonable or unimportant in any sense, they chafe against some golden rules of Global Northwestern literary theory in the New Critical vein (namely, through their intentionalism, instrumentalism, and biographical reading). Southern and Indigenous approaches to literature often have no such preemptory objections, viewing these intentionalist and instrumentalist methods as obviously crucial to the interactional occasions in which stories are told (sitholé 2024), but these approaches are often registered tacitly as incommensurable with Eurocentric literary critique.

In the main, too, literary *theory* has been slow to take up ongoing transformations in the computational sciences, data-mining, Artificial Intelligence, and Machine Translation, domains where the very nature of global multilingualism is being reengineered before our eyes. Because the proprietary work of translation engineers does not squarely address the lay practices and beliefs of any identifiable end user, any apparently coherent language ideology, or any conceptual regime, the rhetorical habits of global supply-side multilingual information infrastructures and platforms remain quite invisible in literary studies. In the chapters to come, the novels suggest ways in which research about literary aesthetics and craft ought to be reconnected with these questions in information science and algorithmic translation systems development, so as to accurately characterize the historic specificity of such networked discourses around multilingual phenomena and their implications for knowledge and meaning in contemporary practice.

What late monolingualism foists most compulsorily onto literature-making is a political economy of multilateral translatability and translatedness. Here it helps to distinguish between translation, translatability, and translatedness—with *translation* being a craft, while *translatability* is a means of production whose commodity or security form is *translatedness*. While the hermetic, diplomatic mode of translation throughout history always required profoundly normative and exacting practices, these tended to respond primarily to the semi-sovereign forces of a host and/or target culture. This bilateral anthropological convention gave rise to Schleiermacher's (1813) methodological question about whether and when it is most suitable to make translations align to domestic or foreign attributes in their translated state.

But that useful binary from Schleiermacher has begun to dissolve amid a late globalism that yearns enduringly to stabilize meaning, style, ideas, and information across scores of languages—not by way of bilingual pairings, but upon an omnilingual grid. The *fremd–eigen* (self–other) dilemma clarifies much less now for us in 2024 than it did even in 1994 for instance, and the notion of a "domesticated" English-to-German translated text does not carry the explanatory or practical weight it once did. As Dorthe Nors's novel *Mirror, Shoulder, Signal* depicts so vividly (as we will see in Chapter 2), the historically robust category of "domestic" has been itself riven through at the most minute levels with globalized instrumentalizations, commodifications, and retrofittings.

The comparatist Başak Çandar helps explain why this state of literary and linguistic affairs since the 1990s has been so difficult for many of us (lay user and expert alike) to come to grips with adequately:

> Having been born in the 1990s, my students had spent their entire lives being surrounded by praises of globalization and ambiguous concepts like "global citizenship." Throughout the discussion, it became clear that their difficulty had more to do with their reflexive assumption that the "worldliness" suggested by the phrase "feeling at home in the world" is a positive and desirable quality. [. . .] Surrounded by so much talk about an increasingly more open and navigable world, students understandably struggled to see the violence that can underpin global connectedness, a connectedness that is also postulated in optimistic terms by World Literature's emphasis on circulation. (Çandar 2021, 144)

Of course, cultures (and literary cultures specifically) have never been pure or protected from one another, having always interlaced with substrates and spectacles of foreignness. But it's a different ballgame now, when the referentialities that are at large in a text issue not so much just from a hybrid and colonial cultural history, nor from one more or less dense cultural tradition, but rather from a globalized template of potentially valuated translatabilities, a grand "omnilingual aspiration," as Kellman (2016) calls it, for political economy broadly.

Such a germinal moment for late (literary) monolingualism, where languages have come to be valued in a newly economistic and industrial way, might seem to suggest a positive opening of consciousness: a move beyond either the linguistic elitism of universities, or the linguistic indifference we may have come to expect from neoclassical economic or Taylorist industrial reasoning. Wouldn't recognizing languages in commerce and global economy be a good thing for literature, bringing new credit to speakers' meaning-making practices in 7000 world languages—rather than just in the industrial-strength leviathan of global English we'd made do with in the late twentieth century (Gordin 2015; Hogan-Brun 2017)? Doesn't this new reliance on language-mediating technologies augur well for a kind of future that might acknowledge how important language(s) are for planetary well-being and justice on various scales?

I do not trust that this is the case, nor do the authors presented in the following chapters. Like other practical fields about which economic reasoning has long been indifferent or ambivalent—homemaking, raising children, sexuality, and affect, to name a few examples—pulling languages back into the fray of financialized market valuation does not bode very well for marginalized speakers and writers, let alone for languages themselves (Mazzucato 2018). Alas, the values we may wish to see vindicated for the "dear meanings" that dwell by virtue of our various languages are often reliably overshadowed by the workings of the global "price system" (ibid.).

As we close this Introduction and turn to the novels, I will attempt to summarize these introductory claims about the current linguistic age of late monolingualism, which I date from 1990:

- "Late" monolingualism is, for the purpose of this book, understood as a historical period—rather than as the empirical state of linguistic proficiency of any individual, nation, or community. The modifier "late" is meant to dislodge the label "monolingual" from its presumptive applicability to individual persons.
- Late monolingualism is a structure that perceives and anticipates global threats to high-modern national monolingualism as a form, and innovates responsive techniques, platforms, and orders to refortify it, to prop it up artificially. These fortifications constitute an infrastructure, retrofitted onto the preexisting affordances of nationalist monolingualism(s), so as to insulate and secure it in perpetuity and with impunity.
- The idea of late monolingualism shares with late capitalism (Jameson, Mandel, Sombart, etc.) a general sense of intrigue about the persistence and non-obsolescence of its respective high modern predecessor form. While energetic notions about hybridity and transnationalism boomed in the 1990s, many scholars, myself included, have been taken aback to witness a deepening and thickening of monolingual administrative, civic, literary, political, and racialized designs instead—precisely in a moment where the dismantling of these seemed most possible and at hand.
- Unlike "late capitalism," the lateness of monolingualism does not—or at least need not—presuppose an underlying Marxian historicist logic of some kind, though neither does it exclude one. Economic systems have been bountifully theorized throughout modernity, but there has been no accompanying linguistic dimension to these historicist intellectual traditions of thought in economics and political economy. For this reason, the "late" in late monolingualism is not expected to correspond to existing historicist models or state forms, whether Marxist or anti-Marxist.
- The infrastructure of late monolingualism is now generally designed and patented by computational engineers and funded by client governments, private firms, lobbied legislators and jurists, and military contractors. Its business idiom is adequacy, compliance, and unobjectionability rather than precision, originality, and accuracy.

- Late monolingualism began to set in practically around 1990, with the first corpus- and algorithm-driven Cross-Language Information Retrieval technologies, which made the multilateral management of language-born information plausible on a large scale. Its earliest practical prototype vision—what Stephen Kellman calls its "omnilingual aspiration" (2016)—was the 1948 Universal Declaration of Human Rights, a document which was deemed juridically original in over 500 languages.[13]
- The infrastructure of late monolingualism is agnostic about the cultural substance of any particular linguistic nationalism, but rather encases the national form in a particular way that ensures free-market ordoliberalism while fending off protectionist and decolonial sovereignty—preempting linguistic activism, untranslatability discourse, Indigenous cultural sovereignty, hard multilingualism (Noorani 2013), linguistic protectionism, and "hard" translanguaging (Li Wei 2017; see definition above, and sitholé and Gramling 2025).

Conclusion: Rematriating Linguistic Sovereignty

Particularly for those whose forebears fought mightily—often against hope and evidence—so that there might someday be a robust contemporary community of speakers and readers, and even a landscape of institutions and publishing houses, who would finally be in a safe position to receive and savor new texts together in their language (originals, translations, and even governing documents in Cree, Bengali, Tigrinya, Bosnian, Yiddish, Scots, Sámi, or Kurdish, for instance), reading a so-called monolingual text in one's favored language may feel, each and every time, like nothing less than a spiritual triumph, with all of the convivial pleasures of survivance that come with it (Vizenor 2008).

I have learned to see monolingualism (in the sense of linguistic protectionism) as a set of potentially potent decolonial strategies, important in Southern and Indigenous literary, linguistic, and political work. Just because French, English, and German literary monolingualism may be seen as bygone, pernicious, nineteenth-century visions doesn't mean everyone else needs to relinquish their designs on the power and promise of strategic monolingualism too. When the Nordic Sámi Indigenous poet, Nils-Aslak

---

[13] Thanks to Dante Prado for pointing out to me Anca Parvulescu and Manuela Boatcă's inquiry, in *Creolizing the Modern* (2022), about a predecessor instance to the UDHR: the *Acta Comparationis Literarum Universarum* (ACLU), edited by Sámuel Brassai and Hugó Meltzl between 1877 and 1888.

Valkeapää issued an explicit interdiction on the translation of two poems from his book *Beaivi, áhčážan* (1991, translated from North Sámi into English as *The Sun, My Father* in 1997 by Ralph Salisbury, Lars Nordstrom, and Harald Gaski), it was tempting for critics to accuse him of being a spoilsport in an age of linguistic hybridity, intercultural communication, and the right to translatedness (see also Domokos 2016).

Particularly moving on this question is Jenny Zhang and Yanti's 2019 methodological study about the status of multilingual research interviews in Nusa Tenggara Timur Province (Indonesia), where the researchers point out that "for many on [their] team, anti-essentialist critiques directly contradicted what they saw as realities: that their languages are ancient, direct inheritances from their nenek moyang (ancestors)" (94). I do hope the critique of late monolingualism proposed in this book does not misrecognize such transgenerational realities of experience and relation in ancestral language. Ultimately, a key prerogative of Indigenous or decolonial linguistic sovereignty (sometimes also negatively connoted as cultural "protectionism") is to rebuke settler concepts and frameworks that—whatever their alleged probative grounding in a long-legitimated settler discourse may be—are found unsuitable to the needs and self-understandings of a contemporary Indigenous community.

Unfortunately, for any of us who cherish the languages we use, late monolingualism is a structure that tends to fake interest in communities and local epistemologies, seeking only to capture them as markets and saturate them with recursive monopsony iterations.[14] Often enough, these monolingualization processes take place under the financial, curricular, policy, or ideological auspices of "multilingualism" or "multiculturalism" and enjoy the cover of these terms and their kind of have-your-cake-and-eat-it-too late style. Late monolingualism retains and in fact emboldens the reassuring comforts and pastoral foreclosures of high monolingualism, even while laying symbolic claim to the presumed virtues of the multilingual, the intercultural, the accessible, and the translatable. Late monolingualism is one

---

[14] The reason I characterize such revenue-generating socio-technological iteration-delivery pathways for harvesting everyday language as a pattern of "monopsony"—a market arrangement where there is only one buyer—is that, though various developers are always vying to purchase access to large batches of our everyday linguistic practices (via our computers and phones), all such competitive buyers still tend to impact us vaguely as one undifferentiated power in the seller–buyer dyad, because we subjugated "sellers" have not yet begun to conceive and organize ourselves in any practical way as actual actors with specific interests and rational priorities in the sale. The 2023 SAG-AFTRA strike was, in contrast, a moment in which a class of sellers of iterative data (i.e., their likeness for AI purposes) first recognized and organized around the conditions of the competitive market, at which point an effective monopsony revealed itself to be either an oligopsony of large buyers or potentially a polyopsony of many smaller ones.

among many "safe space for the privileged" quality-of-life discourses that few real people actually asked for. It is no lay or popular phenomenon, but rather a kitsch product line engineered through elite closure (Myers-Scotton 1993; Táíwò 2022).

Such settler designs on language(s) may be difficult to spot in an age eager to mine the frontiers between languages for revenue, and to promote soft forms of cultural extractivism under color of intercultural understanding. Helpful in this regard is Paul Worley's (2017) concept of neoliberal translation, which identifies a mode of "translation [which] allows for the production and presentation of Indigenous-language texts so long as these are reduced, almost by definition, to being a symbolic supplement to Spanish texts that are actually read" (291). For Analisa Taylor, such neoliberal translation is part of a broader "strategy to manage and redirect the radical propositions of [Indigenous] movements in ways that do not alter the basic power relations between rulers and ruled" (2009, 112).

For attempts to ascertain what kinds of lingualism, monolingualism, translation, and multilingualism do or do not "alter the basic power relations between rulers and ruled" in this moment in history, Eve Tuck (2011) suggests a movement of *rematriation*:

> to uncover the quiet thoughts and beliefs of a community; map the variety of ideas in a community; make generational knowledge of elders, youth, parents, warriors, hunters, leaders, gardeners, fishers, teachers, and others available to other generations; use home languages to express ideas, and to bring new language to new and recovered ideas; and honor all of our relations by engaging in the flow of knowledge in community in ways that reflect epistemology/cosmology and relationships to land. (36)

In the end, many of us in contemporary life truly and rightfully yearn for products made in or for "our" language(s), and our land(s). We hunt passionately for stories written or spoken in that language environment, and prize unobstructed ease of understanding through an idiom we consider to be our own. Whether the socio-aesthetic context be sheer literary enjoyment, or a surprising, passing chat with a new friend, I hold with Deborah Tannen that

> [t]he emotional/aesthetic experience of a perfectly tuned conversation is as ecstatic as an artistic experience. The satisfaction of having communicated successfully goes beyond the pleasure of being

understood in the narrow sense. It is a ratification of one's place in the world and one's way of being human. It is, as Becker calls a well-performed shadow play, "a vision of sanity." (1981, 145)

Ultimately, the specific kinds of pleasurable, transformative, and even ecstatic conversations or literary exchanges that happen between people will always be expressed in a broad range of linguistic forms, ranging from conservative single-language repertoires to the most radical forms of translanguaging practice. There are endless (multilingual and monolingual) ways to have a communicative experience that serves as such a vision of sanity, to tell a story that dignifies and dimensionalizes experience, and to find one's true—though often dispossessed—home in this world through languages. I believe the novels prized, and critiqued, in the chapters to come lend energetic evidence toward this very modest ideal.

1

A Citizen's Compromise

"Let's mark all the things in here," Vanja sang under her breath, letting her eyes wander around the room. "Table, chair, and a pot here; stovetop, fridge, and pantry there. We mark all the things in our care."
"The Marking Song" was part of everyone's life, from the first day at the children's house. When Vanja was younger, marking day at the children's house was the best day of the week.
—Karin Tidbeck, *Amatka* (2017a, 21)[1]

Vanja tillbringade eftermiddagen på sitt rum, insvept i täcket, vid skrivbordet. Genom fönstret syntes bara hustak och drivhusens kurvor långt bort. Om Drivhus 7 bordet framför henne, full av trygga beskrivningar av världen, tryggare och tryggare för varje gång de lästes. Det var som märksången de sjöng varje eftermiddag på barnhuset.
"Nu ska ni märka allting här," sjöng hon lågt för sig själv och lät blicken vandra runt rummet, "stolen bordet och pennan där, kudden lampan och filten där. För nu marker vi allting här."
—Karin Tidbeck, *Amatka* (2012, 84–5)

Karin Tidbeck's 2012 Swedish-language speculative-fiction novel *Amatka* gets us thinking about a world, or a kind of world, in which objects turn to a menacing gloop (kladd) if citizens do not regularly call things by their names and, thereby, "care" for them through linguistic reiteration. Preventing a cataclysmic flood of goo, we're told, means refastening names securely to

---

[1] Even a quick parallel look at the start-text in Swedish, alongside Tidbeck's self-translation of it into English, reveals that the two passages are jarringly unsimilar, the translation having jettisoned major textual portions to other locations within the book. Given that the novel is itself a story about the compulsion to protect the integrity of objects through ongoing normative linguistic reiteration, it will be a key concern of this chapter to understand how the manifest inconsistency of the novel from (source) iteration to (self-translated) iteration—or, in other terms, such wanton relinquishment of translingual equivalence to the nightmare of "goofication"—itself stages a subtle theory of literature in late monolingualism, via the combined macrotext of the novel (O'Neill 2005).

things, by writing/speaking their common label directly upon them—all the time. In the starkly unmetaphorical world of Tidbeck's novel, a key tenet of civic responsibility (and thus, allegedly, of personal safety) is speaking the normative names for things aloud—whether one is alone or in social company—so as to constantly reinstate objects' material integrity.

Of course, getting people to say things over and over, so as to certify and stabilize a proposed object-of-value, isn't necessarily a figment of science fiction. As computer scientist Paul Dourish and colleagues attest in their methodological reflections on Human-Centered Computing, or Human-Computer Interaction (HCI), a lot more collaboration of this sort is demanded of speakers/language-users these days than in previous eras:

> If there is one practice that is characteristic of HCI design, it is its commitment to iteration and to a cycle of prototyping, testing, and re-design in order to work towards solutions that are effective in fitting with user and community needs. [. . .] From that point of view, the practice of iteration comprises, at its most basic, a laying-in-front of users (or their proxies) something that is not-quite-ready. It asks that people take the time to explore something that may or may not be "ready for prime time" or which embodies only in embryo those features and functions that we hope may be of value. Iteration, then, demands a good deal of its audience. Iteration demands patience. Iteration demands forbearance. Iteration demands an acceptance of the not-quite and the not-yet. Iteration demands hope and a commitment to investment now for benefit down the line. Iteration demands that people accept a down-payment now on a debt to be settled later. And iteration demands that people recognize that small steps lead to future benefits. (2020, 3)

While previous eras of materials development and technological innovation did not require, nor desire, this kind of affectively intensive scaled-up participation from citizens—relying instead on postproduction marketing and advertising—Dourish's team points to a newly entangled global culture of iteration since the 1990s, in which we speakers are unceasingly asked to involve ourselves for free in unknown developers' proprietary technological innovations. We are asked to speak, opine, try out, focus-group, troubleshoot, debug, validate, discuss, adopt, finetune, beta-test, accept the terms, provide feedback, and "learn more" (see, for instance, Salas-Zarate et al. 2017 and Baur 2017 on "opinion mining")—and to do all this, in and through our own embodied voices and minds, by dint of our own civic volition to improve what we perceive to be the state of things in our civilizations.

If Dorthe Nors's novel *Mirror, Shoulder, Signal* from Chapter 2 will be anguished by the vertiginous compromises of translating for a late monolingual literary order, *Amatka*'s vigilant anxiety is rather about the pressure to iterate in a social world structured around a looming sense that absolutely no one can afford to be linguistically inattentive, aloof, or indifferent, even for a short elapse of time (see Pipestone Group 2023). In all settings, Amatkans need to speak early, often, and in specific normative, monolingual ways, whether or not they really have a point to make in any propositional sense.

One might think about the kind of test question we human speakers are frequently taught to ask ourselves before opening our own mouths in prickly or boring meetings: *Does it need to be said, does it need to be said by me, does it need to be said right now?* The reason this principle for restraint of pen and tongue does not apply on Amatka is that the primary and urgent reason for speaking at all, ever, is precisely to reconstitute and stabilize an otherwise materially voluble Real World—to terraform or socioform it, in ways sanctioned by Amatka's communal–colonial government. Everyone must pitch in. Today's "language-agnostic" methodologies and analytics on Earth, which many Natural Language Processing engineers are racing to implement in this moment of globalized language-technological innovation (e.g., Ojo et al. 2023), are not a luxury that ordinary Amatkans believe they can afford. Amatkan citizens know they must be on-call, enthusiastic iterative validators for what computational engineers call Named-Entity Recognition (e.g., Zaghir et al. 2023).

On Amatka, linguistic duties-to-care through practices of denotation and annotation are an austere matter of survival—and a fundamental mutual social obligation. We, and Amatka's citizens, are given to understand that the atmospheric and chemical conditions on this world accelerate a general tendency toward physical disintegration, and that it is as much a collective responsibility to keep things well labeled as it is, for instance, to grow food—food that also must be vigilantly relabeled at all times, lest it disintegrate before Amatkans' eyes and stomachs. When this happens, the infectious, gloopy ruins of the commodity are as much a civic threat as is the loss of the commodity itself.

Since things will melt into gloop when they are not called out to and stenciled, continuously, using their agreed-upon and unadorned common names, neglect turns out to be primarily a linguistic vice, and its antidote is a tensely monitored plain-language communitarian monolingualism (whether that be in the novel's start-textual Swedish from 2012 or in its self-translation into English from 2017). Among ordinary citizens, a most banal and omnipresent shortcoming like absentmindedness can metastasize into a socio-logistical, and therefore political, scandal. Any person's momentary failure to relabel things at adequate intervals—to recompose them—has menacing results. Amatka's main character Vanja, a mid-level government bureaucrat, remembers with a shudder how:

> The third shelf on the wall was hers, not that she owned anything other than some washing products and a toothbrush. She reached for her toiletry bag, mumbled "toiletry bag," and opened it.
>
> She twitched and almost dropped the bag in the sink when she saw the contents. The bottom of the bag was coated in a thick paste. It was the toothbrush. She'd been careless. She'd noticed it on the train: the letters TOOTHBRUSH etched into the shaft had begun to lose their definition. Still, she'd thought it would last a little while longer. (20)[2]

When Vanja reaches for her toiletry bag and mumbles "toiletry bag," this semiprivate self-talk is an act of civic devotional reconstitution—not only of one valued object and its proximal surroundings, but of the monolanguage itself that is there to secure them again and again, forever. The act's performativity is temporally complex and emotionally dynamic, because there is always a foreboding, ill-defined time lag between Vanja's re-utterances (perfunctory or enthusiastic as they may be) and the potential negative outcomes of her negligence at relabeling. (Note that sincerity or heartfeltness are never required in such acts of speaking, just constantly adequate manufacture.)

Every mumble of a common name for an object is a kind of iterative deposit into an insurance policy against civic disintegration, a "downpayment" (in Dourish et al.'s terms above), on a future benefit. Here, meaning and its materializations are corpus driven, that is, ensured by the constant, collective, embodied provisioning of "natural language" words by actual speakers (Dourish et al. 2020; see, for example, Tholpadi et al. 2017) into the care of a hidden-hand monopsony. Citizens provide their voices for free, so that they and their inherited colonial project might survive a day longer.

But it is not just chemical and metaphysical conditions that call for linguistic austerity; the hardship conditions colonial Amatkans face have led, allegedly, to social upheavals that prompt even more linguistic austerity from

---

[2] Den tredje i raden av väggfasta hyllor ovanför karet var hennes, inte för att hon hade mer än tvättprodukter och en tandborste. Hon tog tvålasken, mumlade "ask," och öppnade den för att ta ut tvålen.
   När hon såg innehållet ryckte hon till och tappade nästan asken i handfatet. Den var fylld med en formlös massa. Hon hade slarvat. Redan på tåget hade hon tydligt sett att ordet. TVÅL, som var stansat genom blocket, hade börjat tappa formen. Hon hade trott att den skulle hålla sig (17).

the Central Administration, as well as more assurances from the Center about its commitment to justice and transparency in governance. Tidbeck's textual style dramatizes the studied repertoire of practical plain-language strategies (linguistic and apparently nonlinguistic) that such a strong coordinated interest in monolingual and translingual commensuration entails. Much like the publishing industry that has acquired Tidbeck's novel, this practical linguistic world of Amatka is structured around several anxieties about linguistic transparency, which are vigorously inculcated through a civilizing narrative of cause and effect. The necessity of plain, nonmetaphoric language is presented to Amatka's citizens as follows, through the vaguely instructive memory of a tragic event in the colonial past:

> After the tragic events that lay waste to Sunborough, it is the decision of the Central Administration that all names of places and people in the colonies be regulated, effective immediately. Any name that refers to a thing or animal, is immediately homonymic with a word used to denote another meaning in modern language, or in any other way attributes qualities to the place or person shall be changed to an approved name. Approved names shall be simple and mirror the origin of the majority of the pioneers. All place-names will be replaced with a letter combination chosen at random. (199)[3]

In this way, Amatka's civilizers wish to ensure a purely *denotative* world, one that suppresses historical connotations and any wayward, idiolectal, evocative kinds of performativity they may promote. Words on Amatka are always threatening to become loose cannons of meaningful accidence and must be controlled and corralled. Admittedly, such a stance has the potential to offer an ideologically neutral proceduralism designed for true emergency conditions with specific real-time communicative exigencies—rather than, say, for a long-term Stalinist culture or a neoliberal culture of compromise (Smith 2021). This is a militant precautionary measure against non-accidence, of disambiguation, and of linguistic efficiency—not one of overt propaganda, violence against an alien other, or even of disinformation. If we

---

[3] Efter den tragiska händelse som ödelagt Solgård, är det Centralstyrelsens beslut att omedelhart reglera samtliga plats- och personnamn som finns i bruk i kolonierna. Alla namn som hänvisar till ett ting, djur, på annat sätt är en omedelbar homonym till ett ord som används i annan betydelse i modernt språkbruk, eller som på annat sätt tillskriver personen eller platsen egenskaper, skall ändras till ett godkänt namn. Namnen skall vara enkla och spegla den kultur majoriteten av pionjärerna stammar från. Enskilda undantag görs för vanliga namn med utländskt ursprung som kan sägas passa in rent ljudmässigt. Alla platsnamn ersätts med en slumpmässigt utvald bokstavskombination (205–6).

are to take Amatka's Central Administration at its word, everyday language simply *needs* to work this way so as to keep Amatkans' cherished frontier world from physically disintegrating.

Monolanguage as Solutionism

Amatkans' civic compulsion to mark the world in plain, compromissory language is generally taken up not as a burden or imposition, but as the mere opportunity cost for advancement and discovery in a challenging, pioneering world. Citizens respond to this mandate with a spirit of stoic self-evidentness. Whatever state repression and silencing there is in Amatkan society, it is masked by the energetic incitement to speak and speak and speak—so as to hold "our world" together before it's too late. Communication does not just facilitate and soothe good social relations; it vouchsafes the very material ground upon which those social relations are to take place.

Among other things, Earth's late monolingualism angles in this way to fortify its stakeholders against the post-postmodern dread that maybe things themselves (countries, societies, ecosystems) may really be falling apart in a damaging (rather than a liberating or creatively disruptive) way—and that they therefore require an urgent *common language* to save them. Think about the strong tendency among UN sustainability conferences (COPs) around the world to choose English as their conference language, on the implicit premise that we just don't have time for messy, gloopy multilingual negotiations about climate emergency. In this expeditious mode, late monolingualism proposes that humans need a shared, transcontextual idiom—preferably one reigning authoritatively and accessibly across scores of cultures and differences—to solve humanity's grand challenges *now*.

This kind of monolingual solutionism comes in many forms, including some that appear at first multilingual. The 1948 Universal Declaration of Human Rights was such an omnilingual aspiration (Kellman 2016), which sought to "restore" an authoritative moral vocabulary to humanity in the immediate wake of the Third Reich and the Shoah, and to do so by claiming all of the combined totemic power of the 549 juridically equated languages in which the document was eventually produced, from Valencian to Kafi noono.

But as Kellman spells out, the drafting and early adoption period of the UDHR was abundant with contention about whose and which moral categories should get marquee billing, and what constituted an adequate translingual equivalent for "torture," "occupation," "dignity," and the like in Mandarin, Arabic, and Hebrew—let alone for a range of eventual Indigenous-led language adoptions. Despite the idealized and capacious omnilingual–commensurative design the UDHR's planners foresaw, many of the "equal" languages' versions ended up being more like disaffected direct reports to the hypercentral versions in French and English. Their drafters fought losing battles of persuasion about the profound dissensus of meaning, even in a word like "dignity/Würde" when comparing between Latinate and Germanic lineages.

Whether we do or do not tend to agree that humanity needs such clarifying translingual codifications addressing climate emergency and genocide in unison, we will nonetheless likely still want—for different reasons in either case—to critically track the constituencies and operational premises of such drafting conclaves for translingual commensuration, and to be wary of their urgently performative spirit of civic necessity. But, since the Shoah, this kind of purposeful compromise-driven verbal hygiene (Cameron 1995) has ranged far beyond the realm of moral caution alone.

In the late 1970s, for instance, the Swedish manufacturer of telecommunications equipment Telefonaktiebolaget LM Ericsson sought out a private–public partnership with the University of Wales's Institute of Science and Technology. They wanted help producing a new version of industrial language called Ericsson English (EE). Users of this frontier language of commerce would compromise in many of the same ways citizens in Amatka willingly do:

1. Do not use synonyms.
2. Do not make long strings of nouns or adjectives before a noun.
3. Do not add prefixes or suffixes to EE words to make new words.
4. Do not use conversational expressions (idioms, contractions, slang).
5. Do not use unnecessary abbreviations.
6. Do not add new words to the Word List unnecessarily.
7. Write clearly and simply.
8. Use only the active voice of verbs.
9. Use only the simple past, simple present, and simple future tenses. Always use the present tense when possible.
10. EE has only four auxiliary verbs: "must," "can," "will," and "do."
11. Avoid unnecessary negatives.
12. Form questions as in ordinary English.
13. Try not to use too many adverbial clauses in one sentence. If you start a sentence with an adverbial clause, use a comma to mark the end of the clause.
14. Use "which" only as an interrogative adjective. You cannot use "which" to introduce an adverbial clause. You must use "that" instead.
15. Write short sentences dealing with just one idea.
16. "-ing" words are nouns that describe activities. (Crabbe 2017, 34–5)

There is a plausible world in which industrial languages like Ericsson English are the nightmare-of-the-self for elite novelistic literature, and where literature does everything possible to stave off the encroachment of stylistic standardization and simplification. There is also a plausible world in which prestige literatures are distinguished by their stamina and success in holding fast to stances of linguistic–translative resistance, while popular forms succumb.

Neither of these appears to be an accurate characterization of our (un)translatable world in the twenty-first century, however, where elite literary closure is working in different ways entirely, translingual ways that are more friendly to the principles of EE than one might have anticipated. One thinks, perhaps, of Kazuo Ishiguro's operational commitment to use as much visual language as possible in his fiction, so as to ease for his scores of translators the complications of translating complex psychological states (see Parks 2010; Walkowitz 2007). As a (self-)translated literary work, Tidbeck's *Amatka* is an experimental "design noir" response to the generally withering critical dismissal of contemporary literature that inclines toward translatability and steers clear of cultural particularism, and therefore of translational accidence.

Literature in Late Monolingualism is not a book that subscribes to these fault-finding allegations. Rather, it wants to understand what literary authors shrewdly do when faced with such tighteningly hegemonic forces of global free-market translatedness. Do they give up writing? Do they give up writing for anyone outside their immediate linguistic communities (Domokos 2016)? Do they try to shield themselves from certain kinds of critics and criticisms? Or do they foresee other solutions that shore up the late monolingual order in surprising ways?

Writing the (Very Real) Real

Unless we are dealing on Amatka with a condition of collective psychosis, the volubility of most actual objects in that world occurs to its citizens as real and symbolic at once. In an interview with Alison M. Gingeras about time and the Real in the early COVID pandemic, Jamieson Webster suggested that "the time of a catastrophe, traumatic time, works very strangely: in a zig-zag fashion, back to front, slow-motion molasses to utter haste, with aftereffects and shockwaves that inspire a race to cover it all over, to seal the tear in the fabric of reality. Also, the wish to get out of the uncertainty, the anxious wait" (Webster 2020).

Because this is so, because the relation between time, anxiety, and the Real becomes so haste-filled in traumatic time, Webster and Gingeras reflect on how these compromise practices in the name of hardship Realism become so vigorously and proudly owned by subjects. They point to Kristeva's early COVID observation that "the acceleration of our civilization had already arrived at a viral stage, and today this metaphor overwhelms us and enters into the real [*sic*], because it is an internal as well as an external menace— perhaps we do not have strong enough immune defenses and the danger is therefore also inside of us" (Kristeva 2020).

Though Kristeva is speaking about Symbolic virality and its acceleration and Realization through the experience of COVID, the pragmatistic vigilance in *Amatka* about mess versus form bears a similarly intensive message about language. The "real Real" on Amatka is permitted to be nothing but that rhythmic and symbolic reconstitution of pre-sanctioned signs, labels, and signified objects, because the consequence of not doing such reconstitutive work is understood to be so vivid and damaging that it overshadows all other potential signifying commitments. Neglect on Amatka has only this one potential meaning: neglecting to mark monolingually, neglecting to reconstitute sanctioned markings. Here is what such neglect results in:

> It was the suitcase. It had been out of sight under the bed, and she hadn't marked it for several days. It had been so worn, the text on the lid almost erased. She should have scrapped it. Now it was too late. The whitish gloop it had dissolved into had spread across nearly half the floor. It stuck to the sole of her boot. Nothing but her boot between her and that substance. She didn't know what would happen if she touched it, but it would spread to other objects if she didn't act fast. Vanja struggled to untie her laces and kicked the boot away. She rushed down the stairs and collided with Nina in the coatroom. She grabbed Nina's shoulders to stay upright, sending her stumbling backward into the front door.
>
> "What? What is it?" Nina shouted.
>
> "Don't go upstairs, don't go upstairs." Vanja's heart beat out syncopes against her rib cage. "There's gloop on the floor." (64–5)[4]

---

[4] Det var resväskan. Den hade legat under sängen och hon hade inte märkt den på flera dagar. Den hade varit blanksliten, texten på locket nästan utsuddad. Hon borde ha kasserat den. Nu var det för sent. Det vitaktiga kladdet hade sprit sig över nästan halva golvet. Det klibbade fast vid skosulan. Bara skosulan mellan henne och kladdet. Vanja fumlade med banden på kängan och sparkade den av sig. Hon sprang nedför trappan till undervåningen och krockade med Nina i kapprummet. Hon grep tag om Ninas axlar för att hålla sig upprätt.
   Nina slog emot dörren. "Men vad är det?"
   "Gå inte upp, gå inte upp." Vanjas hjärta hamrade mot bröstkorgen. "Det är kladd på golvet" (62).

Vanja's run-in with the whitish gloop here mirrors Jamieson Webster's "slow-motion molasses"—that experience of catastrophic time that moves us to anxious incapacitation as we, like Vanja, countenance the potential unforming of the suitcase. Importantly, Vanja does not know what the actual end consequence of unforming is, but knows from her education to fiercely prevent it. We learn though that, on Amatka, there is always the option to "scrap" an object before it becomes infectiously unformed, but this industry of scrapping requires an abrupt switch of affect from fearful contrition to stoic detachment. In today's monopsony structures for the large-batch multilingual harvesting of linguistic iteration on Earth, there is interestingly no such equivalent yet to these "scrapping" practices for triaging typologically useless language. Later generations of the AI gold rush may begin to find whole kinds of utterances no longer relevant, and it will be important to understand what scrapping certain language and languages entails for speaker–sellers in various socio-industrial relations.

In keeping with Amatka's own governance principles around style, the novel and its self-translation from Swedish into English are sparse and hesitant prose affairs, skeptical of any stylistic immoderations and flourishes that may introduce "linguistic accidence" (Solan 2017, 389; see also Williams 2002) or any ill- or unformed scraps that might mire the conveyance of accessible literary experience. Needing to avoid gloop at all costs, *Amatka* strives, like its characters, to be a plain-language endeavor, helpfully easy to translate and use omnilingually (Kellman 2016) or supralingually (Gramling 2020)—in Spanish, French, English, and beyond. What this fastidiously plain, translative, world-ready mode means for the literary artist in late monolingualism, as well as for the citizen, is etched in clandestine ways into both the start-text and its translations, as will be explored extensively below.

The *Los Angeles Review of Books*' Irene Morrison attempted to figure out the basic critical stakes in the novel's "surreal" project:

> But what is the gloop made of? Is it sentient? Part of the alien earth? Here and elsewhere, Tidbeck is deliberately enigmatic. Surrealism is meant to unsettle, making the novel at home with the kinds of cognitive estrangement so vital to speculative fiction. Rather than the more contemporary light-touch of surrealism found elsewhere in SF [science fiction], surreal events drive the plot of the novel. (Morrison 2017)

Described by *WIRED Magazine* as "weird in all the right ways" (Barron 2012), Tidbeck's fiction gives rise to a world whose wretched grimness is encased in matter-of-fact familiarity and in that familiarity's narrow band of pauper's pleasures for the relatively well-off, like Vanja. But the world of Amatka, despite its katechontic self-fortifications through language and hygiene, is actually a place in which:

> More than half of the farmers had sizable red blotches on their necks and around their wrists. In some cases the rash had developed into full-blown eczema, scaly and wet-looking. "It's the laundry detergent and the soap," Ivar said. "We have to kill off any spores and microorganisms so they don't spread outside the farms. Some of the species are very aggressive. But the fungicides are so strong. People get rashes."
>
> "What happens if the spores get out?" Vanja asked.
>
> "There are some species that tend to invade buildings," Ivar replied. "It's a sort of dry rot. Breaks down structural integrity." (57–8)[5]

Here, a piously denotative culture attempts to conceal the messy, uncontrollable reality of things. Everything, from persons to objects to infrastructure, is subject to this ongoing worry about disintegration, and (even literary) speech itself becomes a total mobilization to combat that prospect on these colonial frontiers. Dissidents are diagnosed as lone wolves, and personal melancholy or silence is dispreferred. One alleged criminal on Amatka is described as having suffered a social malady:

> This man was lonely. He had no one to talk to, no one to confide in. Loneliness is dangerous. Silence is dangerous. Through loneliness and silence, a small feeling of discontent can grow into illness. If only he had had someone to talk to. If only he had felt part of this community, if he had felt a sense of responsibility toward the commune. [. . .] Tonight, we're going to start treating the disease that is loneliness. We are going

---

[5] Mer än hälften av de som satt och åt hade rödflammiga utslag runt handlederna och under hakan. I några fall var eksemen blanka och våta, den omgivande huden fjällig.
  "Det är tvättmedlet vi måste ha till skyddskläderna," sade Ivar. "Vi måste ta död på sporer och mikroorganismer, så att de inne kommer utanför svampkamrarna. Men det är starkt, det tvättmedlet. Folk får eksem."
  "Har ni inte klagat till styrelsen?" Vanja påminde sig själv att ta en tugga av maten.
  "Det är klart att vi har. Men det händer ju ingenting." Ivar gjorde en sur min" (53).
Note that the Swedish start-text omits mention of what happens when the spores get out, moving rather directly on to the matter of complaints to the committee.

to talk about our pain, our thoughts, and through this become closer to one another. (190)[6]

The literary–linguistic world of Amatka is therefore both compulsorily social and vigilant about keeping its monolingual signifying practices effective, clean, and emotionally regulated. Its language is both plain and planed, for the alleged benefit of all citizens' safety, well-being, and thriving perseverance under hardship circumstances. On Amatka, the specter of disintegration has given rise to cultural conventions, rituals, pedagogies, narrative genres, shared memories, and virtues dignifying specific kinds of linguistic behavior, and admonishing others. The total mobilization of these interpellatory efforts makes the distinction between citizens and functionaries, between poets and stenographers unnoticeable.

Such science-fiction visions about the systematic and allegedly necessary instrumentalization of linguistic performativity, in a posthumanist ecological mode, pick up on contemporary apprehensions about civil discourse amid an ongoing global "crisis ordinary" (Brickell 2020)—and about what all this can tell us about globalized (translational) monolingualism in our time (Gramling 2020). Though the novel's tie to current worldly affairs on Earth is left vague in *Amatka*, Morrison sees the novel as one among many postapocalyptic stories about global weirding (see Canavan and Hageman 2016) that spell out what will happen when "Earth becomes unlivable for reasons not fully explained" (2017).

Many critics, like Adrienne Rich, have worried since the 1990s about the "corruptions of language employed to manage our perceptions" (1997, 320). But Tidbeck's critical vision is less concerned with the propagandistic and manipulative harnessing of language by authoritarian minorities than it is about the ways common-sense ideas about the very purpose of everyday language itself are radically reformulated so as to ensure a reliable infrastructure for material supply-chains and their governance. Rather than reserving the expressive liberatory power of language(s) for an elite consecrated few, and "delanguaging" everyone else (Garrido and Codó 2017), Amatka's state makes sure that everyone perceives themselves confidently as

---

[6] Den här mannen var en ensam person. Han hade ingen att anförtro sig till, ingen att tala med. Det är ensamheten som är farlig. Tystnaden. Det är genom ensamhet och tystnad som ett litet missnöje, nåt som hade kunnat lösas med samtal och lite omtanke . . . det är genom ensamheten som det lilla missnöjet kan växa till en sjukdom. Tänk om han hade fått prata med nån. Tänk om han hade känt en gemenskap, ett ansvar inför kollektivet. [. . .] Ikväll ska vi börja behandla denna ensamhetens sjukdom. Vi ska berätta om vår smärta, tala om våra tankar, och på så sätt närma oss varandra (194).

"language people" through and through, responsible for language's careful deployment at every step. But in service of what, and whom? Everything on Amatka is organized around infrastructural security, and therefore around the types of signifying practices that reproduce an integral infrastructure of commerce and provisioning. This is the world's hegemonic ideology. "Marking" is, for residents of Amatka, not merely a manner of rote world-learning, but of collaboratively ensuring that matter will maintain the form and function it has been implemented for—for their safety in a hostile climate. In moments of particular crisis and worry, governmentality in Amatka takes the form of:

> "INCREASED MARKING. In a campaign to improve the commune's well-being, normal activity will be suspended between fifteen and sixteen o'clock for marking of all objects in the area. This will be repeated every day until further notice. Hooray for Amatka's commune!"
>
> "Hooray!" Anders hollered.
>
> "Hooray," Vanja echoed. (174)[7]

Late monolingualism, as we've designated its ascendancy in the early 1990s, is an era of "INCREASED MARKING,"—of the kind of translingual marking, surveying, and calibrating that "will be repeated every day until further notice" (174). Such diligent marking, in translingual commensuration processes, was foreseen by early MT theorists, like Warren Weaver, who proposed that "the real but as yet undiscovered universal language" could be made plain through MT (cited in Hutchins 2000, 11). The outcome and experience of such a shared base vocabulary would be, in his famous analogy, as though people would suddenly be no longer communicating "by shouting from tower to tower" and instead would finally "go [...] down to their common basements" (Hutchins 2000, 19), where *common basement* means an allegedly underlying shared meaning across all languages, rather than the many problematically glossodiverse, mere surface-level expressions of meaning. He admitted that this approach—getting speakers to make their way down to the common

---

[7] ÖKAD MÄRKNING. I en kampanj för att främja kollektivets välmående skall normal aktivitet upphöra klockan 15–16 för märkningsgenomgång av samtliga objekt. Detta ska upprepas varje dag tills nytt besked kommer från styrelsen. Hurra för Amatkas kollektiv!"
"Hurra!" hojtade Anders.
"Hurra," ekade Vanja (176).

basement for the purpose of effective communication—would involve a "tremendous amount of work" (Hutchins 2000, 19).

Amatka fits squarely into the climate-fiction (cli-fi) genre, or more broadly into philosophical fictions of the Anthropocene. But the novel adds a thick linguistic–translative layer to this theory-making premise: a "li-fi" within the cli-fi. It does so, not through a linguaphilic epicureanism, ebullient about incommensurable alien languages, grammars, and communicative repertoires (as Miéville's novel *Embassytown* will be in Chapter 4). Rather, it dilates intensively into the mundane habits of linguistic performativity familiar to us from, for instance, War-on-Terror securitarian monolingualism and the corpus-based computational translation platforms that war has lavishly funded. Linguistic fiction (li-fi) novels, like *Amatka*, suspect that they must themselves do the work of understanding language(s), speech, and translation as a "hidden abode of [global] production" (K. Marx [1867] 1976, 279; see also Stibbe 2015 and Goatly 1996) in the Anthropocene, when other expert epistemic traditions like economics and earth sciences seem unwilling to acknowledge them (for important exceptions, see Dudley 2017 and Farrell and Rabin 1996).

Translating the (Very Real) Real

Tidbeck's exploration is set on a far-off planet that, paralleling twenty-first-century Earth, finds itself compulsorily subscribing to ever-new moments of socio-logistical urgency on ever-new colonial frontiers for crisis capitalization. How, the novel asks, do the phrases we fashion and amplify in a permanently crisis-driven socio-commercial mode act systematically upon objects themselves in the world, and thus reverberate back upon what we think language/Language is, how it works, and what it is for? And how might a Swedish-into-English self-translated novel like Tidbeck's itself go about theorizing the extractive frontiers of urgent, cheap meaning in the age of late monolingualism?

Such a speculative project implicates not only the imagined dynamics of surrealism and physical chemistry, but also the social, civic, and commercial dimensions of speech acts and interpellations in their contemporary practical contexts across securitized monolanguages. Tidbeck's civic nightmare kladd—which she calls "gloop" in her self-translation of the novel into English—is the inevitable eventuality not only when chemical processes in Amatka run amok due to citizens' disattention, but also when citizens inappropriately denote the objects around them, using language that is either incorrect, unplain, or accident prone. This is thus a tutelary discourse for linguistic citizenship (Khan 2019)—about how to properly become a speaking citizen—not through blood or birth, but through legitimate kinds of speaking in the one language the state says it needs to harvest from you in order to maintain its integrity in the face of superdiversity and material threat (Gramling 2009).

In 2015, Rachel Greenwald Smith identified the commensurative mode in contemporary literature as a specifically neoliberal one, where a mutual-aid contract between author and reader stipulates that novels should provide for readers recognizable emotions, models for group affiliation, and vicarious training in the mutual management of affect, as well as tips on how to "use the agency these experiences offer in order to make smart entrepreneurial decisions" (78). Smith has critically developed Jonathan Franzen's notion of "contract writing" to show the ways affect-driven neoliberal novels are often premised on a supply–demand agreement between writer and reader, geared toward upholding the ideological systems in which they are both ongoingly complicit (2014, 37).

Though Smith does not address the contractual nature of writing for translation and translatability, focusing rather on Anglophone compositions, her theorizations assist nonetheless in understanding the moodiness of late literary monolingualism. She writes:

> The contemporary Contract model of literary investment [. . .] is not merely one in which readers generally expect to be rewarded for the time they put into reading a book. Instead, it is one in which readers expect reading to be productive of a specific kind of affective value: the value of connection with others that allows for the growth and enrichment of the self. Just as characters in neoliberal novels develop and grow out of contact with other characters, readers too expect emotional development and growth out of contact with the people who populate the narratives they consume. For a novel to follow through on its promises, in this context, it has to offer means for this connection: through identification, a sense of alliance, and emotional enrichment. (38)

Smith accordingly distinguishes between two kinds of affect, the personal and the impersonal, which novels may contractually provide to readers. It is the *personal* feelings to which the (monolingually) neoliberal novel dedicates its energies: sentimental connections, immediacy, the amplification of recognizable emotions, emotions based on the benefits of networking and entrepreneurship, emotions as a scarce resource, and so on. What the neoliberal novel declines to generate for readers are *impersonal* feelings, which Smith suggests include: art's affective power to intervene in orders, emotional distance and ambivalence, second-order feelings, the feeling that one is feeling, the feeling that one does not know what one is feeling, mediated and contingent feelings across time and space, and emotion as a commons (58)—this all being a range of affective intensity that is properly at home in multilingual experience.[8]

Befitting the spirit of late monolingual cheap meaning, neoliberal novels in Smith's characterization of them help us become the emotionally and economically appropriate, socio-commercially communicative Robinson Crusoes of our day—sharing, speaking, interacting, connecting, and "reaching out" in ways that correspond with energetic socio-commercial wellness and mobility—and help us avoid noncompliant Romantic states like solitude, melancholy, standoffishness, or symbolic opacity. "Individualization," Smith reminds us, "is as key to how all forms of capitalism function as is rigid or unfeeling systematization" (3), and personal feelings have become key to how neoliberal novels help readers manage their affect through the modeling offered within those texts through their fictional social collectivities.

As a key part of such modeling, Smith tells us, compromise

> often seems either obviously good—as when intractable conflicts find a resolution because both parties agree to give something up in exchange for a solution that benefits everyone—or obviously bad, as in the accusation that one has compromised on one's values and is therefore ethically suspect, or disloyal. (2021, 5)

But Smith's understanding is less cynical and agonic than she perceives Franzen's to be. She suggests that, though novels can appear to be providing their neoliberalism-ready readers with the desired affects—of connection, social engagement, resilient productivity, and emotional entrepreneurship—the novels can nonetheless withdraw from the homo oeconomicus-driven contract mid-text, failing to follow through on their promise to compromise (2015). If novels can break with the neoliberal contract of providing readers with the means necessary to perpetuate a certain kind of neoliberal subjectivity, so can the novels of late monolingualism.

Far from succumbing to it, *Amatka* ironizes the mode of affective compromise and emotional transparency that seems to be required of literature-in-translation if it wishes to find its way out of Sweden and into global English, for instance. Smith's primary engagement as regards

---

[8] Admiring Smith's work as I do, I am eager to see a multilingual and translational elaboration on her range of concepts, from compromise aesthetics to personal feelings in the neoliberal contract novel.

"compromise aesthetics" is with contemporary US American culture and society in the context of neoliberalism, and so she does not quite pose the question of how multilingual cultures-in-translation (whether literary, US American, or otherwise) fit in to this picture of a late-capitalist moment that is morally inclined toward compromise as a virtue and an aesthetic. Against the backdrop of its own self-translation by its author, *Amatka*'s macrotext (O'Neill 2005) theorizes the affects of austere (trans)linguistic compromise as an unquestionable socio-commercial virtue, and the way this virtue expresses itself in performativities-under-pressure.

Much dystopian fiction about language and language ideology has tended, since Orwell, to focus on the terrifying vulnerability of everyday civic speech. The power to manipulate social perceptions of reality and social order through a desiccated or inflamed political language, or through totalitarian regulation of language use, can be staged fictionally in imagined societies analogous to those of industrial Liberal capitalism or post-Liberal fascism. Relatively robust, too, has been the modern fictional tradition of radically unimaginable linguistic orders that play out theoretical questions around the anthropological debates regarding "strong" and "weak" linguistic relativity (Gumperz and Levinson 1996). Through this genre, readers have been invited to ponder the potential radicality and normativity of linguistic practice in their own environments—by way of barely imaginable alternative worlds.

Fewer fictional works invite inquiry into a condition of experience in which the functional mutability of language(s) is itself compounded by the technological mutability of planetarily distributed objects, substances, and products, such that the very act of enunciating in a certain way rather than another is tantamount to shaping or upholding the integrity of matter. Though an intriguing philosophical venture under any circumstances, such a compound vision is particularly instructive in an Anthropocene–Chthulucene–Linguacene analytic, where material production and dissolution are not operations alleged to take place against a stable background of nature/order, but where the very construction of material integrity has lost its reassuring, orienting promise.

Tidbeck's novel is interested in this process, which I think of as linguistic infraperformativity—the way languages are made to act upon themselves, upon each other translingually, and upon their own performative reach and amplification, rather than just upon "extralinguistic" social actors or objects of interpellation. From Searle to Bourdieu to Butler, the search in theories of performativity has been one of understanding the power of language upon people and institutions, but not primarily upon language(s) as changing and interwoven subjects/repertoires themselves. The pressure to title books with keyword-searchable, search-engine-optimized, translingually viable titles like *Amatka, Cryptonomicon*, and *Embassytown* is one such matrix in which features of infraperformativity in and upon language(s) are exhibited. Corpus-driven Machine Translation is such an effort, and thus a structural expression of translingual "marking" and linguistic infraperformativity, where the engineering of affordances for cross-language ontologies compels objects to mean similarly from one language to the next over time. Its telos is the stability of the cross-language pathway or "synset," as much as it is the accuracy of the desired search request equivalence. Of course, language, politics, and land have always been practically and locally inextricable in all cultures, but the Linguacene is a historical period where the systematization of multilingualism truly changes the planet and geopolitical order, or multiplies changes long underway. A range of scholars have described globalizing conditions since around 1990 that have tended to accelerate profound changes in the use, learning, reform, and valuation of so-called individual languages (see, for instance, Duchêne and Heller's 2012 collection on *Language in Late Capitalism*).

One of the motives urging *Literature in Late Monolingualism* into being was the suspicion that Anthropocene scholarship has just had too little to say about languages, monolingualism, multilingualism, and translation—and that this is likely an analytical problem. It is not a problem simply because languages are important and need defending (which would be an ethical, representational, or political argument), so much as that languages and translingual matrices have been utterly catalytic in erecting, establishing, and maintaining global industries throughout the Anthropocene period, however it might be periodized.

This analytical weakness has been in effect since Marx showed himself rather reluctant to consider language as a means of production of any kind; prospects for such materialist argumentation around languages have mostly gone downhill from there. The colonial, practical materiality of languages in translation—how workers receive instructions from foreign managers, how value is conveyed from source to market, how companies insinuate themselves in locales through languages and translation, the occlusion and banning of Black, women's, and Indigenous languages from the work of commerce and science—have, however, been essential to sustaining the industrial accelerations that define modernity. And yet it has been relatively easy for Anthropocene scholarship to whistle past language(s), as though they were only perhaps the icing on the cake of modernity, if anything at all.

As an experiment in this problematic, *Amatka* wagers to conflate cause-and-effect in physical chemistry with the workings of (infra)linguistic performativity, pushing the notion of the speech act to its metaphysical extent.

It is a hypothetical entailment: if we are to understand, feel, and interpret the symbolic world in accordance with what signs do, with what we do with signs, and with what signs do with us in various languages, we ought to be able to apprehend this reality in its most vivid, fantastical, and indeed mundane terms. But beyond allegorizing performativity, which many literary and poetic texts have done for millennia, *Amatka* presents an infraperformative society: a world that has decided that it has particular securitarian needs from language, and thus instrumentalizes monolanguage(s) for coordinated material, strategic ends.

Katechontic Insecurities and Anxious Transplantations

For us readers still on Earth, Tidbeck's translingual gloop (kladd) is not just some funny quirk the author Gösta Svensson (from Nors's novel in the next chapter) might have drummed up as a Unique Selling Point to market Nordic books for global translation. Gloop/kladd is much more of a material reality for us humans than we perhaps like to talk about; we cover it up and stave it off with things like preservatives, refrigerated shipping, and other kinds of prophylactics. Our planetary infrastructural ecosystems, not terribly unlike Amatka's, have always been riven with what environmental engineer Peter Haff calls the enduring "problem of solids transport on the Earth's surface" (2012).

Since at least Madeira's fifteenth-century sugar plantations, global supply-side manufacture logistics has been, if nothing else, an extensively practical laboratory for this problem of maintaining and manufacturing material integrity over time and space, lest globally shipped commodities turn into noxious gloop in their shipping containers. It has only been in late monolingualism since 1990 that languages have effectively joined the ranks of those valuated wares that are systematically traded upon a global infrastructure, and which themselves therefore become susceptible to Tidbeck's specter of gloopification too.

Though processes of global linguistic stabilization, preservation, and commensuration have their roots in early colonial modernity—with the transcontinental consolidations of multilingual meaning around indigo, silver, jute, breadfruit, sugar cane, wood, coal, Jesus Christ, and enslaved persons (Colón, Añón, and Teglia [1493–1504] 2010; Cortés and Añón [1519–] 2010; Hanks 2010; Ma 2017)—its rhythmic processes have accelerated asymptotically in the intensely iterative age since 1990. Colonial endeavors of translocal linguistic commensuration (Hanks 2010)—which had begun in the earliest plantation "factories" in the fifteenth century, continued amid colonial Christian evangelization efforts, and were enshrined only later in seventeenth-century monolingual conceptions of well-developed languages—is not a discontinued effort. It is only now in the twenty-first century reaching a new velocity of fortification and systematization, to which Tidbeck's and Nors's novels (see Chapter 2) aim to respond.

To get some further clues on this predicament, we can turn to *Amatka*'s author Karin Tidbeck herself, a multilingual literary creator who self-translated this novel from Swedish to English. Tidbeck shares how, when translating her own novel, she sought to adhere to the constraints that conditioned the world of Amatka, where no metaphors, homonyms, or synonyms were permitted to circulate. "Since they were 'forbidden' in the book," explains Tidbeck, "I had to write them out of the prose as well. So, making that happen in English was difficult because English is a different language in that way. It's difficult to tame when you're not a native speaker, and I'm not a native speaker" (Tidbeck 2017b).

What we seem to learn from Tidbeck here is that *Amatka* was a literary-translational performance piece, an exercise in the multilingual pla(i)ning of language—both in the craftsperson's sense of planing a surface, as well as in the socio-commercial sense of rendering plain language for cross-cultural commerce and provisioning. Because the original text of *Amatka* obliged itself to such a stern linguistic constraint, endemic to its fictional world— an asperity against metaphors, allegorical-poetic phrases, and ornamental complications, themselves one of the biggest flies in the ointment of plain-language campaigns and Machine Translation—Tidbeck's self-translation into English had to find its way into inhabiting such a serviceable asperity as well. What's good for the original goose is, it appears, good for the translated gåskarl. Is this ascetic gambit what Doris Sommer (see Chapter 2) would call a "bilingual game" (2003)—or is it a hunger game of the monolingual?

As an additional-language user of English, Tidbeck had to be particularly industrious in her translation of *Amatka* to sweep away any metaphorical language in English that may not have appeared to be connotative or metaphorical at her first glance. In a kind of phenomenology of self-translation, she thus lived and relived this disciplined—sometimes cruel, sometimes resilient—linguistic piety in the composition process, which her own protagonists were also subjected to within the world of the novel.

Taking this riddle of audience-design further, Tidbeck gave the novel a title "Amatka" that was at once translingual, ethnically unidentifiable, untranslatable, and yet optimal for search engines—a veritable grail of compromise virtuosity for products of all kinds in late monolingualism. In naming this world of stoic commensuration "Amatka" (itself a symbol for translingual compromise), Tidbeck knew what she was doing all along, and which literary–aesthetic luxuries she would need to cut her losses on for the commensurative symbol "Amatka" to do global resilience in the ways she needed it to. Delightfully, Tidbeck rebuffs such allegorical interpretation outright—as she must:

> I don't write metaphors. Swedish mainstream readers really want to see my work as a metaphor, because that's how they learned to read speculative fiction. It has to be a metaphor for something else. But I don't write metaphors. I write ideas. What you see is what you get, pretty much. I wonder if that's a way for readers to keep their dignity. They can say, "I'm reading this because it's a metaphor," because they can't say, "I'm reading this because it's science fiction." (Tidbeck 2017c)

If, in Amatkan society, what you plainly see is allegedly what you get, and what you speak is what you produce, this recursive matter-of-factness is, given its macrotextual outreach through translations, an arduous infrastructural performance of translingual commensuration: an artifact of the profound, stoic sacrifices that must be made in order to preserve its own persistence as a literary commodity. It is a postmultilingual fantasia.

To put the matter in different terms that Tidbeck would certainly disapprove of: if the mine is an upside-down city (Brechin 2000; see also Wu 2015), the plain-language monolingual novel guards against its own cavernously multilingual preproduction underside—of commensurations, compromises, elisions, and impoverishments. Rather than a presentation of the novel as a metaphor for something else, *Amatka* is the perfected realization of a primary mode of late monolingual readiness, literary and otherwise: offering acquiescent linguistic compromise and, in parallel, acquiescence to being linguistically compromised. This is such a grand metaphor in *Amatka* that it's almost impossible to close-read in the text.

A clue about this cavernous underside, assiduously covered over by linguistic plainness, comes forth in the ostensibly easy translatability from Swedish to English of the very substance that threatens Amatka's civic integrity. "Gloop" in English may very well be an excellent and serviceable one-to-one translation of "kladd" in Swedish from a Machine Translation perspective, but it has none of the kladdig connotational extensivity that kladd does. Kladd means sticky goo, but it also means a doodle or a draft, as in a draft of a message, of a piece of art, or of a proposal. If you doodle on a piece of paper, it is in Swedish a kladd. If you write out a first version of something, it may be a kladd as well—as in a gooey "quick-and-dirty version."[9] In this sense, kladd is intimately related to writing, and to versions of attempted meaning, in a way that English gloop or goo simply is not.

Of course, this translingual implicature surfaces and becomes part of the close reading of the *Amatka* macrotext (the original-and-translations together, O'Neill 2005), regardless of Tidbeck's allegedly aloof intent as author or translator. By translating kladd as gloop, Tidbeck herself cleaves off the intensive meaning-making craftiness of kladd, scrapping it with no remorse. It is this quiet cleaving-off that is therefore proposed as the spectacular cost of any text's entrance into global Anglo-monolingualism in translation. It's not that the English "gloop" is wrong as a choice in translation, but that it is a deeply partial compromise that obscures/withholds as much as it conveys. That withheld meaning tells a great deal about the linguistic performativity at work in the novel's world too; kladd in Swedish (unlike gloop in English) is always potentially a kind of meaning-making activity—a drafting process, a doodle, an approximation, a becoming—rather than a certified, validated, securitized symbolic entity in pursuit of global motility.

Beta-Testing Translatability

Lest I give the impression that this mode of compromise-toward-translatability is a fault of the text or its author, I should resurface some of the brilliant and crucial aesthetic compromises struck in previous ages, which I explored in *The Invention of Monolingualism* (2016). Few to no musicians today view Johann Sebastian Bach's compromise for flexibly playable and combinable tonality in *The Well-Tempered Clavier* as a scandalous failure; well-temperament and, later, equal temperament were an enabling, historic step that ushered in a different world of aesthetic repertoire-building. These were an invention and an innovation—opportune and opportunistic at once. They were infrastructural genius. *Amatka*'s macrotext offers a draft, a kladd, for what such compromise can ambitiously herald and become for late monolingual literature, though the novel—in contrast to Miéville's *Embassytown* in Chapter 4—ends up studying the politically repressive rather than the enabling outcomes of such compromise.

When removed to a crisis-normative place like Amatka, the otherwise obviously elitist indefensibility of linguistic prescriptivism is able to shirk its

---

[9] Thanks again to my UBC colleague Lena Karlström, the Swedish language and literature scholar and teacher, for talking me through these connotations.

notoriety (as a pernicious caprice of social domination and colonial moralism). This is because, on Amatka, linguistic appropriateness (Flores and Rosa 2015) is tested in real time against the behavior of always potentially menacing material objects—*Gegenstände*, which stand opposite the speaker in a tense relation of perlocutionary becoming. Excellent verbal hygiene in that world (Cameron 1995) is thus a forensic, extralinguistic gauntlet-run, testing not the speaker's class identity, social standing, obedience to power, or expressive genius, but merely their fitness for subjectivity in this material world at all. A credible fear about the world's apparent physical instability ensures general, equal-burden adherence to linguistic purism much more reliably than any centrally espoused, classist "language ideology" was ever likely to do.

Here, perhaps again, Amatka turns out to be more like Earth than we at first want to admit. What does it mean to ensure the material integrity of resources on a colonial frontier anyway, and what communicative norms are alleged to be required for such a resilient endeavor? Alison Bigelow (2020, 1–2) details how the sixteenth-century Spanish soldier–historian Gonzalo Fernández de Oviedo y Valdés labored to commensurate Indigenous Central American mining vocabularies with everyday colonial Spanish. Oviedo foresaw that, in order for the colonial interest in gold and silver to persist rather than dissipate, he needed to convey information about the mineral-washing practices of Indigenous and African women in the West Indies "'en lengua o estilo delos que son mineros platicos' (in a language and style of those conversant about minerals)."

Bigelow shows how Oviedo's subjugative commensuration of Indigenous practice and knowledge into colonial idioms served to erase that practical knowledge entirely from the scientific record over time, through further colonial habits of practical disembedding, conceptual decontextualization, and symbolic refunctionalization. As Sherwin K. Bryant (2014) argued, enslavement and Indigenous subjugation aren't solely systems of labor and resource extraction, but also of epistemic theft under color of intercultural translation. Mining industries and plantation owners "conveyed these [Indigenous, Afro-Indigenous, and Afro-Latinx] ways of knowing by coining new vocabularies, repurposing existing expressions, and fashioning new forms of communication" (Bigelow 2020, 13).

Unfortunate for potential efforts to account for these practical linguistic aspects of extractivist industries in the Anthropocene has been the fact that twentieth-century historians of science, such as Modesto Bargalló, often dismissed Indigenous practical vocabularies in matters of mining gold, silver, copper, and mercury in the progressive retelling of colonial history. Instead of taking seriously colonized Indigenous people's expert practices of accessing and processing resources in service of their occupiers' capitalization efforts, and acknowledging the linguistic expressions for these practices, histories of science have more often assumed the colonizers' scientific idioms to be accurate and definitive, even amid their political efforts to articulate an anticolonial counter-historiography.

Curiosity about the role of language(s) in political economy, and its linguistically mediated material conditions over various empire-building eras, has not garnered a great deal of interest among critics who read Tidbeck's novel, where the enthusiasm remains centered on aesthetic inquiry about Language as a creative human faculty. Leif Schenstead-Harris, for instance, situates *Amatka* within

> a long tradition of investigating the central powers of language. [. . .] Most recently, philosophers such as Giorgio Agamben (2017) or Daniel Heller-Roazen (2017) have forwarded similar constructivist theses about language in texts such as, respectively, *The Fire and the Tale* or *No One's Ways*. In Tidbeck's *Amatka*, however, the thesis is posed in the sinuous shape of fiction's eternal question to its reader. Language is gradually, unsettlingly slanted, made diagonal, and put to question. Reading the novel is a remarkable exercise in which the borders of perception and communication fluctuate and bend. (2017, n.p.)

Though I agree with Schenstead-Harris on these points, and with Irene Morrison further above, *Amatka* is, I think, also ambitiously a study in the relationship between colonial capitalization and compelled translatability. The book wonders at length about the pressurized construction of monolanguages under supply-side manufacture—logistical conditions that are—on Amatka, as in any colonial outpost—multiply extreme and urgent-feeling.

Whether Amatka's citizens are, in the end, future space travelers from Earth or not, they are also certainly colonial pioneers involved in a total mobilization of high-stakes production and linguistic normativity that is socially overdetermined at all levels of interaction. Amatka is a company town, a colonial fortification, and a polity spectacularly under alleged siege by a range of frontier hardships against which its civic order fortifies at every turn. Its civic and linguistic pedagogies ensue from such a sense of metaphysical, existential siege (Donald 2009).

Through its meditation on the hardship of self-translation and the self-translation of hardship, *Amatka* re-dramatizes the monolingualizing anxieties both of early modern colonial settlement and of twenty-first-century literary publishing. As Prakash Kumar (2014) puts it: "The protean knowledge that was assembled in the first plantations in the Caribbean in the mid-seventeenth century had roots in various peasant traditions on the Indian subcontinent and elsewhere in the world" (720). Throughout the modern era, global Indigenous vernacular linguistic, epistemic, and symbolic repertoires needed to be ignored in order for colonizers to stabilize and "mark" objects that would be permitted to cross, or would be dragged across, the Liberal "production boundary" (Mazzucato 2018) into global supply-side manufacture.

By 1785, for instance, a European like George François Grand, First Collector of Tirhut (Bihar, India), was able to get away with claiming that he himself had fortified and exported an authoritative global dye color made out of various plants around the planet, from *Indigofera suffruticosa* in Guatemala to *Persicaria tinctoria* in China: "I introduced the manufacturing of indigo after the European manner, encouraged the establishment of indigo works and plantations, and erected three at my own expense" (Kumar 2013, 724).

Engineering efforts toward "Human-Centered Computing" and "user-centered design" (Dourish et al. 2020) for global translation platforms carry on in this grandiose five-century-long tradition of corralling meanings through stabilized forms of participant design that require constant overwriting, buy-in, and reiteration from multilingual user groups across the world. Engineering-oriented disciplines are only now beginning to tap into feminist and Indigenous critique to rethink how, as they see it, "questions of polyvocality and ambiguity might be seen from different methodological stances, how bodies and politics and histories are made visible or suppressed within particular methodological frames" (1). Historically speaking, though, it is an understatement to say that such supply-side efforts have been slow to notice how these extractive processes of meaning-gathering and data-mining place a profound affective and practical burden on language users and their knowledge repertoires, particularly on users of marginalized languages.

It would be easy enough to read and appreciate Tidbeck's novel as an imaginative study in linguistic repression alone, brought on by the politics of weird atmospheric conditions, and to do so would indeed render a fully-formed and satisfying argument. But such an angle would not befit the current book's overall investigation into literature in late monolingualism in any more than an oblique way. It will take us some more work to get to precise insights about how this novel works specifically on the plane of multilingualism and translation in the age of late monolingualism, rather than solely on the plane of authoritarian language politics.

What distinguishes late monolingualism in the 1990s onward from high or colonial monolingualisms of the nineteenth and twentieth centuries is its will and capacity to commensurate and transplant meaning effectively and quickly—and to do so at a scale and reach that even the most ambitious

Enlightenment language engineer could not have foreseen. Since 1990, a vested interest in commensuration between languages—which has been an ongoing colonial technique of conflating settler and Indigenous epistemologies through language for at least four hundred years (Hanks 2010)—has been reanimated and reapplied to computational engineering processes of entity-recognition: the establishment of synsets and cross-language ontologies that marshal commensuration between concepts in one language and concepts in scores of others (Saif et al. 2015; Huakang Li et al. 2017, for instance). This is a strongly centripetal iterative process, in which outlier data (a symbolic object's connotations, endemic meanings, and historical intensions) hardly register as counterevidence in the bright light of their too-big-to-fail counterpart concepts in charismatic superlanguages.

Consider as a historical prototype of such threatening symbolic disintegration the production of breadfruit, an early colonial food mass-produced for enslaved workers for the purpose of reproducing them and their labor power in the cheapest way possible. A researcher of early American literature, Juliane Braun, documents how the colonial Anthropocene has entailed global hyperprojects of linguistic commensuration and material production, like breadfruit. In 1793, in "the most ambitious botanical transplantation scheme the British Empire had ever attempted" (Braun 2019, 643), the West Indies company brought over a thousand Tahitian breadfruit tree saplings to St. Vincent, Barbados, and Jamaica "to provide a low-cost, low-maintenance food for the enslaved" (644).

Here, the breadfruit tree itself is not so much Braun's object of historical inquiry as are the standardization and stabilization of its symbolic distinctiveness and market-valuated distribution globally, and therefore its part in an effective and coordinated colonial project of labor extraction and the cheapening of life. Tidbeck's is a late monolingual novel that queries the dynamics of these twin supply-side practices: disembedding and refunctionalizing meanings into "strategically deployable shifters" (Urciuoli 2000, n.p.) on the colonial frontier while reconstituting and fortifying resource objects under a commensurated translingual sign.

The Birth of the Linguacene

In the introduction to this book, I argued that the thirty-odd years since 1990—a window spanning the rollout and refinement of algorithmic Cross-Language Information Retrieval capacities—have ushered in a new age in matters of language and meaning. Of course, I adapt the concept of a historical period called the "Linguacene" from the designation widely accepted in the natural sciences—and now widely used in the humanities and elsewhere—of an age called the Anthropocene, which some geologists tend to date to 1712 and the invention of the Newcomen atmospheric engine, though debate continues on the periodization and its validity. The Anthropocene, as geologists and stratigraphers have understood it, is that era of geological time when human societies' burning of coal, natural gas, and oil began to exert a structural impact on the planet, on its biospheres, and on conditions for the persistence and well-being of humans and other species.

I define the Linguacene as an era of human history, a late subset of the Anthropocene since around 1990, in which the minute, technocratic coordination among planetary languages and their meanings has become a viable precondition for global industrial and commercial traffic. It is an era in which such multilingual coordination among 60–170 major planetary languages becomes a primary location for the extraction of new forms of capital and control—an era in which, therefore, such supply-side, algorithmic coordination among languages itself begins to terraform the world through the industrialization of translatability, which, in turn, shapes the future of our species and all others, and in which a form of reactionary, neocolonial, and small-c conservative multilingualism itself begins to co-participate in terraforming Earth.

The historical processes I have characterized as late monolingualism are distinct in scope and purpose from the appellation Linguacene, though overlapping in several regards. I believe the Anthropocene as an analytic has long needed a linguistic component, and theorists have been hesitant to provide it. This is not a mere matter of disciplinary perspective or empirical focus, but a broad analytical problem, which these novels attempt to help solve.

The word Linguacene is thus in some ways designed to shift the focus for a moment away from the Anthropocene—not out of any disagreement with its own merits, nor out of fatigue with its centrality in scholarly conversations. Rather, the thrust of an argument about the Linguacene is one in favor of a more honest and rigorous dealing with language/translation as that symbolic order which has propelled, enabled, and accelerated many of the material processes described under the historical heuristic of the Anthropocene.

All of the human industry and activity that has led the planet to where it is today have had to be linguistically articulated—often in a colonizer's language, exported in the form of translation and language brokering, filtered through complexly multilingual and stratified education and industrial systems in colonized lands, and controlled and monitored in scores of subjugated languages. Else there would have been little likelihood, for instance, that the East India Company would have so effectively broken the commercial customs of the textile industry in the late seventeenth-century shadow of the Mughul Empire in Bengal. Genocidal displacements of Indigenous nations to make room for cotton and tobacco industries in the American Southeast did not succeed without massive communicative enterprises involving multilingual translation between colonial and Indigenous languages (Brickhouse 2014).

Whereas Anthropocene discourse often looks to the Newcomen steam engine as a pivotal point in the establishment of the age of anthropogenic climate and geological change, a Linguacene approach would add to this account the intensity of translations leading up to the invention itself. Harry Kitsikopoulos (2013, 307) tracks the way Hero of Alexandria's aeolipile, as documented in his *Pneumatica* (62 CE), was the subject of frequent translation in fifteenth- and sixteenth-century Italy, moving northward via Regiomontanus, Salomon de Caus, Jacob Besson, Hieronymus Cardan, and others in Italian, French, German, and English so that seventeenth-century England could house a growing discourse on steam power.

This is not to say there were not successful efforts around steam power prior to these translations (see Gerbert's hydraulic organ in tenth-century Rheims), but that the traffic in discourse was intensified through multilingual translation such that the combinatory powers of innovation were accelerated in the seventeenth century. The founding of the Royal Society in the 1660s was brought to us by, among others, John Wilkins, whose *Mathematicall Magick* was inspired in part by the excitement of Hero's steam technology, from Greek (Kitsikopoulos 2013, 313). This multilingual discursive means of production is a much different way of conceptualizing the Anthropocene than subscribing to a tacit indifference toward language as a materially enabling condition.

But, given that all of Britain's industrial advancements and innovations were tied to domestic resource crises (wood, for instance) and that the solutions for those crises were linguistically and fiscally forged on the multilingual imperial frontier, language was never external to the key dynamics of political economy. In this sense, we should likely add multilingual epistemic prospecting as a fourth dimension to Di Muzio and Dow's three major omissions, or silences, in the historical account of global capitalism— alongside "the financial revolution and the creation of the Bank of England; the transition to coal energy; and, last, the capitalization of the state as it relates to international warfare, colonialism and Atlantic slavery" (2016, 2).

One doesn't need to leave "Europe" to find evidence of such industrious silencing of Indigenous and colonized epistemologies and multilingualisms in the historical record of global capitalism. Consider the nineteenth-century British-owned Alten Copper Works, a copper mine by a remote fjord near today's town of Alta, Norway (Hiss 2017; see also Nielsen 1996), which recruited a multilingual workforce from Cornwall, Northern Finland, and Indigenous Sápmi. As Hiss puts it:

> The ACW directors became active policy makers and brokers between national politics, migrant workers, and the surrounding communities. Against the agenda of national politics, they protected their employees from assimilation policies and supported linguistic diversity. With economic success as the primary rationale, their engagement in diversity issues displays manifold ways of positioning. The company knew how to exploit the linguistically diverse situation to their advantage: Maintaining ethnolinguistic diversity among the workers (contrary to national policies) helped them to keep wages down and secure a flexible supply of laborers. (698)

The success of the ACW hinged on its ability to recruit and (dis)organize labor groups—from southern Scandinavia, Finnmark, Sápmi, and Cornwall—in such a way that they could not effectively mobilize for higher wages.

So why not course-correct and reframe matters in this way, complementing existing Anthropocene debates with a bid for a more linguistically and translationally aware set of inquiries and historical analyses? Establishing the practical linguistic underpinnings of Anthropocene processes would and will be a crucial complement—and indeed reframing—of how we talk about the structural relationship between industry and effects. It will be a major improvement to acknowledge the materially consequential, mediating function that languages have played in accumulating the specific kind of Anthropocene we live in today.

What such a complementary analysis will not deliver, in ways that Stephenson's *Cryptonomicon* aims to do in Chapter 4, is to account for the period in which language itself moved from industrial enabler of economic globalism in the eighteenth to early twentieth centuries to what it has become since 1990: a newly separate domain of motile commodities, now bearing financialized value (in the economic sense) which clients effectively seek to harness for proprietary purposes. The technical affordances that yielded such an effective commoditization of language—by way of certain kinds of monolingualisms, multilingualisms, and the like—were born in the 1940s, experienced variously comical booms and busts throughout the ensuing quarter century, and hit their stride only in the 1990s with corpus-based Machine Translation and Cross-Language Information Retrieval.

It's a reasonable, even prudent, hunch to want to scale back these days on the number of words around us that end in cene. Proposing the term postprint, and apologizing for the "posty" coinage in the same breadth, N.

Katherine Hayles admits: "Yes, I know, it's a drag, but it honestly seems the most appropriate term to describe where we are now" (2021, 2). I feel similarly circumspect about introducing, from a literary and linguistic point of view, the Linguacene. Apologetic, sure, but not hesitant. The lessons learned from the debate among Capitalocene, Plantationocene, and Anthropocene approaches in the humanities and social sciences are many, even if stratigraphers are not overly invested in the political dimensions of these distinctions.

Donna Haraway's addition of the Chthulucene (2016) has been instructive too, in that it points out the ongoingness of troubling change and transformation that will increasingly characterize future life on this planet. The advancements of the Linguacene are therefore also part of the unpredictabiility of the Chthulucene. There are good arguments that not every discipline needs a cene of its own, and that their proliferation only muddies inquiries we urgently need to make clear. (Consider Steve Mentz's *Break Up the Anthropocene* (2019), the final chapter of which is the "Neologismcene.")

As is likely evident by now, I am struck though by the profound underestimation of the practical centrality of languages that pervades, and indeed structures, entire fields of analysis around Anthropocene phenomena. Economics has had bleakly little to say about language—from the seventeenth-century physiocrats all the way to Neoclassical approaches—and yet Appadurai (2016) argues that the entire 2008 financial collapse was in fact a crisis of *language*, not just of markets. Something is now happening to the world-language system that makes processes and cultures easier to manipulate, hollow out, functionalize, disempower, preempt, and dominate. These puzzling new regularities for manufacturing consent are most often attributed to neoliberal governmentality, without much room for a specifically linguistic analysis of the changes in how we expect ourselves and our fellows to track the relationship between cause and effect, the domestic and the foreign, the here and the there, the sincere and the artificial, the discursive and the material, and the free-spirited versus the free-marketed.

The Linguacene is, unfortunately, an era in which the vagaries around the expectations we have of our languages (and of each other's languages) widen the space of potential manipulation and extraction. I have therefore proposed the concept of late monolingualism to help theorize a recent historical period (from 1990 to the present) in which transnational supply-side innovators idealize, sell, and demand translatability at all costs, often in order to secure traditional national borders, even while accelerating transnational freedom-of-movement for capital-driven enterprises. Late monolingual phenomena indeed accelerate and exacerbate Linguacene phenomena.

I adapt this concept of the Linguacene in order to suggest that the global large-scale industrialization of translation and multilingual extraction is redoubling global industrial damages, rather than counteracting them with, for instance, "green" innovations. Though we are traditionally accustomed to thinking about translation and translatability as a virtue, capable of improving communication between cultures and of breaking down inequities, barriers, and injustices, the Linguacene is a historical period in which translatability is effectively put in the service of industries that tend to exploit and create global inequities, rather than tacke them.

The focus on materiality and practical action in both of these domains of knowledge has detracted from their willingness to consider the linguistic–symbolic features of materiality and practical relations. Major thinkers in Anthropocene discourse like Andreas Malm have called for a renewed line of thinking about literature and the textual archive as regards fossil fuels, but they fall short of thinking about language(s) as part of the engine fueling extractive industries (Malm 2017, 126). For instance, works of "fossil fuel fiction" like Lawrence's *Lady Chatterley's Lover* ([1928] 2015) may be seen to provide a window onto the oil economy (Cole 2020, 289), but not as readily as part of a linguistic assemblage that actually propels and necessitates that economy. Languages are allowed to be key witnesses to economy, but not part of it. It is time for critics to break that plate-glass window separating language from the rest of political economy—if for no other reason than that global industrialists did so already some forty years ago now.

Recycling in the Linguacene

Amatka is not just a world of colonial mining and planting; it is in fact also full of books, libraries, and paper—much of which is now being bulk-recycled to make new paper for medical records, conveniently effacing its complex and difficult precrisis language and literature, which the recycled paper had once stored and held. This world's literary paper is being transformed into more practical, informational, communicative paper for plain language. It's not that Amatka's Central Administration and its functionaries don't want stories, poetry, literature: they simply want a new *kind* of literature that affirms the collective civic contract, the compulsive iterative conviviality seen as necessary for the world's resilience.

The culture of marking on Amatka is not entirely one just of cherishing what is, of dealing with what the world has offered—which could be viewed as a devotional or ecological orientation of some kind. Rather, much of Amatka's human labor and industry is also dedicated to scrapping: taking formed objects in various states of perfection or decay and voluntarily annihilating them to benefit other purposes. So, alongside and parallel to the specter of negligence that is gloop, there is the fastidious virtue of scrapping objects at the right time and for the right reasons. Consider the following exchange between Nina and Vanja, which concerns the use of mushroom proteins to make supplementary paper during an apparent shortage.

"Something's going on with the good paper," Nina said. "It's the same thing over at the clinic. We get less and less good paper, so we have to start committing things like schedules and routines to memory. We've even had to start using mycopaper for the medical records."

"But that won't work."

"No. We've had to bring more people in just to retype the records before the old ones reach their scrap-by date."

Vanja glanced at Nina. "But why? Do you think we're running out?"

"They say the good paper is needed elsewhere." (59)[10]

Multiple transformations appear to be afoot here. Fast-decaying paper documents have to be retyped, requiring more human labor to do so. Non-decaying paper is needed for an undisclosed purpose, leading to reliance on faster-decaying paper. We also learn that objects in mass circulation come with a scrap-by date, though sometimes this date can be extended through remarking. There are apparent exceptions to the material–linguistic volatility of the world, as the colonizing forces who settled Amatka had brought with them a kind of building concrete that was not susceptible to the performative power of individuals' linguistic disattentiveness or disobedience:

> The commune office of Amatka had rounded corners and small recessed windows. Like all central buildings in all colonies, it was

---

[10] "Det är nåt med finpapperet," sade Nina. "Det är samma sak på kliniken. Vi får mindre och mindre finpapper. Vi har fått börja använda mykopapper till journalerna."
 "Det går ju inte."
 "Nä. Vi har fått ta in mer personal bara för att kopiera journaler på nytt papper innan de gamla måste kasseras."
 Vanja tittade sidledes på Nina. "Men varför?" "Håller det på att ta slut?"
 "De säger att finpapperet behövs på annat håll" (55).

built from concrete, that rare material that the pioneers had brought with them. And like all other things from the old world, concrete didn't need marking to keep its shape. It was solid, comforting. The plaque next to the entrance read *Central building constructed and erected year 15 after arrival. Long live the pioneers! Long live Amatka's commune!* (24)[11]

The plaque on the concrete, indissoluble structure introduces us, broadly speaking, to the literature of Amatka—to its functions, signifying methods, and repertoire of messages. As befits literary culture, there is true enthusiasm for Amatka's writerly traditions, a sense of anticipation and a desire to share. Literature is duly enchanted as an indispensable key to the essence of Amatkan society and its historical experience:

"Poetry," he said. "If you want to get to know Amatka, you must read our poetry. This one was written by Berols' Anna. Very concise, very typical of our culture." He offered Vanja the book.

She turned the book over in her hands. *About Plant House 3* had been published twenty years ago: three hundred and sixty-five poems describing Plant House 3 in minute detail. Vanja opened the book to a random page.

at five twenty-two   among the beets
The shift from   blur to acuity
The long furrows   of chalky earth
The sound of water   absorbed by roots

"Is it popular?" Vanja asked.

"Very, very," the librarian replied. "Not as popular as *About Plant House 5*, that's the most popular one by far, but it's on loan at the moment.

---

[11] Det höga huset i Amatkas mitt hade trubbiga kanter och små insjunkna fönster. Mörka fuktränder strimmade den ljusa ytan. Det påminde ett ögonblick om en tvål med stansning som höll på att korka igen. Plaketten som satt vid sidan av ingången löd *Koloni 5, Amatka, centralbyggnad uppförd och rest år 15 efter ankomsten. Leve pionjärerna! Leve Amatkas kollektiv!* (19).

But you can read them in any order you like. They're written so that the reader can start anywhere." (36)[12]

Vaunted for their concision, accessibility, and random-access handiness, these poems train readers in how to "shift from / blur to acuity" on every new morning. The predominating mythos about Amatka's literature is not, for instance, the reasonable apology that hardship has made expression terse. The aura around literature is not an ethnographic or autoethnographic mood, nor even historicist in any explanatory way. Rather, what is being cultivated is a dehistoricized celebration of essential axioms: clarity, clarification, the expulsion of vagueness and doubt, a culture of vigorous, mutually confirmative head-nodding.

But it would be inaccurate to suggest that this axiomatic project feels only like cheerless drudgery for citizens of Amatka, including new Amatkans, like Vanja, whose colonial vocation it is to Recognize and Name Entities (Zaghir et al. 2023). Vanja expresses a certain sincere amenability, even delight, about the precarious objectivity she is tasked with reconstituting every waking moment, through language. Describing her education and training background as that of an "information assistant," she accounts for her employment history before arriving to Amatka as follows:

"I wrote pamphlets for the education unit. You know. Those little manuals." "'How to Stay Healthy' and 'General Clothing Maintenance,' that kind of thing?" "Yes, exactly. It was sort of fun, actually." (41)[13] Vanja fits the description of a pleasant bureaucrat with few complaints, eager to be helpful, and engaged in pragmatic, informative tasks of benefit to the vision of popular community her government espouses. Vanja is a positivist, an

---

[12] "Poesi", sade han. "Om du vill lära känna Amatka, då ska du läsa poesi. Den här har Berols Anna skrivit. Mycket konkret, mycket typisk för vår kultur." Han satte boken i Vanjas händer.
Hon vände på boken. *Om Drivhus 3* var utgiven för tjugo år sedan: en femtio sidor lång beskrivning av Drivhus 3 ned till minsta detalj. Vanja slog upp en sida på måfå.

klockan fem och tjugotvå bland betorna
en skiftning från grånad till skärpa
de långa fårorna av kalkhaltig jord
ljudet av vatten som sugs upp av rötter

"År den populär?", frågade Vanja.
"Mycket, mycket", svarade bibliotekarien. "Inte like populär som *Om drivhus 5*, det är den mest lästa, men den är utlånad för tillfället. Men du kan läsa dem i vilken ordning du vill. De är skrivna för att läsaren ska kunna börja var som helst" (33).

[13] "Jag skrev pamfletter åt utbildningsenheten. Du vet. De där små handböckerna."
"Håll dig frisk och Allmän klädvård, sånt där?"
"Ja, precis. Det var ganska roligt faktiskt" (37).

ameliorator open to compromise, an infrastructural helping-hand through language. This does not mean, though, that she has never been curious about the substratum of meaning-making potential, below these "fun" and important tasks of marking and writing informational pamphlets. As we will explore below, the entire macrotext of the novel threatens to dissolve into gloop as she witnesses the dissolution from within.

Letting Things Fall Apart

To briefly summarize, the key prerequisite for Amatkan citizens' persistence on their colonial frontier is linguistic iteration—the willful fortification of symbolic norms upon objects that are fragilely averse to this ecosystem. Amatkans transplant and iterate incessantly, willfully laboring to bring entities into being that are preposterous against the apparent natural dynamics of their new world. This hardship of always potentially infelicitous transplantation and iteration engenders a social world centered around "what one does not stop (not) translating" (Cassin 2004, xvii). This is exactly the vocation and predicament Tidbeck has taken up by self-translating her literariness from Swedish into a plain-language global English.

It is this wary culture of marking and iteration in *Amatka* that points us toward a commensurative and reconciliatory mood in literature's late monolingualism. The collective virtue of keeping things well marked through an idiom of compromise and communal self-sacrifice is inculcated in childhood on Amatka and suffused with positive feeling. Amatkan monolingualism is no mere nationist–mnemonic device (Fishman 1968) for a lost or threatened cultural heritage, nor a repressive political program; monolanguage on this frontier is a hydraulic system built to stoically achieve the apparently impossible: survival on an allegedly hostile, improbable planet. Stabilizing globalized concepts means reiterating them across language frontiers in a constant recursive loop of marking and validating.

As an ever-present term of art in Amatkan society, though, "marking" is deceptive because it suggests an authorial action—marking something that was previously unmarked—rather than the derivative action of copying a preexisting authoritarian label. This subsumption gives Amatkans an ongoing sense about their own individual centrality in assuring their destiny, where what they are really doing is relabeling a destiny issued to them by the planet's Central Administration.

In reading this novel as a macrotext (O'Neill 2005), it is essential to grasp as philosophically conjoined concerns Tidbeck's desire to be read beyond

Sweden and Swedish, on the one hand, and her making of a novel that is about a world where material objects respond to language on the other. Late monolingualism is an era and a structure in which the enunciation of meaning and the materialization of objects are steered by global linguistic–technological infrastructures of an unprecedented kind: autocorrection, autotranslation, autoformatting, named-entity recognition, cross-language synsets—all of which also help steer the traffic in publishable meaning. Tidbeck described her literary subjectivity in the world-language system, in a 2017 interview, as follows:

> When I was nineteen, I worked in a science-fiction bookshop in Stockholm. There was, and still is, this magazine called "Locus," which is the SFF [science fiction and fantasy] industry's main magazine, and I would read that during lunch break. And I had this revelation that "I wanted to be in here. I want to have my book reviewed in here. I want to have an interview here. And I want to be on the shelves in the book shop . . . in English." The thing is, Sweden has a very small readership. It's very difficult to get books published, it's very difficult to sell books, it's extremely difficult to sell speculative fiction. So, I realized that the market was so small that I had to switch languages, but I didn't switch until I was in my early thirties. (Tidbeck 2017b)

Vanja is, like Tidbeck, a plucky author-from-elsewhere trying to find her footing in an exacting, insufferable, and self-justificatory new linguaculture full of dubiously manufactured (self-)translations. At the outset of the novel, Vanja's relocation to this new world prefigures Tidbeck's need to make do as a self-translator from Swedish to English under duress from external forces that, by disguising linguistic ideology in free-market metaphysics, achieve the "effective depoliticization of the economic" ("wirkliche Entpolitisierung des Ökonomischen"; Grandner and Traxler 1984). Vanja has been seconded (i.e., translated) to a frontier world where the purpose of language use is alleged to be sheer and vigorous survival, by way of commercial authoritarianism and linguistic "preservation" on a stunningly concrete timescale.

Consider Vanja's childhood consciousness, as she is working in a storeroom of objects, unaccompanied:

> Vanja had been [. . .] tasked with marking pencils and rulers, and she took to the job in earnest. *Pencil pencil pencil pencil pencil pencil*, she had chanted, touching the pencils one by one, until the stream of words inverted and made a sound like *cil-pen cil-pen cil-pen cil-pen cil-pen cil-pen*, and the row of pencils had shuddered and almost turned into something else, and she realized that this is how it happens, and her

whole chest tingled. Right then, the door to the storeroom opened, and Teacher Jonas was in the doorway. He looked at the row of pencils, then at Vanja. "I saw that," he said. Then he grabbed her by the arm and steered her into the classroom. (22)[14]

Given what we've been told about Amatka's weird climate, it is not clear in the retelling of this moment what transformation is actually taking place in the storeroom. What is the material consequence of the words Vanja is actually uttering? Has the sound of the words even changed? Has she begun, for instance, to audibly emphasize the second syllable of *pencil*, against conventional usage? By all possible measure, the phonological-prosodic shift is minute, and it appears in this imagined world to be materially consequential, making the pencils start to shiver and threaten to become *cilpens*, whatever those might be. But Vanja's enunciation here is also a criminal and antisocial act, one ambiguously perched on the border between intention, prosody, and surveillability. Teacher Jonas, she expects, "was going to tell the others what he had seen, and she would be sent away. The silence seemed endless" (22).[15]

But there is more to this scenario than just a memory of titillating linguistic transgression. Swedish readers may have already felt alarmed at the fact that the original text and its (self-)translation cited in the epigraph of this chapter—a passage which introduces the "Marking Song" to *Amatka*'s readers—are profoundly unsimilar, suggesting that the translingual underside to the text is falling apart before our eyes. Tidbeck's clandestine joke appears to be that, right at the moment when rebellion against normative regularity is thematized in the novel, whole paragraphs and passages are removed and "misplaced" into other, far-distant sections of the translated text in English. Though the novel appears to be about the compulsive and compulsorily purist regulation of plain meaning in the supply chain between Swedish and English, under conditions of linguistic and metaphysical crisis in Amatka and commercial globalization on Earth, the joke is on us readers of the English version.

---

[14] "Vanja hade stått inne i ett förråd, satt att märka pennor och linjaler. *Penna penna penna penna penna penna,* hade hon rabblat, med fingret på varje penna, tills strömmen av ord blev bakvänd och det plötsligt lät som *napp-e napp-e napp-e napp-e napp-e napp-e, och raden av pennor hade sk*älvt till och nästan blivit någonting annat, och hon förstod att *det är så det går till,* och hela bröstet pirrade. Just då öppnades dörren till förrådet och läraren stod i dörröppningen Han såg på raden av pennor, på Vanja, och tog henne sedan hårt i armen och ledde iväg henne till klassrummet" (85–6). Thanks to Lena Karlström for helping me compare the Swedish and English versions.

[15] Lärar Jonas "skulle han tala om för de andra vad han hade sett, och hon skulle skickas bort. Det var tyst en lång stund" (86).

Tidbeck has of course insisted that she is no allegorist, and she is studiously disinterested in our reading too much into her self-translation practice. But even a quick look at the differing page numbers between the Swedish and English for the passage about cilpens just above shows us something fishy, something far afield from alleged plain-language transparency and (trans-)lingual purism. The passage is jumbled, misplaced, hidden elsewhere in the English book than it was in the Swedish. If late monolingualism demands that literary utterances be made translatable for plain-language global distribution, such that the speculative valuation and supply of the commodity can be managed across a range of end-user language markets without delay or barrier to its uptake, Tidbeck has climbed right into the middle of this logic and started rearranging things without telling anyone.

Think about what is going on with the pencil/cilpen iteration above, an act of reproductive securitarian *marking* gone awry. It is the kind of anticipatory annotation that computational engineers in Machine Translation and Cross-Language Information Retrieval labor to perfect through Named-Entity Recognition (Zaghir et al. 2023)—one that has, however, gone to kladd in the mouth of the wayward citizen, Vanja. This simple word pencil has gotten out of control in the act of enunciation—and is then flipped around recklessly in the (self-)translation too (Waterhouse 2011). It was not a premeditated intervention on Vanja's part, but once it began happening, she herself was transformed by what the transformation revealed to her.

When I began to track and contrast the Swedish and English versions (both made by Tidbeck), I noticed that this memory of the cilpen in the storeroom was not in the English where it had been in the Swedish. It had moved about sixty pages ahead. The same is true for the memory of the marking song in the epigraph to this chapter; whole paragraphs are moved, not just a page or two, elsewhere throughout the manuscript—scattered, tossed, centrifuged. Importantly, this redistribution occurs in the self-translated novel's narrative only at those moments when the overweening stringency of marking practices, or the insurgency of decreation, is at hand (Phipps 2019). As self-translator, Tidbeck misbehaves whenever the text and its protagonists—which she always knew she would end up self-translating—misbehave too.

What we're dealing with here, as close readers, is therefore not one or the other text, an original or a translation, the source/start-text or the Anglogenic rendering, but rather the meaning-making interstices among them—what O'Neill calls the "macrotext" (2005), or what Lezra understands, less auspiciously, as the dynamics of the void at the center of "the market system of credit–debt global capital [as] a translating machine" (2015, 175; see also Wennerlind 2011). Where O'Neill envisions such an integrity of multiple original and translated texts as a holistic recovery, as a methodological salvation in a globalized literary world, Lezra and Tidbeck seem to anticipate it as a decrepit ruins, left behind by decades of automated ordoliberal conceit and expediency around the industrialized hunt for "equivalency."

A Sovereignty of Self-Translating

Asserting and preserving the labeled integrity of perishable objects has been key to managing crises on colonial frontiers since the fifteenth century. Commensurating potentially divergent meanings into a normative concept has also been essential for consolidating any discourse that might perpetuate that concept and its associated objects beyond the current context of situation, thereby ensuring perpetual xenos rights over local goods on behalf of far-off imperial masters. Though Slobodian, and Hayek before him, views xenos rights as primarily an aspirational attribute of capital and property, I believe we can usefully extend it to linguistic, symbolic, and discursive holdings as well. Slobodian writes:

> The category of xenos rights helps us think about individuals having protected rights to safe passage and unmolested ownership of their property and capital, regardless of the territory. It is a right that inheres to the unitary economic space of dominium rather than the fragmented state space of imperium—yet it requires the political institutions of imperium to ensure it. (2018, 123)[16]

Drawing on Slobodian's conception, I use the notion of "discursive holdings" in a linguistic sense to describe the ways foreign linguistic capital is able to establish semiotic and discursive dominium within domestic languages, edging out endemic meanings in supply-side institutional and corporate communications (on such Anglophone corporate holdings in, for instance, Italian greenwashing advertisements, see Caimotto 2019).

Such commensuration processes have always involved deliberately manipulating and otherwise suppressing inconvenient empirical evidence,

---

[16] In *The Globalists*, Quinn Slobodian glosses Carl Schmitt's 1950 conception of dominium versus imperium in the postimperial world order. "Schmitt proposed that there was not one world but two. One was the world partitioned into bounded, territorial states where governments ruled over human beings. This he called the world of *imperium*, using the Roman legal term. The other was the world of property, where people owned things, money, and land scattered across the earth. This was the world of *dominium*. [. . .] The division of dominium and imperium was more fundamental than the purely political distinction of foreign and domestic" (2018, 10).

as the merchant–naturalist John Ellis (1710–96) repeatedly did in order to persuade the Royal Society and British Admiralty to fund his plant translocation schemes around the cheap, hyperproductive, low-maintenance, labor-reproducing crop of breadfruit (Braun 2019, 658). There is no reason to suppose that such suppressions of empirical difference were more pivotal to colonial discourse in the fifteenth or eighteenth century than they are today in the neocolonial designs of "language-configurable" translation technologies.

In Tidbeck's novel, the demand for denotative simplicity and plainness in Amatka's language is cherished as a brass-necked triumph of its colonial founders, which is then retrofitted to act as a kind of mythical autochthonous ethnic pride among settlers. But, throughout, Amatka's origin story is one of linguistic compromise rather than of linguistic sovereignty. Its ancestral pioneers are revered for having had the stamina and insight to cultivate the disciplined monolingual simplicity entailed by their new environment. That legacy is, however, portrayed as affirmatively communicative, not harshly repressive. One way to understand the symbolic intensions of this pioneer settler-colonial lineage on Amatka is to view it as the ancestry of late monolingual literary translation itself.

From Jean Bodin to Carl Schmitt, political theorists of sovereignty have regarded the sovereign as that which does not get translated, or which can withhold translation discretionarily. Though the untranslatability of French's *souveraineté* was asserted pursuant to the 1539 Ordinance of Villers-Cotterêts in order to resist Latin, Hebrew, and other classical languages, this early modern multilingual theater of rigorous reconceptualization has "been all but ignored by modern scholarship, including Nancy, Derrida, Balibar and Schmitt" (Keohane 2015, 250). And yet, in Bodin's 1576 theorization that "[It] belongeth unto the royaltie of soveraigne majestie, to be able to compel the subjects to use the language and speech of him that ruleth over them" (Bodin [1606] 1962, 181), suggesting an alternate conceptual history to translating and nontranslating, which Tidbeck takes up in imperious, clandestine ways.

When we read Tidbeck's English self-translation of the novel, we find that there are in fact other titles in the Amatkan library than just the stoically informative Amatkan literary classics like "*About Eight Mushroom Chambers* by Idars' Ivar, *About Bodily Variations* by Torus' Britt, and a thick volume bound in red and marked only with the words *About Trains*" (38). Once, while helping a new friend Ulla to mark her belongings, Vanja came upon something unexpected:

> Wedged between a copy of *About Bodily Variations* and *A Biography of Speaker Hedda* was a slim volume with the word *Anna* handwritten on

the spine. No *About*, just *Anna*, as if the book was named Anna. One couldn't name a book anything other than BOOK, or start the title with anything other than "About . . ." Naming an object something else, even accidentally, was forbidden.

Vanja drew the book out and opened it. Poetry, on what looked like good paper, handwritten in faded blue ink:

> we speak   of new worlds
> we speak   of new lives
> we speak   to give ourselves
> we become

Ulla gently took the book out of Vanja's hands. "That's personal, dear," she said. (46)

When Vanja asks Ulla, about this "personal" volume, "What does she mean, to become?" Ulla's response is: "Nothing, go on with the marking, dear" (46). Here Vanja has obviously struck a nerve, as she asks Ulla about "becoming," and Ulla quickly admonishes her to drop the question and return to the work of reiteration. Ulla's possession of a potentially contraband book is not only controversial due to its ideological bearing—that is, its exploration of "becoming"—but also due to the valuable paper upon which it is written. But here, again Tidbeck is playing a trick: the passage is not present in the Swedish original text at all, and by permitting herself to compose entire new scenes for the English, she is allowing this book *Amatka* to "become" as well, to insert itself into an otherwise dull, global canon of sanctioned titles in Amatka's library.

Tidbeck is inventing and investing in a new conception of translatability and linguistic justice here (Van Parijs 2011), in the midst of a project that seems militantly docile about translatedness. Keohane's formulation is helpful to this end, as he reconciles the alleged muscularity of sovereign untranslatability with the actual work of translating, which he regards as follows:

> The translator would not be the sovereign who combines absolute power and excess over legality, [. . .] but the judge who combines a respect for the singularity of idioms with a respect for the general laws of translation. [. . .] This position would therefore agree that there is something before and beyond the laws of translation, but what we might call the *anomos* quality of untranslatable would not constitute a sovereign exception,

it would be the exceptional appeal to justice. [. . .] Translation would consequently be the reasonable transaction between two obligations— respecting the generality of the law (the translatable) and the singularity of justice (the untranslatable). (Keohane 2015, 256–7)

Viewing untranslatability as an "exceptional appeal to justice," rather than merely as an exception to rules, allows Tidbeck as a self-translator in late monolingualism to return to untranslatability discourse some of the vigorous moral and aesthetic imagination that has always been germane to it. In Chapter 2 on Dorthe Nors's Danish-language novel *Mirror, Should, Signal*, we shift the focus to individual subjects who attempt to translate in this historical age, and the vertiginous experience of disorder and vulnerability that they sense in such attempts.

2

A Translator's Vertigo

A vast exchange is commencing. Sonja can't claim otherwise; nobody can. It's barely visible yet, but it will be, and when it comes, it'll be vast.
—Dorthe Nors, *Mirror, Shoulder, Signal* (2017a, 183, translated by Misha Hoekstra)

Det bliver en stor udveksling. Sonja kan ikke sige andet, ingen kan sige andet. Den er nænsten ikke synlig endnu, men det bliver den, og når den kommer, bliver den stor.
—Dorthe Nors, *Spejl Skulder Blink* (2016, 186)

I've noticed my reluctance over time about the warm request with which Doris Sommer begins her paradigm-making 2003 book *Bilingual Aesthetics: A New Sentimental Education*, which was: "Come play bilingual games with me." What could ever be wrong with such an inviting call, or with the prospect of exploring a new game together? Hasn't the "ludic," that realm of playful exploration, long been a key practical methodology and analytical lens embraced across all domains of developmental and pedagogical inquiry, from business management to early multiliteracies and additional-language learning (Warner 2024)—and across any cultural sphere one might name that is amenable to fun and pleasure?

There is great persuasive power in Sommer's evocation of an underappreciated realm-in-waiting called bilingual aesthetics, where revealing and revelatory games are being played in more-than-monolingual literary ways, a realm that hearers of Sommer's call ought to experience without delay, before we collapse under monolingualism's grim and fortified self-satisfaction. There is in Sommer's phrase, moreover, the congenial feature, rare in academic books, of an invitation to do this "with me"—offering conviviality and good guidance when sought.

But I also admire Sara Ahmed's *Feminist Killjoy Handbook* (2023), and the killjoy in me yearns to acknowledge a problem in the association of multilingualism with play, games, creativity, and resilience. Considering the huge number of books and articles on this association *multilingualism=play* in the last two decades, it is clear that one of the few grand virtues that is readily ascribed to multilingual practices is indeed "creativity," whether in the collaborative design of refugee resettlement programs, in translanguaging practices between multilingual pals, or in community arts initiatives. Multilingualism is almost reflexively praised as creative, but it strikes me that such an attribution can obscure how rarely multilingual stories, truths, and utterances are ever also presumed *credible*.

In the worst cases, the association of multilingual stories with creativity and games can scuttle their bid to be heard as trustworthy, serious, or truthful in a given context or moment, while "plain language" monolingual texts arrive with built-in, unearned surplus presumptions of transparency, rationality, and informativeness. Increasingly, in this era of Artificial Intelligence, the prospect of multilingual credibility is an outcome reserved just for those well-paying corporate or state clients who can secure made-to-order localization/optimization services with which to curate the tone and receptivity of their messages to global monolingual end users. How can we make future institutions, publishers, and curricula hear and read the multilingual, code-mixing practices of diverse speaking subjects as propositionally *credible*—at least as credible as we grant for the least creative instances of monolingualism, to which institutions routinely ascribe credibility?

Ordolanguages and Otoliths

There are novels and memoirs whose authors—having rummaged around in the secondary and critical literature of their day for the conceptual resources they need for a particular kind of story, but find they're coming up empty-handed—go ahead and make the theory for themselves, in and through their own literary texts.[1] Dorthe Nors's *Mirror, Shoulder, Signal*—like Tidbeck's *Amatka* in the previous chapter—is one such extended and complex theoretical assertion. We take up this second novel so as to locate the literature of late monolingualism in the intimate primacy of one woman's rebellious but compulsive relationship to a global political economy of commoditized literary monolanguages. It documents Sonja's compromised alienation from the contemporary Danish-language spoke of the domestically fortified,

---

[1] In Gramling (2012, 2016a), I advanced a related claim about the ad hoc theory-making efforts around mono/multilingualism among Holocaust memoirists like Primo Levi when faced with such a theory deficit.

presumptively monolingual, but anti-protectionist language infrastructure for global commerce I have termed *ordolingualism* (Gramling 2020; see also Introduction, p. 7, for its definition).

In that critical spirit, Nors's novel delves into this broad symbolic domain of "orders" and "disorders" to explore Sonja's particular and compromised life in and with monolanguages. Sonja's vocation as a translator has trained her to be confidently productive in certain commercial orders of linguistic manufacture, while plagued with despairing purposelessness in the midst of other sociolinguistic experiences that fall outside of the productive relations of late-capitalist literary industry.

It is this tense nexus of subjectivity that proves wretchedly difficult, for Sonja and other multilingual literature-makers, to grasp and theorize—and to do so in a text conditioned by monolingual constraints. This difficulty is registered in oblique, embodied ways throughout the novel. Beyond (and while) being a literary translator from Swedish to Danish, Sonja suffers from bouts of Benign Paroxysmal Positional Vertigo (BPPV) or "otolithic" vertigo. Though dizziness and vertigo do not themselves add up to a "mood" in our sense of a late monolingual mood in literature, they are a mood-effecting circumstance for those who experience them: a confusing somatic syndrome that disorders one's sensemaking confidence in the world. Vertigo sporadically annoys subjectivity, it disrupts, it disconsoles and disabuses one's equilibrium, it threatens our credibility and "standing."

In the human ear, the "otoliths" are the organs that register our sense for gravity and linear acceleration, according to how we're oriented in space. At erratic intervals throughout Nors's novel, something in the translator Sonja's sensemaking habitus is perturbed, and she is compelled into unwelcome moments of fearful recognition:

> *The disorder,* she'd thought, and went to see the ear doctor, who proceeded to sling her around. "It's not dangerous, you know," he said on cue. "It's just some tiny stones inside of you that are breaking free." (55)[2]

This is a telling moment where Sonja's concern about her ongoing experience diverges from, and is overshadowed by, experts' advice, and where those experts' explanations are designed to sound both harmless to her and, ultimately, beneficent. When interacting with almost everyone in the novel, Sonja's desire to understand and share about the nature of the disorder

---

[2] Skavanken, havde Sonja tænkt og til ørelægen, som derefter kastede rundt med hende. Det er jo ikke farligt, sagde han som ventet. Det er bare nogle små sten, der river sig løs inden i dig (55).

she experiences results in disinterest, perplexity, or diminishment. She is encouraged over and over to banish this embodied experience from the slate of relevant, discussion-worthy things, despite the ubiquity of therapeutic wellness culture around her.

Edward Said's conception of late style, we'll recall from the Preface and Introduction, foresaw an involuntary, tense relation between aesthetics and bodily condition, one that can trigger acquiescence or defiance in equal measure. Nors's novel is an extended inquiry into that lived, embodied, and moody relation within late monolingualism, which is expressed in Sonja's constrained creativity as a commercial literary translator, particularly through the prism of her occasional dreaded dizziness, and her midlife resolve to learn how to drive an automobile despite the vertigo—hence the title *Mirror, Shoulder, Signal*.

The novel thus places us, and Sonja, within three modern orthopedic discourses, which intersect. First, there is the curative medical discourse addressing the vertigo, which seeks to restore Sonja to her proper bodily relation to perpendicularity and linear acceleration, and to mitigate the vividly disordered sense for gravity and bearing she occasionally experiences. Second, there is her driver's ed teacher and superego-intimate Folke (literally "the People"), who seeks to practically integrate Sonja into the orderly, arbitrary, consequential, and bindingly global symbolic conventions for automotive traffic. Third, there is Sonja's literary translating from Swedish to Danish, which compels her to reproduce gruesomely femicidal texts that have the added nationistic[3] (or soft-nationalistic) function of re-marking, to use an Amatkan term, for imagined end-user readers a strong distinction between two long-kindred and conditionally intercomprehensible standardized written Nordic literary languages, Danish and Swedish.

Each of these discourses magnanimously tutors Sonja, and us, how to "stay in our lane" in contemporary sociolinguistic life—that is, how to be a good, contact-averse ordolingual (Pratt 1991). Each teaches us toward proper dealings with a particular kind of naturalized linearity and grammaticality in traffic and communication, and brushes away any subjective impulse to improvise according to one's singular, local, embodied hunches about meaning and meaningfulness—whether as a translator, speaker, or mover in space. Sonja's inclination to begrudgingly endure these three normative, alienating, and enabling discursive apparatuses—rather than to dismantle them, or forgo them altogether—informs her social experience throughout

---

[3] Joshua Fishman called nationism the "very operational integrity" of the nation. "Nationism—as distinguished from nationalism—is primarily concerned not with ethnic authenticity but with operational efficiency" (1969, 113).

the novel, and haunts her with curiosity about alternatives to the symbolic pieties of late monolingual life.

Trading on Femicide in Clean Monolanguage Containers

The textual inquiries that form the core of *Literature in Late Monolingualism* continue on with this vexing killjoy problem around literature and multilingual subjectivity, by way of a Danish-language novel about being a translator of Swedish-language novels. Sonja's work as a translator in *Mirror, Shoulder, Signal* is likely not the kind of energetic activity that Sommer had in mind when she invited us to come play bilingual games. Being a translator is for Sonja a productive but depleting livelihood that, throughout Nors's novel, hovers in that ambiguous and stressful realm between what Arlie Russell Hochschild (1979) called commercial "emotional labor" and private "emotion work."

Mirror, Shoulder, Signal is not a ludic book that promotes translation and translingual practice as a liberatory artisanal field for any and all; it is an anxious story about living, feeling, and laboring (literarily), not just between two languages—which people have done for millennia—but between two globally marketed and securitized monolanguages.[4] The novel expresses a nonplussed aphasia toward Sommer's warm invitation, a perplexity whose unrelenting stamina, and disarming self-awareness, gives rise throughout the text to an emerging theory about literature in late monolingualism.

Here is how Sonja, the narrator, herself feels about the literature she translates for Denmark's ruling, middle, and leisure classes. (Note that Gösta Svensson is the name of "her" Swedish noir crime novelist, and Kate is Sonja's sister, who lives in the rural northwest of Denmark.)

> They don't read anything else, the politicos. In that sense they're like Kate. Both Kate and the politicians brag about the number of crime novels they read. Even though Kate goes around Balling with no idea of improving herself, she imagines that these books are edifying. That's why she tells Mom she's proud that Sonja has a finger in the pie. "Gösta throws light on society from below," people say. "It's just like Sudoku," the politicos say. A crossword puzzle with sperm and maggots, and they're bringing it to the cottage. Sunk in their wicker chairs, they read about

---

[4] See Introduction for these definitions.

body parts in black plastic bags. They'll rub themselves in SPF 50 and wallow in evil like it's a party. (59–60)[5]

Scorning Danish politicians' likening of the serially femicidal, thanatophilic Swedish crime novels she translates for them to Sudoku, Sonja has clearly grown crestfallen about the fact that—though bilingual games could and should be able to enrich a sense of relational meaning-making across languages and cultures—the political economy at hand induces instead a horrifying translingual anaesthetization process. If it is in fact a "game," late monolingual reading about the "Sweden nobody knows (det Sverige, ingen kender)" (65, 66) is the mere game of winning clean and untroubled dominium over the messy symbolic value of translingual others.

It is also, as we'll explore further below, a game of collecting and amassing xenos rights (Slobodian 2018) over meaning in others' languages. Drawing on Quinn Slobodian's work (2018, 2023), we can define linguistic xenos rights as the prerogative pursued by powerful clients to control the meanings and usages at work in others'/other languages from afar—for instance, US corporations' attempts to control what Italian subsidiaries or peer corporations mean when they use a particular Italian phrase or discourse (see Caimotto 2019 on "Anglicisms in Italian Environmentally Friendly Marketing"). Literary artists, too, like Gösta Svensson and his high-powered promoters in Sweden and beyond wish, and intend, to exert enduring xenos rights—in this case, over the Danish language Sonja articulates to represent him.

There are, then, three written, revenue-generating monolanguages in the mix, by way of which various actors are trying to speculatively exert xenos rights: 1) a presumptive readerly Danish monolanguage, published in Sonja's and Nors's books, 2) a presumptive compositional monolanguage in Svensson's[6] Swedish books (as a start-language for the endless gravy train of noir translations), and 3) the speculative Anglophone target monolanguage

---

[5] De læser ikke andet, politikerne. På den måde ligner de Kate. Både Kate og politikerne praler med, hvor mange krimier de læser. Selvom Kate har gået rundt i Balling og ikke haft til hensigt at løfte sig noget videre, bilder Kate sig ind, at krimierne eleverer hende. Det er derfor, hun siger til mor, at hun er stolt af, at Sonja har fingrene nede i den slags, *Gösta kaster lys over samfundet set fra neden*, siger folk. *Det er ligesom at løse en sudoku*, siger politikerne. En kryds og tværs med sperm og maddiker, og de skal have den med I sommerhuset. Nedsunket I fletstole skal de læse om ligdele i sorte plasticsække. De skal indsmøre sig i solfaktor 50 og dyrke det onde som fest (59–60).

[6] Unlike the usage throughout the novel's social discourse, where the Swedish author is routinely called by his given name Gösta—as though he is just everyone's friendly neighbor from down the street, and thereby trustworthy and "our kind of people"—I shall refer to him throughout this chapter by his surname.

of Misha Hoekstra's eventual internationally distributed translation—which I foreground, in part, on the conviction that literary translations are themselves always primary texts too, rather than just renderings of originals.[7]

Each of these written monolanguages is, I'll contend, a complex product, more specific in its design than the mere expression of an allegedly natural, ethnic, or national entity called "a language." Rather, in late monolingualism, each published literary utterance of monolanguage is an iterative supply-side product that emanates from a certain composite projection of global linguistic order, anticipated by authors and sanctioned by presses and distributors as a kind of clean shipping container for meaning.

In and beyond the world of Nors's novel, this continuous and lucrative production of monolanguage is predicated upon certain ongoing wagers about (a) the (non)intercomprehensibility of Nordic languages, (b) the prospective cultural translatability of such a text out of Danish or Swedish, and, relatedly, (c) the Anglophone reader's anticipated readiness to purchase and promote this novel. J. A. Y. Smith (2017) has coined the term *translationscape* to account for these various intersecting dimensions of translingual production and prospecting.

Literary Translation's Sunken Place

There are many thoughtful ways to read *Mirror, Shoulder, Signal*, some of which have to do particularly with language, and some of which don't. The interpretation we are working through here is most invested in the way Dorthe Nors tells a killjoy story about multilingualism by way of a literary translator, Sonja, who is both baffled at and enervated by the specific world-literary and linguistic market-order for which she is contracted to create translations.

It is also through this market-order that Sonja has acquired her ongoing financial stability as an adult linguistic citizen of Denmark and of the European Union, with all the personal privileges, vested interests, and identity compromises that such a stabilization reproduces in her. Is her resulting

---

[7] Both high and late monolingual textual products (see Introduction) tend to trade on an assumed ambivalence among readers about whether it is optimal to present an author (like Kant or Benjamin, or Svennson or Nors) as being just as cognitively original and capacious in English as they were in German, Swedish, or Danish, or whether emphasizing their translatedness supports one or another promotional project around the author. This wager is reflected most legibly in whether or not the translator is mentioned on covers and promotional materials, or whether translation is essentially erased from existence so as to elevate the primacy of an implicitly omnilingual thinker as authoritatively conscious in each word of the work.

experience of linguistic subjectivity—we are led to ask—an expression of good civic order, or of bad personal disorder? Is it a proud success, or rather a *skavank* (blemish/defect/fault) that makes her impeachable and potentially performance-unready?[8] It's hard to tell for us, and for Sonja herself: there seems to be little end in sight as far as Sonja's own financial stability is concerned, because the domestic Danish market's demand for the prolific, brutally femicidal Swedish Nordic noir crime novels she translates is also evidently insatiable.

And yet Sonja senses, or is beginning to sense, that "a vast exchange is commencing" ("[d]et bliver en stor udveksling") around the political economy that conditions her linguistic subjectivity, whether or not any of her readers might be taking note. Throughout the novel, this "commencing exchange" is registered through political, economic, semiotic, affective, corporeal, infrastructural, and relational indicators, though its bearing and end point remain tantalizingly unrevealed, as befits the text's emergent theory-making endeavor around its late monolingual mood.[9] Where Flannery O'Connor's natural landscapes dangled with ominous moral portents, in Sonja's twenty-first-century world it is the terraformed postindustrial landscape of Denmark that does so—shuddering with the prospective chaos of alternate worlds for meaning-making across languages.

Translating Monolanguages

What is it that might make a multilingually inclined author or translator, like Sonja, moody and disorderly in the carrying out of her vocation under current publication circumstances? Multilingual literary artists, like Nors and her main character Sonja, may of course desire a lot more from their current linguistic landscapes and subjectivities than the textual formats of their industry allow them to pursue under late monolingual conditions. They may desire—against "their" texts' conventional dispreferences:

---

[8] Hoekstra's English translates skavank as disorder, which introduces into a reading (based on that English text) an analytical binary between order and disorder. Skavank, deriving eventually from the Lower German for a wound taken in battle, foregrounds the wound itself as a socially legible blemish and therefore detriment.
[9] An "udveksling," in Danish, can mean exchange and transaction, but also a shakeup, for example, of personnel, resources, and roles. I thank Ann-Kathrine Havemose for consulting on both of these terms, skavank and udveksling.

- that literary texts might display the actual sociolinguistic diversity of the speakers in our communities and in our midst;
- that literary texts might showcase the human experience of linguistic change, orthographic mutation, multimodal expression, and stylistic opacity in their complex social contexts;
- that literary texts might highlight and investigate the everyday human experience of language learning, literary and technical translation, interpreting, and the like;
- that literary texts might evoke, guide, and educate knowledge about the feeling of being linguistically included or excluded—that they might render palpable the worldly experience of linguistic borders, frontiers, intimacies, and distances;
- that literary texts might make plain the infrastructures that move meanings from language to language, from linguaculture to linguaculture—bilaterally and multilaterally, quickly and slowly, beautifully and violently;
- that translation itself might be permitted, even encouraged, to "get out of control" before our eyes (Waterhouse 2011);
- that literary texts might have the effective power to portray how meanings from powerful other languages—those of a colonizer, governing authority, or transnational interest—exert a presence in the text and in the actions of its characters (i.e., exert xenos rights), as well as to depict practices of resistance and motivated mistranslation (Brickhouse 2014).

Sonja knows there's nothing about literature that essentially resists doing any of these things, and that nothing about these things is essentially unfeasible in literary texts. But the mandate of a clean, prophylactic monolingual piety—which rigorously quashes these desires—tends to prevail, deep and effective, in the literary industry where Sonja is laboring decade after decade. *Mirror, Shoulder, Signal* documents the way this controlled order of late monolingualism plays out in the embodied experience of one outwardly successful commercial translator.

I am interested in *Mirror, Shoulder, Signal*'s stamina in expressing the quietly defiant struggle of one literature-maker toward a credible multilingual subjectivity-in-the-flesh, from deep within the labor–industrial relations that—whether or not we asked for them—produce, or iterate, translational monolanguages for uptake and consumption in contemporary social life. The courage of the novel's contemplations lies in its ways of running against the affective grain of both the translatability industry (Gramling 2020) and defying the tempting conceit of linguistic indifference (Pipestone Group 2023).

Just as with Sonja's vertigo though, most of her interlocutors disregard these preoccupations she has about allegedly pernicious (dis)orders in language and translation as a woman's obsessive overthought: impractical and irrelevant to how things really are. Sonja's critical ruminations, despite this ongoing dismissal, further blemishes, rather than bolstering, her overall social and socio-commercial credibility in an entrepreneurial urbane scene. She puts the predicament this way in a letter to her sister Kate, who lives in the rural West of Denmark:

> Over here [in Copenhagen], the big thing is to find your market segment and blend in, to not stand out, to become a chameleon and then flee all other social relations. I miss sticking by someone. Like a burr. I want to be as unshakable as kin, for over here it's all teflon. (97)[10]

The particular implications of this wish to be unshakable are clarified through Sonja's profession as a literary translator, where her predicament within late monolingualism lies in being both party to its reproduction and increasingly desirous of its dismantling. Surrounded by the signs and impacts of relentless global anti-protectionist neoliberal economics, she can either stick with meanings and their contexts or blend in with the idiom of commercial optimization.

Troubled in this way, *Mirror, Shoulder, Signal* does flirt fretfully with a "discourse of retreat" (Gifford 1999, 45 ff.) into monolingual Danish national epistemes, while remaining transfixed on the traces in and around Sonja of ordolingual commerce via globally marketed translated discourse. The author Dorthe Nors sketches out the ambivalent intension of her particular literary–national mode as follows:

> I write in a minimalist style that is rooted in a Danish literary tradition— the subtleness, the way we undertone content, and the way psychological material is dwelling under the lines. I'm also trained in the Swedish tradition. I studied Swedish at university and there's a lot of Swedish existentialism in what I write. So, form: Danish. Content: Swedish (to simplify it enormously). (Nors 2017b)

---

[10] "Herovre handler det mest om at finde sit segment og så matche, aldrig stikke ud, blive en kamæleon, og så ellers flygte fra alle relationer. Jeg savner at blive hængende på nogen. Som en burre. Jeg vil være uafrystelig som biologiske relationer er det, for det er teflon herovre" (98).

Despite these "unshakable" commitments to Danish, Nors's writing also strains toward the antipastoral (Gifford 1999), as regards her anticipatory audience-design and her critical approach to cultural translation. The novel seems intent on fending off the halcyon idealization of the Danish countryside, and of supposedly untranslatable Danish cultural experiences. Describing how she works with the so-called untranslatable Danish ethnos of hygge (a "hugging," cozy interrelatedness), Nors writes:

> I don't want to wreck hygge. I just try to do hygge justice. And hygge is much more than the coziness of interior decoration, a laid-back lifestyle, and a happy-go-lucky approach to life. "Hygge" is also a social control mechanism. It's a way Danes keep unpleasant things at bay and make sure that nobody "spoils the fun." Hygge depends so much on consensus that it can be difficult to deal with for outsiders. At times hygge can even be dangerous. But I don't want to wreck hygge. It's lovely (and a bit weird) to walk through life in knitted socks. (Nors 2019)

On display here is more of Nors's killjoy criticality and craft, resisting an understanding of Danish's hygge as merely a reflexive convivial assent to norms of ideological coherence and positive community affect. Picturing an audience who will most frequently read her work in translation, she wants the collective concept of hygge to find full and complex expression in that readerly experience, and not to end up being an item for cheap meaning, consumed serially "just like Sudoku" (59–60). This ambition is one of the grand wagers of the novel, which seeks to theorize the ominous systematic cheapening of meaning in late monolingual traffic.

Before continuing in this line of thought on the dilemma of multilingual literary dispositions under the regime of late monolingualism, or rather as a way of doing so, I'll allow myself a moment to reflect on my own positionality and practice in these systems too—as a literary translator, like Sonja, who publishes novels with trade presses that distribute internationally. Sonja, the literary translator, is profoundly uncomfortable with the fate of "blending in to [her] market segment," wanting instead to "stick [. . .] by someone [. . .] [l]ike a burr." What does this ideal, this commitment, feel like for a working translator, when it triumphs or fails?

I found myself recently finishing page proofs on a book-length literary translation from Turkish into English, while also composing this chapter about *Mirror, Shoulder, Signal*, and wanting like Sonja does to stick to choices, to words, like a burr—not out of sheer recalcitrance and idiosyncrasy, but out of a particular belief in the broad multilingual, multimodal, epistemic capacities of the future readers I'd imagined for the book I was trying to make. Sonja's malaise in the novel brought to the surface several of my own intuitively attempted refusals in the face of the loose bundle of supply-side marketing and compositional norms I'd been asked to subscribe to, in the course of that literary translating and publishing process.

Though our press copy-editors for the Turkish-to-English novel translation were otherwise relatively light-handed with my and my co-translator's style in the target language of English (as long as the resulting manuscript was unequivocally in English monolanguage, save for a few cameos), I was struck by how the press imagined our potential readers to be far more epistemically narrow, and far more monolingually cloistered in their potential curiosities, than I found reasonable to presume. There was in the press's communications throughout the editing process an evangelical idealization of a frictionless, fast consumability for this world-literary text, preemptively cleansed of any moments that might prompt a reader to (desire to) Google something about said world, or to slowly sound out a borderline unfamiliarity.

What did the press, as a complex corporate team managing a supply chain of (cheap or dear) meaning, assume readers would or could (not) come face-to-face with about Turkish, Kurdish, Persian, and Yazidi (i.e., "greater Mesopotamian") concepts, metaphors, gestures, and historical references? What epistemic ideology and market stratagem of hyper-Anglophone monolingualism did they tacitly rely on to intuit this? It felt as if the press colleagues were trying, even in this cosmopolitan realm of "world literature," to measure our translation with the old adage "If English was good enough for Jesus..." (Pratt 2012).

Though there was no explicit house policy on these matters (see Eldridge 2023 on style guides and multilingualism), many of the press's suggested emendations to our various drafts seemed designed to overprotect readers from the multilingual world and its potential referential equivocations, to fortify a literary "monolingual international" (Anderson and Donato 2015) as a proxy buffer against the hardship of encountering something even momentarily opaque. In my postproduction dealings with the press, I felt as if I was spending a limited ration of indulgence tokens for items deemed beyond the English monolanguage, the overuse of which was alleged to threaten avid readers' access to an unencumbered, pleasant, immersively worldly read. Spending one token too many would, it seemed, block my readers' consciousness from being able to immersively inhabit this other world the text generously created for them (Ryan 2001, 14–15, 104).

Is that what translations, or literature, are supposed to do—whether they are sold at an airport or rather at a university bookstore? It's not as though our translation was thick with ambiguous cultural references that arbitrate elite taste through shibboleths on every page, nor even with what Schleiermacher suggested belonged to the practice of foreignization (Bernofsky 2014). What I sensed simply was that the press was designing readers, and designing *for* readers, who, they presumed, needfully subscribe to wall-to-wall monolingual expectations: namely that a single named language—here in our translation, English—is presumed credibly sufficient and ultimately optimal for managing all the meanings necessary for a worldly and capacious human life. My co-translator and I were not trying to get readers to pretend to know more than they did, nor certainly to know Turkish and Kurdish language or culture. But neither did we assume that their readerly practices and curiosities as "end users" of literature needed to be pre-limited to a monolingual epistemic and cosmological aperture. From whom and what, exactly, were they being protected?

The Translation Superhighway

Literary translation in late monolingualism is, in my own professional experience as in Sonja's, often structured around an invisible contract to pre-design an attenuated set of optimized meanings for a certain kind of imagined monolingual end user who is alleged to be living encased in an ordoliberal world market-order (on neoliberal forms of the "contract novel," see R. G. Smith 2014, 37; and Chapter 1). Translating is therefore not now primarily a craft that negotiates the critical dilemma of so-called domestication or foreignization of meanings in a world of differences, as it might have been when Schleiermacher ([1813] 1838) proposed these methods. Now that the postimperial, post–First World War era has redesigned global political economy around ordoliberal free-market principles for anti-protectionist meaning-transfer and orderly, inobtrusive decolonization after empire, principles which were not yet in effect in Schleiermacher's time, the contract is rather to reproduce a globalized discursive equilibrium of controlled parafamiliarities.

I regard *Mirror, Shoulder, Signal* as a linguistic antipastoral (Gifford 1999, 1), an inventory of the ways in which long-idealized depictions of the (Danish) cultural landscape are being dismantled by traffic in the kind of globalized, translingual meanings that Danish readers ostensibly prefer to consume in alienated form, hence the "vast exchange ... commencing" (Nors 2017a, 183). As a Swedish to Danish translator (working with two historically sibling languages), Sonja finds herself producing and reproducing for readers, who very well know better, the commodity of cosmopolitan monolingual feeling (Gramling 2009), a supply-side concoction for which Nordic publics have never really clamored.

In their nationistic-tutelary way, Sonja's translations help to retain and remake the kind of clean, untroubled, ordolingual borders between Swedish and Danish life and language (something which no one but jingoist shills have asked for, since the days of the Kalmar Union), amid the affective encroachments of economic globalization, ultimately to the benefit of those encroachments. What such supply-side ordolingual traffic management requires of her is regular delivery of functionally equivalent, pansemiotic sets of meanings—here, those housed in Svensson's femicidal crime novels—which can travel parallel to one another and be substituted for one another without difficulty or delay, when needed. This is the kind of translation that Sonja does, and it troubles her; it feels like a blemish on her character.

And yet, "domestic" and "foreign" are no longer particularly effective analytical concepts in this global political economy of ordolingualism in which contemporary translators like Sonja work, though the power of those categories as administrative performatives for exclusion is ironically intensifying in the political sphere of immigration/asylum. The linguistic order that Sonja and I, as literary translators, have inherited is rather an anti-protectionist one that has been ongoingly pre-stabilized to suit free-market monolanguages in their commercial interaction with other free-market monolanguages. Loss of linguistic sovereignty is the price we have paid for this stabilization, and Sonja's desire to reacquire and reimagine it, to "stick [. . .] by someone [. . .] [l]ike a burr," registers in her as a threateningly vertiginous blemish or disorder.

Here's the way Sonja accounts for her own pious, constrained subjectivity in the transposition of her star male author's writings from Swedish into Danish. The scene unfolds as Sonja is trying to recover, in as inconspicuous a way as possible, from an alarming bout of vertigo and double vision. Notice the affective interplay among details of involuntary bodily movements, gestures of tautological stoicism, banal cosmopolitanism, fidgeting, free-market ideology, the tyranny of consistency, behavioral fastidiousness, claustrophobia, and commodity quality control:

> She closes her eyes, opens them again: still two. She takes a deep breath, because it might have something to do with oxygen. A gulp of cola, and Vesterbrogade buzzes with sunlight. *It is what it is*, thinks Sonja, and she tells Molly that Gösta's going according to plan. She doesn't want to talk to her about back home. That would be like talking to Marie about Indre Mission. That kind of thing's a waste of time, and Gösta's engaged in dissecting the Sweden nobody knows with a fine scalpel, diligently strewing the body parts in a decipherable pattern nearby the entire way from the Artic Circle to Bornholm. Sonja is a party to the process, she's

deep into its linguistic manifestations, and since Gösta's publisher is busy launching Gösta every time he's written something new, Sonja's also busy editing Gösta, so that the blackbirds he's conjured on page ten don't turn into great tits by page fourteen.

"It's also important for a novel that a character have the same name throughout the entire work," Sonja says. "Unless the name change has something to do with the plot, that is."

"Can't you try and translate other authors?" asks Molly. "Some that mean something to you. After all, there ought to be a few Swedish authors who'd like to give readers something besides blood and guts."

"Free market forces," says Sonja and moves her legs; there's really not room for them under the café table. (65)[11]

Sonja scrubs her literary products for terminological consistency, with a nationistic fastidiousness (Fishman 1968) parallel to that with which Gösta Svensson offers a forensic diorama on "Sweden" from the Arctic Circle down to Bornholm. These two processes of symbolic provisioning—Svensson's incessant nationistic installments and Sonja's translative distributions—go hand-in-hand "according to plan"; it feels to her like a "waste of time" to imagine alternatives to this set of supply-side procedures.

Of course, one of the things Svensson is succeeding famously at doing is selling Sweden to literary tourists through the prurient power of sexualized violence, and Sonja knows she is spending her own career helping him to do so. Critiquing Jameson's conception of so-called Third World Literature, Shu-

---

[11] Hun lukker øjnene, åbner dem igen: stadig to. Så tager hun en dyb indånding, for det kan også være som at tale med Marie om missionen. Den slags er spild af tid, og Gösta er i gang med at dissekere det Sverige, ingen kender, med en fin skalpel, og han er flittig til at strø ligadelene i et aflæseligt mønster fra polarcirklen og næsten ned til Bornholm. Sonja er med i processen, hun er langt inde i dens sproglige forekomster, og fordi Göstas forlag har travlt med at få skudt Gösta af sted, hver gang han har skrevet noget nyt, har Sonja også travlt med at redigere Gösta, sådan at de solsorte, han har fremmanet på side ti, ikke har forvandlet sig til musvitter på side fjorten.
  —Det er også vigtigt for en roman, at en figur har det samme navn gennem hele værket, siger Sonja. —Medmindre navneforandringen har noget med plottet at gøre, altså.
  —Kunne du ikke prøve at oversætte nogle andre? Nogen, der betyder noget for dig. Der må da være svenske forfattere, der vil læseren noget andet end vold og blod, siger Molly.
  —De frie markedskræfter, siger Sonja og flytter på sine ben, de kan ikke rigtigt være under cafébordet (65–6).

mei Shih puts the aporia this way in their account of "Global Literature and the Technologies of Recognition":

> When the signified is predetermined, allegories are easier to write or create and to understand and consume. A predetermined signified is produced by a consensus between the audience in the West and the Third World writer or director. It is a contractual relation of mutual benefit and favor that works first to confirm the stereotyped knowledge of the audience and second to bring financial rewards to the makers of those cultural products. In other words, allegory works and sells because it makes the non-Western text manageable, decipherable, and thus answerable to Western sensibilities and expectations. (2004, 20)

Despite the framing Shih takes on from Jameson "between the West and the Third World," the claim applies well to how smaller literary monolanguages relate to their global ordolingual distribution channels. Sonja's and Nors's explicitly felt predicament is the repetitive, immobilizing dread of producing texts that are contracted to supply moderated doses of national allegory about another's "society from below" on an ordoliberal field of global parafamiliarities.

How can works like Nors's appear to satisfy a covenant with readers to uphold monolingualism and its affective promises about unfettered access to the foreign meaning-making world, and then break the contract anyway, midstream? By cross-figuring the decision-making experience of translation work with the decision-making discourse for automotive traffic, Nors establishes a practical–affective repertoire around the lived tension between alleged freedom of mobility and controlled infrastructure—upon which this possibility of breaking the contract can be then imagined and tested in an ongoing, minute way.

What Mary Louise Pratt (2002) coined under the phrase "the traffic in meaning" twenty years ago remains a potent and suggestive image. If we allow this metaphorical phrase to expand into its properly complex and worldly infrastructural dimensions, it is no unified phenomenon or simple slogan.[12] Traffic can be bustling, hulking, jagged, streamlined, violent, stalled, quiet, loud, smelly, antiseptic, peopled, mechanical, efficient, illicit, or wayward (see, for instance, Robbins 2007). There are many lanes—off-ramps, shoulders, breakdown lanes, sluices, guardrails, and embankments—all simultaneously copresent and all in various states of use and disuse, of repair and disrepair.

---

[12] As ever, I'm indebted to the Chilean educator Malena Samaniego Salinas for her inspiring thoughts on this metaphor.

Thousands of years of energy and innovation have gone into steering and enclosing the trafficking of dirty, pungent, living, and perishable things into containers that mask, preserve, or neutralize these various qualities of the contained substance. Supply-side manufacture has learned how to disprefer "perishable" items that do not traffic well, or at least predictably, over long stretches of space, time, and other frontiers. Though this systematized prophylaxis has historically applied to foodstuffs, crops, energy, minerals, and livestock primarily, there is no good reason to exclude linguistic and symbolic meanings from the analytic of potentially "perishable" items in the traffic, which an infrastructure might ultimately decline as unsuitable for transport.

Nors's novel is an extended study in the subjective experience of participating reluctantly in a certain kind of securitized, risk-averse traffic-in-meaning—and of one driver-in-training's sense for why capitulating to such safe behavior in traffic feels ultimately still so preferable over other kinds of arduous mobility and transformation. Among other things, the novel's title, *Mirror, Shoulder, Signal*, replays for us—and for its main character—an internationally shared mnemonic device that simplifies complex embodied knowledge about how to safely change lanes while driving an automobile.

This mnemonic is concurrently then an allegory for how, in an age of what I call ordolingual commerce, one comes to the conclusion that one can and must translate "safely" by using compulsory supply-side functionalities, as if switching language tabs on a Wikipedia entry. Like the other three main novels treated in this book—Stephenson's *Cryptonomicon*, Tidbeck's *Amatka*, and Miéville's *Embassytown*—*Mirror, Shoulder, Signal* test-balloons in its very title a safety concern about leaving behind potential (un)translatabilities, and does so against the backdrop of an age of global literary production whose business model is premised on no less than omnilingual diffusionism (Kellman 2016).

In the critical reception of Nors's novel, interest in this anxious critique of (translational) monolingualism that is set forth on nearly every page has been fascinatingly absent, and this gap mirrors the ways Sonja's experts and peers within the novel want to steer her away from thinking too much about language—which is, after all, her métier. Nors has described how she learned to cultivate a relationship to the gradual merging of translated and original language as her work became more popular, and how her compositional practice has "really changed" in her life (Nors 2019) because of the translations. And yet, when *Rumpus* asked her to reflect on the state of translation in Denmark, and the way this novel articulated a conversation about it, she thanked the interviewer for the delightfully unexpected question:

No, there have been no wider conversations about the state of translation or the psychology of translation in connection to the book. The psychology of translation is really interesting, though. What happens when you live through the work and voice of someone else? But I was never asked about that in Denmark. Thank you for asking. There is an interesting translation theme waiting to be excavated from that book. (Nors 2019)

So, although Nors herself attests to this major change that translatedness has brought to her compositional life, she also notes how this dimension is only an inchoate or potentially neglected theme in the critical conversation around *Mirror, Shoulder, Signal*. This set of ironies suggests to me even more strongly that the novel advances its own version of "a new sentimental education" (Sommer 2003) around late monolingualism, around its confusing effects for readers and writers, and its as-yet uncomprehended impact on this age of literary writing—despite the obviously topical role that translating fiction plays in the novel's plot.

The Femicide at the Heart of the Translation System

It is not happenstance that what is at the center of Sonja's successful translation career is women's "suffering from elsewhere": murderous misogyny is the symbolic lynchpin of the Swedish political nationalism (Fishman 1968) being translated and avidly consumed by Danish politicos throughout the novel. Sonja reflects in passing on a television psychologist whom she could easily imagine appearing in one of the future Svensson novels she'd inevitably be asked to translate. This psychologist, she recalls stoically,

> liked to put women in a centrifuge. He'd had the centrifuge constructed for his experiments. A woman would sit strapped into the middle, and Gösta would have loved the contraption. If Gösta knew it existed, he would immediately write it into a scene. A woman, strapped tight and preferably naked, with something in her mouth. But never mind Gösta, because then the psychology professor centrifuged these women. The women were spun around, up and down. They spun in ellipses, and yes, they were strapped in while they spun. Then afterward, when the centrifuge had stopped, the women were asked to do exercises. In the exercises, they were supposed to orient themselves spatially. They were supposed to coordinate distances and solve math problems and walk a straight chalk line. The women were terrible at it, and the professor

concluded that women were poor at orienting themselves in space. Then he put a black man in the centrifuge. He centrifuged the black man for a long time and achieved the same result: black men were extremely bad at orienting themselves in space. In fact, there was only one group of people who oriented themselves worse, and that was black women. (89)[13]

The image of the centrifuge dramatizes late monolingualism's tendency to select market-ready "exhibitionist" stories (Pandey 2016) and violently distribute them throughout the free-market world-language system with as much velocity as possible. Sonja foresees that such exhibitionism will tend to upvote stories of authoritarianism, misogyny, precaritization, impunity, racialized social hierarchy, and humiliation pageantry, because those are the meanings that sell otherness and diversity the cheapest.

In "Art That Scars" (2018), the comparatist Başak Çandar argues alongside J. M. Coetzee's short 1986 essay "Into the Dark Chamber" that

> the dark torture chamber tempts the novelist to imagine what goes on in the room, thus triggering the novelistic fantasy. The danger is that this fascination often turns violence into a spectacle at the expense of the victim. In fictional torture narratives this becomes especially problematic, because the trauma of torture arises not just from the experience of extreme physical pain, but also from the humiliation of the exposed body—its privacy completely violated, its private functions made forcibly visible. (1342)

Svensson, Nors's tireless scion of this pruriently violent procedure of spectacularization, knows this formula well and will gladly and efficiently provide the supply-side "content" for the centrifuge to distribute translingually in the name of Nordic Noir (see also Melamed 2011). After all, one of the specters that Sonja, Nors, and Svensson all dread may be haunting novels

---

[13] [H]an kunne godt lide at sætte kvinder ind i en centrifuge. Han havde fået bygget centrifugen til sine forsøg. Kvinden sad spændt fast inde midt i den, og Gösta ville have elsket det apparat. Hvis Gösta vidste, det apparat fandtes, ville han straks skrive det ind i en scene. En kvinde, fastspændt, nøgen helst, og med noget i munden. Men til side med Gösta, for så centrifugerede psykologprofessoren kvinderne. Kvinderne blev kørt rundt, op og ned. De snurrede i ellipser, og de var jo spændt fast, mens de snurrede. Så bagefter, når centrifugen stod stille, blev kvinderne bedt om at lave øvelser. I øvelserne skulle de orientere sig rumligt. De skulle koordinere afstande og løse matematiske opgaver og gå lige på en kridtstreg, Kvinderne var elendige til det, og professoren konkluderer, at kvinder var dårlige til at orientere sig i rum. Så satte han en sort mand ind i centrifugen. Han centrifugerede den sorte mand meget længe og nåede frem til det samme resultat: Sorte mænd orienterede sig uendelig dårlig rumligt. Faktisk var der kun en mennesketype, der orienterede sig dårligere, og det var sorte kvinder (89).

in late monolingualism is the imminent "charges of repetition and yawns of familiarity" (Shih 2004, 16), most notoriously sloganized by Tim Parks's 2010 essay "The Dull New Global Novel." Ostensibly unconcerned, Svensson himself pontificates that the remedy for this specter of dullness is to script into the novel certain kinds of formulaic translatable singularities:

> A Gösta seminar [in Stockholm], where Gösta was supposed to tell people how his books should be translated. And as if that wasn't enough, he'd also wanted to tell them how the books should be written, and at one point he told them that the crime commissioner ought to have a quirk. *Kiwrk* is how Gösta said it. The commissioner ought to have a *kiwrk*, an idiosyncratic penchant for chewing matchsticks or collecting toy cars. On top of his *kiwrk*, the commissioner ought to drink and have family problems, preferably with a daughter. Gösta was sharing this sort of thing with his translators, translators who covered large swaths of Europe. Most of these translators had been educated at venerable universities, but the knowledge they'd acquired there was of no use anymore. (136)[14]

Note particularly this last sentence, where it is suggested that everything the assembled multilingual Svensson translators had once learned from their own advanced philological training at university—about, for example, particularity and aesthetic originality—appears to have quaintly obsolesced, because the production of literature now requires a standard set of supply-side formulae for producing controlled otherness, formulae that Svensson himself is invited to pedantically prescribe at the helm of his very own "Gösta seminar."

Men Depoliticize Language for Me

Instead of taking up critically multilingual projects through literary means, those philologically trained translators at the Gösta seminar are conscripted

---

[14] Et Gösta-seminar, hvor Gösta skulle fortælle folk, hvordan hans bøger skulle oversættes, men ikke nok med det; han ville også fortælle, hvordan bøger skulle skrives, og på et tidspunkt fortalte han, hvordan en kriminalkommissær skulle have et "quirk." *Kvørk*, sagde Gösta, Kommissæren skulle have et *kvørk*, altså en idiosynkratisk hang til at tygge på tændstikker eller samle på legetøjsbiler. Ud over *kvørket* skulle kommissæren drikke og have problemer i familien, helst med en datter. Som en god far fortalte Gösta oversættere fra store dele af Europa om den slags. De fleste af disse oversættere var uddannet på hævdvundne universiteter, men deres viden var der ikke længere brug for (138–9).

as thanatophilic otherness machines for amassing xenos (copy)rights. This revelation dawns on Sonja gradually and somatically:

> Actually, Sonja's not hungry. If she scrutinized herself, she'd find a spot of queasiness. It's not late pregnancy, ha! Or the stomach flu. It's the large quantities of coffee that she ingested during an especially violent chapter of Gösta. All that flesh decomposing; the angry ejaculations, the mutilated vaginas, the ritual adornment of evil. Every summer, journalists ask the members of parliament about the reading material they're bringing to the cottage. And they're bringing Gösta. (59–60)[15]

In a study of contemporary Yucatec Maya literature—from Noh Tzec to Briceida Cuevas Cob—Paul Worley has described a homologous dynamic of such linguistic exhibitionism, faced by Indigenous authors under conditions of neoliberal multiculturalism since the 1980s. Worley describes a mode of

> neoliberal translation [which] allows for the production and presentation of Indigenous-language texts so long as these are reduced, almost by definition, to being a symbolic supplement to Spanish texts that are actually read. [. . .] Moments of irreconcilable otherness are translated into the terms and structures of the neoliberal multicultural nation-state, thereby reaffirming that nation-state's norms and values. (Worley 2017, 291)

Worley hastens to add that "this mode of translation is not a conscious matter of selection for many of the indigenous writers who translate their own work, nor is it a straightforward assimilationist project of governments that may patronize them" (292).[16]

Though Worley is clear that this "mode" is not assimilationist in the traditional sense—and that its format as a "semiotically absorbed object" (296) is "ripe with decolonial potential" (2017, 295; see Arias 2012, 212–13)—he shares with Charles Hale two key arguments about neoliberal translation. First, it is part of a broader "cultural project, which contributes

---

[15] Egentlig er Sonja ikke sulten. Når hun mærker godt efter, har hun en snert af kvalme. Det er ikke en sen graviditet, ha! Eller Roskildesyge. Det er de store mængder kaffe, hun har indtaget over et voldsomt Gösta-kapitel. Alt det kød i opløsning. De hidsige ejakulationer, de lemlæstede skeder, og måden det onde pyntes med ritual på. Hver sommer spørger journalisterne folketingspolitikerne, hvilket læsestof de skal have med i sommerhuset. Og de skal have Gösta med (59).
[16] Arguments of this sort have been advanced, for instance, in the case of Rigoberta Menchú's *testimonios* (Arias 2006).

both to the rising prominence of Indigenous voices and to the frustrating limits on their transformative aspirations" (Hale 2007). Second, it is part of a broader economic agenda that "openly recognizes, if not outright celebrates, the rights of all people within a given nation-state even as it simultaneously erodes the rights of labor and slashes state-funded projects in order to facilitate economic exchange" (Worley 2017, 292; Hale 2006, 75). Furthermore, Worley argues, neoliberal translation is embedded in a transformation of citizenship in which "these victories have been achieved at the precise moment when neoliberal policies have altered, if not all together devalued the meaning of citizenship itself" (292; see also Moksnes 2012, 10).

This mode of neoliberal translation plays, in Melamed's view, a prominent role in conveying literature "as a way for dominant classes to know racialized others intimately [. . .] [L]iberal antiracisms have made it possible to disseminate highly ideological truths and information bits as authentic and substantive knowledge" (2011, 16–17). Sonja's confrontations with the Gösta industry's inner workings diagram a forensics of translated discourse as it circulates homeostatically to and fro through global free-market orders, from domestic state actors and policymakers to transnational content-providers and embodied translators, who together form and stabilize a particular political economy through monolanguages. Gradually, Sonja's questions to herself mirror Çandar's:

> How can a representation subvert this exposure, when it cannot help but expose to the readers the exposed body? In Coetzee's understanding the problem is less linguistic than conceptual. State violence and torture are the mechanisms of a compromised and unethical system. How can the novel, then, represent these mechanisms without perpetuating and becoming complicit in this unethical system? Or, how can these representations convey torture as the product of a systemic immorality, rather than a culmination of individual acts of evil? How can such representations avoid turning violence into a spectacle, an object of curiosity or fantasy? (Çandar 2018, 1342)

The traffic in cheap meaning is indeed not a literary or poetic problem alone; it works at the level of any relationship that seeks to establish reproducible, accessible, commensurated meanings from one language to the next, regardless of what that harvest/target language is. It seeks to replace "dear" meanings—cherished and endemic ones forged through lineages of "hard multilingualism" (Noorani 2013)—with mutable, tradeable, expendable ones. The kind of disposable cheap meaning to which Sonja increasingly calls alarmed attention is not merely the translingual commodity of mass-produced images, sentiments, tropes, and dramatic twists, superimposed from one production context to the next, as quarterly revenue benchmarks require. Sonja is prompted to apprehend these emerging questions in part because of the naggingly enfleshed defect/disorder (*skavank*) she experiences against her will, the vertigo, and the impending feeling of vulnerability and anticipatory dread that it furnishes her in everyday life, especially as she wagers to become a motorist. The vertigo, like Svensson's killers, is always around the corner, though the doctors and politicos, respectively, assure her that she is in no danger whatsoever.

Rather, this agony is at its most potent when it takes place through exchanges (udveksling) within intimate relationships. Kate and Sonja are two sisters who aggravate and alienate one another in part because of Sonja's university training in literature. But it is Sonja's work translating misogynistic Swedish crime novels into Danish, which her sister and other family members read voraciously, that regains Sonja some standing within the family. The following passage vividly detects the particular affective alienations at work in late monolingualism. Notice the role of fear and intrafamilial anxiety, which is ultimately assuaged by a global traffic in displaced violence:

> It's as if Kate's afraid of something in Sonja, though Sonja doesn't think of herself as a person to fear. *And if there's someone who scares me, it's Gösta*, Sonja thinks, regarding the manuscript on the desk. *His rapes and his sales numbers scare me.* Yet Kate's not afraid of Gösta. That sex criminal who might lurk behind the front door when she comes back from a late shift at the nursing home? Kate tackles him lustily in the pages of Gösta's books. If there's one place the two sisters can meet, it's in Gösta Svensson, because Sonja's in fact the reason that Kate can now disappear, in Danish, into an ordered universe of evil. With Gösta, Kate can sniff death without it actually concerning her, and the hatred she must feel for herself can find an outlet in the killings that always form the prologue of Gösta's stories. She's also told their mother that she feels proud that Sonja knows Gösta. "Kate is fond of you," Mom's told her on the phone. "She thinks it's great about that crime writer fellow." (29)[17]

---

[17] Det virker, som om Kate er bange for noget ovre i Sonja, men Sonja synes ikke, hun er noget at være bange for. Hvis jeg er bange for nogen, er det Gösta, tænker Sonja og betragter manuskriptet på skrivebordet. Jeg er bange for hans voldtægter og hans salgstal. Men til gengæld er Kate ikke bange for Gösta. Den seksualforbryder, der måske gemmer sig bag entrédøren, når Kate kommer hjem fra en sen vagt på plejehjemmet, håndterer hun lystfyldt i Göstas bøger. Hvis der er et sted, Kate og Sonja kan mødes, så er det i Gösta Svensson, for Sonja er selve grunden til, at Kate nu også på dansk kan forsvinde ind i ondskaben som ordnet univers. Hos Gösta kan Kate lugte til døden, uden at den egentlig angår hende, og det had, hun måtte føle til sig selv, kommer rigeligt til udbetaling i de aflivninger, der altid er ouverture til Göstas historier. Kate har også sagt til mor, at hun er stolt af, at Sonja kender Gösta. *Kate ER da glad for dig*, har mor sagt i telefonen. *Hun synes, det er flot med ham det krimimanden* (26).

What kind of intrafamilial alienations are being expressed here through the proxy theme of translated literature? More specifically, what kind of transnational political economy ensures that Kate's fondness for her sister is based not on their sisterhood, but because of the kind of supply-side function she plays in the reproduction of certain cheap meanings, delivered regularly to Denmark from elsewhere?

There is likely a historical reason why it feels easier for Kate and Sonja to interact by way of a foreign author marketed to them from abroad, that is, through a controlled unfamiliarity. This comfortable kind of alienation had been engineered for them nearly a century ahead of time. In his economic history *The Globalists: The End of Empire and the Birth of Neoliberalism* (2018), Quinn Slobodian argues that a small cabal of economic intellectuals and institutional designers active in Central Europe from the 1920s onward were extraordinarily successful in shaping the cultural globalism that guides much of contemporary thinking for institutional design in statecraft, publishing, and other spheres well beyond economics.

They did this through strategies of controlled postimperial decolonization that touted the value of national self-determination while severely curtailing it at the same time. Inspired primarily by the Austro-Hungarian Empire, which devolved language and culture matters to the constituent nations while retaining authority over trade and economic policy at the imperial state level, these "ordoliberal" thinkers wanted to export from the Danube Basin a container-model for borderless free-market relations, unobtrusively ornamented by vibrant national identities and their languages.

Rather than a synoptic model of control and world planning (with the graphs, charts, or formulae popular in 1920s economics), the mostly Germanophone intellectuals of the Geneva School of ordoliberalism represented a somewhat subtle (but all the more effective) approach to order and adjustment, which eschewed aggressive interventionist counter-models like the Bretton Woods system. Their cosmology for "the world economy" was of a sublime, unknowable unity that had to be respected by strong pro-market laws, always at the expense of emerging national autarchies in Latin America and Africa.

The international trade theorist Gottfried von Haberler saw the world as a homeostatic unity, as a developing economic organism, and catalogued the obstacles that disrupted that unity (customs, duties, tariffs, protectionism). This view of things was often called the Haberler method, based on his 1936 report characterizing the entire world economy as a sublime object of inquiry. In this sense, the Geneva School were not planners so much as deplanners, and their deplanning explicitly sought to undermine national self-determination, particularly later in the 1960s Global South.

Slobodian shows how the mostly Germanophone intellectuals of the Geneva School of ordoliberalism sought to protect dominium from imperium, that is to protect the free flow of capital and foreign-owned property over the objections of any local territorial protectionism. This principle, of a dual world-government that protected dominium (i.e., private property), became a major contribution of the Geneva School to the American New Right in the 1960s and 1970s. New Right proponents like Bill Buckley, in turn, used neoliberal economic conceptions about then-decolonizing Rhodesia, for instance, to defend racial segregation in the immediate wake of the *Brown v. Board of Education* decision in the United States. Asserting dominium, therefore, was never about "property" alone; it was also about white supremacy, the wielding of symbolic power from afar (Kramsch 2020), and the prerogative to cast political subjectivity in economistic terms.

Geneva School neoliberalism was "ordoliberalism" made global. Ordoliberalism was born of the Habsburg "dual" government—not in the sense of the Hungarian and Austrian dual monarchy, but of the economic and the cultural realms, sequestered from one another jurisdictionally. The logic went like this: while all of the nations of the Austro-Hungarian Empire would be allowed to keep and govern their languages, flags, and cultural emblems, the empire's economy was run entirely by the central state. This Habsburg-inspired model is essentially that which neoliberals wished to transmit systematically throughout the rest of the decolonizing world—to restore the world to the dual-government structure that had worked so well for empires, where features reserved for dominium (economics and property) predominated over those devolved to imperium (culture, language, national institutions, education, and domestic statutes).

These men didn't just have ideas and theories: they were effective at diffusing them into the institutional design of bodies that would later (or immediately) adopt their impulses to varying extents, including the European Union, the World Trade Organization, and the Doha Round. One of the ordoliberals' key principles, which they borrow from none other than Carl Schmitt, is the underlying political necessity of the "effective depoliticization of the economic" ("wirkliche Entpolitisierung des Ökonomischen"; Grandner and Traxler 1984)—that is, the legally secured exemption of economic processes (and their impacts on culture) from political intervention of any sort.

It was, of course, precisely this kind of autonomous prerogative for political and economic control (in a previously imperial polity and policy landscape) that newly emerging postcolonial nation-states demanded in Africa, Latin America, and elsewhere—including urgent measures like redistributive justice; colonial reparations; permanent sovereignty over national resources and monetary policy; increased, uncoercive, and reliable aid; stabilization of commodity prices; and regulation of transnational corporations (Slobodian 2018).

Thanks to these male ordoliberals from Central Europe, though, we can trace this political imperative of effective depoliticization of the economic into all aspects of contemporary life: the insistence on personal responsibility and fiscal discipline; the imperative of individuals to compete with one another and themselves for ever decreasing resources; the lack of consequences for impunity among predatory lenders and data breaches; the triumph of *Citizens United* and unbridled wealth disparity; and the narrowing of public discourse to a mere trickle of patriotism, viral memes, and unaffordable superconcerts. All of this and more—including the logic of late monolingualism itself—can and should be traced, at least in part, through the economic cosmologies of the ordoliberal Mont Pelerin Society's (MPS) halcyon visions of Habsburg dual government.

Speech Has Horsepower and Direction

One of the key tenets for such a model for globalization was the protection of xenos rights, Slobodian's term for former imperial land-owners' entitlement to continue to exert dominion over properties owned abroad, even if the territory where those properties are located is now in constitutionally decolonized nation-states' hands. Mines, plantations, agricultural and strategic sites, oil fields, foreign military installations, infrastructure features, and today data-hubs are places where the principle of foreign dominium is permitted to override the principle of local imperium.

On its own, this neocolonial reassertion of dominium, which has been relatively continuous with and unimpeded by decolonization processes, is an important theme in literary work the world over. But there is a further plane that Slobodian's conception of xenos rights permits us to consider, and that is the linguistic and more broadly symbolic and discursive plane. Though neocolonial violence is exerted through dominium claims in Indigenous and decolonized lands, whether these be claims made by interests (private or state) headquartered in former imperial states or by entirely new colonizers (i.e., China in East African mines, for instance), dominium over property and relations of production is only one expression of xenos rights.

Slobodian does not extend the inquiry to xenos rights asserted for excavating (cheap) meaning and other symbolic resources—that is, when neocolonial interests demand, implicitly or explicitly, to control not necessarily the surface-level words that circulate in local languages in decolonized territories, but rather the meanings and discourses that these local idioms are coerced into bearing.

In Nors's novel, it is for instance the mythologized discourse of femicide that enjoys unbridled xenos rights in other languages, thanks to Sonja's lucrative compensation as a reluctant matrix of its reproduction.

Customarily, this question is handled under the rather vague aegis of "cultural globalization." But what does it look like when a firm, state, or industry is able to compel a local community of practice, using "its own language," to make and utter meanings that comport with the concerns of that firm, state, or industry headquartered overseas? That it prioritize or answer the questions that firm, state, or industry poses? From "individual initiative" to "zero tolerance" to "terrorism" to "sustainability" to "fiscal responsibility" all the way to conceptual orthodoxies like "the economy" or individual "language(s)," xenos rights of meaning are asserted when one agent seeking to export such an interest or discursive framing requires an external mirror image of itself elsewhere, which it can then reimport and verify as evidence of familiar universal values newly re-witnessed in an unfamiliar idiom.

Homi Bhabha (1984) had touched upon such relations when he described the process of colonial mimicry and mimesis. But what is still outstanding now, a half century since his theorization of mimicry, is a systematic account of how these processes obtain in the relations of production among literary translation, AI-mediated information management, and international publishing. How do literary authors encounter this phenomenon of symbolic xenos rights which, I contend, is a key stabilizing function of late monolingualism?

If earlier forms of nationalized monolingualism in the postcolonial language planning process (see Fishman 1968) strategically adopted and normalized counterpart words in local languages that would correspond with those of global hypercentral languages, the post-1990 automation of Cross-Language Information Retrieval has turned this equivalence-building procedure into a totalizing infrastructure that is meant to cover as many languages as can be found and named as such. Literature in late monolingualism, and Sonja within it, lives in the busy shadow of this escalated rush on linguistic and symbolic xenos rights.

These questions have long been foremost in Nors's mind as a writer. She spells out the challenges as she sees them:

> Denmark is such a small country. 5.6 million people. We're a tribe. We've learned since we were children that we're small and weak compared to big neighbors like Germany, but we've also learned that the best thing about us is that we're Danish. We're so proud of being Danish. That pride makes it hard to be international. Danes are very proud of other Danes doing well in the world. Danes doing well in the world should however

only talk about Denmark in certain ways, when outside Denmark. You should never say anything controversial about the Danes, even though you are a Dane yourself. If you get international success, you are both elevated back home and excluded. "You are no longer one of us!" It's hard to balance, if not impossible. But I am Danish, and I am international. I love my country, I love the landscape, the language, the humor—but I couldn't live without having access to other regions of the world. It works for me because I was blessed to find homes for my literature in the US and the UK (and after that in many other countries). I have a great editor in Denmark who supports me both at home and abroad. It works because of the literature in itself and because of the people who read it. (Nors 2019)

Despite the measured tone of this assessment, Nors attests to some crushing cultural constraints she experiences as regards what literary utterances are supposed to do in order to be publishable. I have called this set of behavioral constraints ordolingualism—an economistic model of multilingualism (and translating) modeled after the ordoliberal economics and political economies of the unevenly postcolonial 1930s through 1970s, described above. It is a bundle of practices and principles that aim to adjust languages into supple relations with one another in a global order that minimizes protectionism, diminishes decolonial opacity, subdues linguistic sovereignty, and removes other subjective and local barriers to free access on capitalization frontiers. Key to ordoliberalism and ordolingualism alike is that they tolerate and promote cultural expression (imperium) only to the degree that it does not hamper free trade and private control (dominium).

Further to this process of adjusting meanings multilaterally, and to its impact on Nors's compositional subjectivity, *Rumpus* magazine asked Nors about her collaboration with her English translator Misha Hoekstra:

The manuscript goes back and forth a lot. I participate in the translation in the beginning. When it comes to the English language, Misha Hoekstra always has the final call. When it comes to the Danish language, its dialects, and at times very subtle and slightly hidden meanings, I always have the final call. These two levels of language have to merge. After the first drafts of the manuscript, I leave the work to Misha. We started working like this five years ago when my books weren't sold to that many countries. I had the time to dwell on the process back then. I learned a lot from that. Now I have translators working on my books in all kinds of languages. Even Chinese! And Catalan! My writing life has really changed. (Nors 2019)

It is relatively common for authors to talk fondly about their close collaboration and compromises with their translators in this way. But when Nors speaks here about the two levels of language having to merge, there is a striking attunement to the ordoliberal concept of imperium and dominium, where international commodity traffic (the second domain) must not be impeded by cultural particularity (the first domain), and that these two domains must be coordinated into a hierarchical harmony. They cannot be simply left to their own devices, as the spirit of a "free" market might suggest.

Translation, in Nors's story, is alas, as we've noted, not the wide, creative, embodied, and expressive aesthetic craft and sovereign intellectual prowess activated by transposing complex meanings from one language to another. In fact, it is barely celebrated in the novel at all. Rather, translation is desublimated in Sonja's story—constrained to the act of safely moving volatile commodities from one lane of linguistic traffic to another in a securitized, fast-moving, and controlled infrastructure, lest a costly and threatening accident occur, the nature of which is rarely specified. It is a late, pliant, and fearsome mode of resigned production, with none of the ludic affect of games and creativity many of us expect to see in the arena of multilingual practice.

To Sonja's increasing dismay, translation is a security-minded activity that prizes the reinforcement of borders and the assurance of stakeholder dividends. It encourages language-making subjects to stay ever equidistant from the counterpart objects around them in other lanes, that is, from other bounded monolanguages, otherly territorialized linguacultures, and otherly languaged literatures. Blurring lines between Swedish and Danish, for instance, would run counter to the design of that revenue-generating infrastructure.

These prophylactic behaviors are what the ordoliberal free market in translation requires: the future-proofing of a supply-side global multilingual infrastructure (Krystallis et al. 2020). In the 1990s, rapidly transnationalizing commercial interests had good reason to be worried about the complexity and recalcitrance of a multilingual world that now threatened to constitute the lion's share of their (deregulated) competitive market, and corporations had begun to apprehend the process of linguistic globalization as a "chaotic, dangerous and bewildering prospect" (Kelly-Holmes 2010, 196). Managers in logistics and development needed a supralingual idiom, not necessarily English, but something possessed of enough ordering power so as to "bring harmony to the world" of marketing (196).

Such a future-proofed linguistic infrastructure for global trade seeks unobjectionable outcomes that are relatively indifferent to linguistic vividness, expressive precision, and accurate local meaning (features devolved to imperium), if these cause any friction in the linguistic supply chain. It rather aims to secure managerial flexibility and constant value-creation throughout the linguistic or literary commodity's operational life. Translation becomes a kind of future-proofed bounded rationality (Krystallis et al. 2020, 8), with its own compulsory security-minded mnemonics like "mirror, shoulder, signal." As a translating subject who yearns for various kinds of unstructured and intuitive mobility, Sonja is always profoundly ambivalent about this alienated, allegedly accident-proofed version of her vocation. Equally prone to hedge in favor of its orderliness as she is to dilate in subjective intensity, she expresses this anxious, frustrated perfect ambivalence to Folke:

> "I just want to learn how to drive, okay? I don't want to have my hand held. I don't want to be massaged, hugged or interrogated, to be hit on or coochie-cooed. I want to learn to drive that car so I can drive over there!"

Sonja can point too, and what she points at is Avedore Power Station, but also behind it, at Denmark and the world in general.

> "I want an ordinary Class B driver's license, and all the other bullshit you people dish up is stuff I got wise to a long time ago. I'm over forty, and I've learned it the hard way, so don't push your Gestapo on me." (167)[18]

Far from "sticking [. . .] by someone [. . .] [l]ike a burr," like she'd said she wanted, Sonja here identifies with the kind of mobility that ordolingualism and ordoliberalism offer: freedom of trade and commercial opportunity, unconstrained by context-specific cultural and linguistic differences and the difficult movements between them. Frustrated with the superego-figure Folke, who is teaching her to drive, Sonja wants to bat away everything else, including him, that feels hellishly intimate in her midst—paternalism, condescension, sexism, wanted and unwanted human contact, history, invasions of privacy, fascism, intimacy, culture, context—in favor of just "learning how to drive," that is, just participating successfully in the profession of trafficking in no-burrs-attached ordolingual literary translation.

---

[18] –Jeg vil bare lære at køre bil, okay? Jeg vil ikke masseres, jeg vil ikke holdes i hånden, krammes, udfrittes, anmodes og dikkedikkes. Jeg vil lære at køre den bil, så jeg kan køre i den retning!
Sonja kan også pege, og det, hun peger på, er Avedøreværket, men bag det Danmark og verden som sådan.
–Jeg vil have kørekort til kategori B, og alt det andet pis, I kan finde på, har jeg lært for længst. Jeg er over fyrre, og jeg har lært det på den hårde made, så du skal ikke komme her med al din Gestapo (171).

As such, this region of Sonja's psyche and persona does not seem to want "contact zones" (Pratt 1991), transgressions, or other kinds of intersubjectivity, intimacy, or particularity to push in on her translation success, to desire something from her. The irony for Sonja—and a predicament of some ethical trouble for her—is that the Nordic noir novelist she translates from Swedish to Danish, Gösta Svensson, has made his name and fame precisely by narrativizing paternalism, condescension, sexism, wanted and unwanted human contact, history, invasions of privacy, fascism, intimacy, culture, and context. Sonja's language is the clean shipping container that transports the gruesome commodity, a container that reads *Nordic Noir* on its exterior.

Here, we can pause to note, as Sonja seems to do increasingly throughout the story, that there is nothing essential about human languages—nor about working with them—that entails that a translator prioritize prophylactic infrastructures and safety regulations when trafficking literary meaning, nor that they respect international coordination and commercial supply-chain procedures the way Haberler told us to. This is a twentieth-century invention. If such preemptive securitarian priorities determine linguistic practice (monolingual, translational, or multilingual—as may be the case), those priorities and practices are learned historical contingencies born out of late empire, globalized state power, and ordoliberal political economy—rather than being immanent features of language/languages themselves.

This is one of the implicit wagers of Nors's novel, in which Sonja, a translator of brutally femicidal fiction from one Nordic monolanguage to another, becomes anxiously unmoored from her controlled ordolingual habitus as a commercial translator by bouts of revelatory vertigo. Meanwhile, the novel's title presents an austere securitarian mnemonic about rules for proper movement under conditions of escalating peril, a rule of thumb that teases but also thwarts the always potential transformation of Sonja's subjectivity—to change from being one kind of translator-languager to another, of becoming sprogkyndig in a fundamentally different way. Consider this incipient discomfiture Sonja feels while driving a car:

> It's awful being a disappointment to both yourself and others, and Sonja's solution is to talk. Speech has horsepower and direction. With speech, she can do what she can't do with the car: she can throw it, and if she just jabbers away, she'll become a person in [her driving instructor] Folke's eyes.

"I completely forgot to tell you, but it's me who translates Gösta Svensson into Danish," she says. (80)[19]

What is it about being a free language user, a languager, that differs drastically—or ought to—from being a competent motorist? And what is at stake for Sonja here in blending metaphors captured by, but by no means proper to, the discourse of automotive transportation (horsepower) when she discusses her subjective experience of speech and translingual practice? There is within Sonja a vigilant apprehension about what uncontrolled linguistic behavior in the "traffic in meaning" around her might bring about. Like her doctor has said of her disorder, though, "It's not dangerous, you know. [. . .] It's just some tiny stones inside of you that are breaking free" (55).

But, of course, the doctor's condescending summary minimizes the experience of skavank (defect) that Sonja is trying to figure out; the pathophysiological explanation helps little because what matters to Sonja is the vertigo's unpredictable impact on her ability to move as a credible being in the world. And few other people in the story are interested in helping her explore this dysalignment further, though they're happy enough to come compassionately to her aid when she falls.

A Late Style for Cheap Meaning

These experiences of disordered effects and affects are where the rubber meets the road for deciding what kind of translator Sonja will become, or remain, over time. It's one thing to tell a translator to be free and creative despite the commercial consequences of doing so; it's another to experience the mercilessly rigid habitus of the translatability industry for yourself—as a drip-drip-drip of rejections, dismissals, condescensions, and corrections that add up to an ordolingual tutelage of delanguaging (Garrido and Codó 2017, 44). This invisible rigidity is what the highly successful professional translator Sonja finds herself struggling against incessantly in various realms of practice, as in this scene where she attempts to learn how to use the stickshift:

---

[19] Det er slemt at være en skuffelse bade for sig selv og for andre, og Sonjas løsning er at snakke. Sproget har motorkraft og retning. Med det kan hun, hvad hun ikke kan med bilen: Hun kan kaste med det, og hvis munden løber, bliver Sonja et menneske for Folke.
 –Jeg glemte helt at sige, at det er mig, der oversætter Gösta Svensson til dansk, siger hun (80).

"You have to imagine an H with two segments poking out of the middle, and then we do like this..."

You cannot make diagonal movements with the stick, Folke explains. You cannot go from second to third by taking a shortcut. You *have* to follow the construction of the gearbox. That all makes sense to Sonja, but she has a hard time concentrating with Folke's hand on top of hers.

"There," he says, and lifts his hand. "Now we'll try it in real life."

Mirror, shoulder, signal: Sonja tries to use her body, but the car's too big. (79)[20]

This scene is, in a practical and symbolic sense, a typography or penmanship lesson about how to make a letter H, and how not to—the rudiments of creative writing. With his hand on top of Sonja's, Folke lets her know that an H-making movement that involves diagonal gestures offends against the machine, grinds the gears, and prevents one's seamless advancement as a motorist. Of course, without Folke's hand on hers, she is also a maker of H's in her translation work, where a similar sensation of intimate paternalistic control nonetheless applies. Sonja wants to learn how to drive so as to be safely mobile in all the middle-class ways an automotive infrastructure foresees, to get away from Gösta and Folke entirely, instead of being sheltered by cosmopolitan, pedestrian Copenhagen where her university literary training took place. But what she unwittingly experiences in that effort is a new alphabetization process that, in her mid-forties, retrofits and encases her literacy in newly compulsory safety protocols.

There's of course nothing about being a translator in one's mid-forties that entails developing a "late style," in Said's sense. Still, Nors's philosophical fiction is about belatedly deciding one needs to capitulate to moving in a specifically ordered way in a particular version of the "Real" world on offer, and consecrating that practice as having been the proper one all along. It is about acquiescing to drive (and translate) in this individualist–ordolingual

---

[20] –Du skal forestille dig et H med to stritter i midten, og så gør vi sådan her:
   Man kan ikke lave diagonale bevægelser med gearstangen, forklarer Folke hende. Man kan ikke komme fra andet til tredje gear ved at skyde genvej. Man er nødt til at følge gearets konstruktion. Det giver mening for Sonja, men hun har svært ved at koncentrere sig med Folkes hånd over på sin.
   –Sådan, siger han og løfter hånden. –Så prøver vi ude I virkeligheden.
   Spejl, skulder, blin: Sonja forsøger at bruge kroppen, men bilen er for stor (80).

way, despite the subjective counterevidence and disordered effects that result along the way.

Driving, and translating, in an ordered, ordolingual way is thus a Bourdieusian *illusio* (Heidegren and Lundberg 2010): a strategic entry into a certain game with conventionalized, rationalized, financialized rules—and then an endeavor to forget that one has selected this particular rule-bound game over other potential meaning-making activities. It is about learning to take on, reluctantly and against one's better judgment, a resigned "late style" in the (literary) traffic in meaning, a style that strategically misrecognizes all other kinds of traffic. Here is a bit of the backstory to that elected strategic *illusio* in Sonja's case:

> Folke's thrilled. He forgets to advise Sonja on her driving. That doesn't matter, because it's going better with the gears, while Folke leafs through the books. He wants to know if translating's hard. He also wants to know if there's any money in that shit, and he wants to know where Sonja learned Swedish. In this way, she gets a chance to tell him that she's the first in her family to go to university. Her sister's a home care assistant and her brother-in-law works at a wind turbine plant. Sonja also succeeds in saying that her father's a farmer, and that she comes from a parish that lies so far west that Folke's probably never been there.
>
> "Nope, never been that far from Copenhagen. I've been to Croatia, Germany, and large stretches of France. But nothing beyond that. I only go places you can drive to in a car." (81)[21]

Folke is plainly a Scandinavian name suggesting "citizen," "folk," and "people," and his driving tutelage for Sonja performs an interesting mix of mansplainy lay expertise in infrastructural nationism (Fishman 1968) and sheer superego. Folke is the common-sensical, curious, responsible, urbanized, monolingualized, and, therefore, timely modern subject against which Sonja's untimely, critical, uncooperative, and once-rural subjectivity nurtures its suspicions about a disorderedness within ordolingual nationism.

---

[21] Folke er begejstret. Han glemmer at advisere Sonja om kørslen. Det gør ikke noget, for det går bedre med gearet, mens Folke bladrer løs i bøgerne. Han vil vide, om det er svært at oversætte. Han vil også vide, om der er penge i lortet, og han vil vide, hvor Sonja har lært svensk henne? På den måde får hun anledning til at fortælle, at hun er den første i sin familie, der har gået på universitetet. Hendes søster er hjemmehjælper, og hendes mand arbejder på en vindemøllefabrik. Sonja får også fortalt, at hendes far er landmand, og at hun stammer fra et sogn, der ligger så langt vestpå, at Folke nok aldrig har været der.
    –Nej, så langt fra København har jeg aldrig været. Jeg har været I Kroatien, Tyskland og store dele af Frankrig. Men aldrig længere væk. Jeg kommer kun steder, hvor man kan køre til I bil (81).

Late Literary Monolingualism as Antipastoral

Though relatively unaddressed thus far, climate disaster and climate anxiety are a major roving feature of dithering attention throughout the literature of late monolingualism—arguably in interlocking ways throughout all four novels explored in this book. This is no mere matter of historical coincidence and loose contemporaneity. Rather, late monolingualism itself plays a materially accelerative role in anthropogenic climate disruption, which these novels perceive acutely, if also ditheringly. The novels make such a wager, theorizing—often through oblique means—what this relationship between monolanguages and climate disaster may be in our time.

I've just now suggested that climate is a "dithering" object of attention in these novels. I do so in the sense that Kim Stanley Robinson proposes, in his own science-fiction novel *2312*, where the age 2005–60 is periodized as a dithering "age of indecisive agitation." In a similar way, Donna Haraway suggests that "[p]erhaps the Dithering is a more apt name than either the Anthropocene or Capitalocene! The Dithering will be written into earth's rocky strata, indeed already is written into earth's mineralized layers" (2016, 102). Though dithering is etymologically linked to shivers and trembles, it is in contemporary usage indeed a kind of linguistic and communicative behavior—a hemming-and-hawing, a hedging, a stuck-in-discussion equivocation—and, I suggest, an indulgence in late monolingual pastoralism that idealizes a protected cultural serenity against all counterevidence.

Consider Sonja's conversation with her sister Kate, where she muses about the sky above Copenhagen:

> [H]ere on the thickly peopled side of Denmark, a violent storm is raging.
>
> "Probably from some of that climate stuff," [Sonja] says, even though Kate once told her that she doesn't believe in that climate stuff because climate change is a question of faith, like joining the Jehovah's Witnesses, even though her husband travels the world over in the service of wind energy. That's how it is with so many things, and just to say *climate stuff* is to open a rift between the sisters Hansen." (155)[22]

This rift between the sisters arises here from what the philosopher Jonathan Ichikawa (2024, 2) calls "bad failure to believe," and its potential opposite, "epistemic courage." Kate makes what Sonja sees as the mistake of, as Ichikawa

---

[22] Herovre i den tætbefolkede side af Danmark star Himmel og jord i det.
 —Det er nok noget klimahalløj, siger Sonja, selvom Kate engang har sagt, at hun ikke tror på klimahalløj, for de der klimaændringer er et trosspørgsmål på linje med Jehovas Vidner, og det selvom hendes mand rejser kloden rundt med vindenergi. Sådan er der så meget, og bare det at sige 'limahalløj' danner en kløft mellem søstrene Kate og Sonja Hansen (159).

calls it, "focus[ing] too much on bad belief," of zeroing in on things that are apparently a question of faith (trosspørgsmål), and making a virtue out of disbelieving them. Writes Ichikawa:

> Bad belief is a problem, but it's not the only problem, and its cousin— bad failure to believe—can be just as destructive, and is going far less noticed. Many people focus on the mistake of believing things people shouldn't believe. [But there is also] the converse mistake: the mistake of not believing things people should believe. (2)

There is a core tension in the social world of *Mirror, Shoulder, Signal* among differing stances of credulousness and incredulousness, and in how these accrue different valences of civic credibility or blemishedness for those who hold them. Kate's cynical disbelief in things that appear to be unsubstantiated matters of faith—like "climate stuff"—radiates a glow of pragmatist market-driven credibility, whereas Sonja's moody dissidence—and therefore "disorder" (skavank)—renders her uncredible and suspect. Though a successful and well-paid translator of monolanguages, whenever her linguistic experience of the world falls into the multilingual interstices or leads her into political assertion, her credibility is continuously impeached. Sonja is in effect expected—to cite a lyric from The Chicks—to just *shut up and translate*.

Luna Filipović (2007) invokes the potent metaphor from forensic linguistics of "language as a witness" to show that the presence of multiple languages in evidentiary evaluation and testimony can aid in ascertaining truth, for instance in court proceedings. Far from confusing matters, two or more languages that offer differing typological axes of expression can together create a vector, marshalling the truth-telling power of individual languages-in-concert, and can help advocates come to the defense of people who find themselves in peril. Sonja finds herself a linguistic witness to emerging truths that are vulnerable to common-sense monolingualist dismissal at the hands of Folke and Kate—that is, "climate stuff" and the kind of perishable multilingual meaning-making dispreferred for, i.e., banned from, her traffic in translations of Svensson into Danish.

There is profound discomfort throughout Nors's novel with how to speak about the Danish landscape, and appreciable scenic vistas are routinely disabused of their alleged naturalness in an antipastoral reflex:

> Amager Nature Reserve stretches out toward the airport, planes are aloft, and a freeway bridge spans the horizon, though she can hardly hear any traffic. *They should have sent a poet*, thinks Sonja.
>
> "Gorgeous, eh?" says Folke.

"Yeah, some nice mounds," says Sonja.

"They're scrapheaps. Garbage!" cries Folke, and he puts a hand to his beard. "Garbage, ha!"

[. . .] "That's the remains of the Gestapo headquarters downtown, the Shell house. They didn't know where else to cart the shit, and so someone came up with the idea of just hauling it out to the dump at South Harbor." (165, note that "They should have sent a poet" is in English in the original first paragraph, citing the Soviet spacecraft designer, Sergei Korolev, in global Anglophone translation)[23]

The nation and its landscapes are never permitted a foundational naturalness in the text, but are always the ruins of other historical disasters that have been covered over and rehabilitated. There is no hygge-loving Denmark underneath it all, just garbage, complicity with fascist colonizers, and failed protectionism.

In this dithering linguistic–communicative sense of (anti)pastoral, it is not so much a matter of "literature that describes the country as providing an implicit or explicit contrast to the urban" (Gifford 1999, 2) so much as literature that describes the domestic meaning-making repertoire (imperium) in implicit and explicit struggle with the allolingual discourse regimes (dominium) that are felt to be encroaching upon them. Nors's novel offers no "celebratory attitude towards what it describes, however superficially bleak it might appear to be" (Gifford 1999, 2). And just as Leo Marx declared "no shepherd, no pastoral" (Gifford 1999, 1), such a text needs a translator, or otherwise multilingual languager like Sonja, to play the dramatizing subject for this antipastoral, a figure who both presents and undermines any "idealisation of the reality of life in the country" (Gifford 1999, 2).

In its sense for the disordered global business of making literature in late monolingualism (originals and translations alike), one of the symbolic figures Nors's novel brings to bear is the exclosure (udhegning): an arena that is protected from the unwanted encroachment of others. The actual employment of exclosure is a pastoral gesture, designed to both ward off

---

[23] Et sted ovre til venstre strækker Amager Fælled sig ud mod lufthavnen, der er flyvere i luften, og der er en motorvejsbro i jorisonten, men man kan næsten ikke høre den. *They should have sent a poet*, tænker Sonja.
 —Flot, ikke? Siger Folke.
 —Jo, det er nogle fine høje, siger Sonja.
 —Det er skrotdynger, Skrald! Siger Folke og tager sig til skægget. —Skrald! HA!
 — [. . .] Det er resterne af Gestapos hovedkvarter, Shellhuset. De vidste ikke, hvor de ellers skulle køre lortet hen, og så var der nogen, der kom på, at de bare kunne køre det ud på Sydhavnstippen (168).

and nostalgically preserve the near-wild world, while the literary figuration of exclosure is a distinctly antipastoral one, shoring up for readers' critical awareness the infrastructures that uphold such a nostalgic distance. Like Kafka's famous "Parable of the Leopard," *Mirror, Shoulder, Signal* wonders aloud about the role of such infrastructural features in the symbolic landscape, and the kind of dreaded porosity that they index. In the novel, exclosures are the subtle intersections of economy, ecology, and ordoliberal consciousness. While learning to drive, Sonja digresses about an old boyfriend from back home in Jutland, nicknamed Bacon Bjarne:

> "No, the farming operations have gotten so huge. [. . .] They buy up everything around them [...] as long as he can make the payments on his outrageous loan from the credit union, it means nothing to [Bjarne] if the infrastructure goes south. My dad always said that people are strange vermin, and he's right. But the deer are still around. There are so many deer that they have to make exclosures for them."
>
> "Exclosures?" asks Folke, indicating with his hand that she's too close to the other cars' ears.
>
> "They're the opposite of enclosures, like they have for cattle."
>
> It's good to talk and drive at the same time. (82)[24]

Bjarne's subsidized and failing rural farming enterprise is a product of coordinated agrarian credit foreseen in European farming subvention policy, and yet the enterprise is porous with its own industrial–ecological externalities. In asking for an explanation for this unfamiliar word and phenomenon "exclosure," which an urbanite like Folke would have no need for, he nonetheless simultaneously performs exclosure by gesturing a warning that Sonja the driver is coming too close to the other cars; he thus dramatizes and conjures an exclosure for her as an entity in the traffic in meaning, suggesting that she can only stay safe in the traffic if she maintains a constantly vigilant calibration of her counterparts' distance-in-motion.

---

[24] —Nej, landbrugene er blevet så store, siger Sonja. —De opkøber alt omkring sig. [. . .] så længe hank an betale af på sine uhyrlige kreditforeningslån, betyder det ikke noget for ham, at infrastrukturen knalder sammen. Min far har altid sagt, at mennesker er noget underligt kravl, og det har han ret i. Men kronhjortene er der stadig. Der er så mange kronhjorte, at de laver udhegninger for dem.
 —Udhegning? Spørger Folke og viser med hånden, at hun er for tæt på de andre bilers ører.
 —Det er det modsatte af de indhegninger, man har til køerne, svarer Sonja.
 Det er godt at tale og køre samtidig (82).

This gesture suggests that the concept of exclosure, alleged to belong to rural farming, is in fact foundational for all of the national economy and its symbolic infrastructures for cultural inclusion and exclusion. Sonja laconically confirms this by noting as an aside above in the last line—almost as an intertitle to the reader—that communicative discourse and infrastructural mobility are best practiced in tandem, so as to cultivate the most expert agility and proficiency at both kinds of ordoliberal behavior. Involving oneself in automotive infrastructure (e.g., translating ordolingually) sharpens one's ability to produce desired discursive products, in interactions designed to facilitate and fortify certain kinds of socio-commercial relationships globally.

Exclosures for Whom?

Nors's novel bears witness to the suspicion, and the experience, that literary composition and production have been neither outliers nor exemptions to this process of the ordolingual and ordoliberal anti-protectionist restructuring of the world market. It is tempting, consoling, and heartening to think literature inherently resists these geopolitical habits. And, indeed, novels often find ways to provide such consolation by curating their translatedness and multilingualism in a particularly evocative, performative, or diluted way (Pandey 2016, 104) that permits readers linguistic access to a manufactured cosmopolitan scene (Pandey 2016, 105; Myers-Scotton 1993, 107) and/or a pastoral one. Pandey describes a spectrum in which

> writers [. . .] who in "claiming the right to difference" (Bandia 2006, 354) engage in deliberate acts of non-translation—an intentional use of opaque and deep multilingualism. [. . .] At one end of the cline, we encounter anti-translation strategies aimed at encoding an intentional incomprehensibility—opacity. At the other extreme end of the cline, we encounter strategies aimed at complete transparency—linguistic strategies intent on proffering complete cultural and linguistic equivalency. (Pandey 2016, 107–9)

It is in this conjuncture that the translator Sonja's transformation into an efficient, effective, safe driver—who *stays in her lane* and changes lanes in an optimal way—becomes conceptually interesting. As a literary experiment in this predicament of disorder in a global system of monolanguages, the novel asks: What will be the aesthetic, hermeneutic, narrative, and representational complexities that prove possible in this age, and in future ages, where translatability is ever more prophylactically honed, prized, bought, and sold? Chapter 3 focuses on the twentieth-century emergence of cryptography as an intensive boom in this kind of industrial revolution around access to multilingual commodities, as fictionalized in Neal Stephenson's mammoth *Cryptonomicon* (1999).

3

An Engineer's Contempt

> "I'm not sure what a technocrat is," Randy said. "Am I a technocrat? I'm just a guy who went down to the bookstore and bought a couple of textbooks on TCP/IP, which is the underlying protocol of the Internet, and read them. [. . .] Does that make me a technocrat?"
> —Neal Stephenson, *Cryptonomicon* (1999, 83)

> It is as if a reader has only two mentors to choose from when deciding how to assign value to literary art: Paul Volcker on the one hand and Harold Bloom on the other.
> —Rachel Greenwald Smith, *Affect and American Literature in the Age of Neoliberalism* (2015, 37)

Over its 101 unnumbered chapters, Neal Stephenson's millennium-ending novel of lament, *Cryptonomicon*, appears intent on being a hostile text, one difficult to like. It is recalcitrant, indulgent, stingy with its affections—reserving praise for such treasured obscurities as Interlibrary Loan, Tolkien's dwarves, and staple removers, or for the sort of scientistic elegances (like symmetrical precision) that promise to long outlive the frailties of the human condition. As such, *Cryptonomicon* seems to like languages (or, rather, to suffer them) a fair bit more willingly than it likes the people who speak them, whether the language in question is Tagalog, American English, humanities academic jargon, or a programming language of some sort. Whenever the novel's protagonists—all, in some way, engineers of global information infrastructure—come face-to-face with actual human beings practicing their language(s) in inefficient, embodied, less-than-genius ways, these men get huffy, embarrassed at the indignity of it all, nostalgic for perfectibility.

If we are not outright dissuaded by such a front, *Cryptonomicon*'s thousand pages do thrust upon us a generously telling spectacle about late monolingualism, and specifically about one of its primary moods: contempt. On the surface of it, the novel is about two intergenerational male lineages of savants, the Shaftoes and the Waterhouses, who make and break codes in geopolitically pivotal ways amid the seismic transnational rumblings of, first, the 1940s and then the 1990s. This temporal frame is emblazoned most vividly in the novel by way of a controversial academic humanities conference, organized by Randy Waterhouse's girlfriend and rising-star humanities scholar Charlene, which she has titled "The Intermediate Phase (1939–45) of the Global Hegemony Struggle of the Twentieth Century (Common Era): War as Text."

But just beneath its grand conceits about geopolitical brinkmanship, and its urge to tell a heroic history about the misunderstood engineers who've acted as its hidden hand throughout, there is also all throughout the novel a perfectly ambivalent struggle to chronicle the obsolescence of embodied human language(s). And, no less so, to grieve the impending loss of literary storytelling by way of those languages, felt amid the 1990s frontier gold rush for "global hegemony" over information—in this case, global dominion over the logistics of meaning-making through instantaneous information transfer infrastructure.

Perhaps exactly because of its stark attentions to the technological means of production for globalized meaning at millennium's end, Stephenson's thousand-paged tome was never likely to attract easy admiration on any scholarly world-literature scene. At least not on one that believes in the importance of prizing "world against globe" (Cheah 2014; see also Kadir 2004), that is, thinking beyond the mere global circulation of revenue-generating literary commodities.[1] (It's also likely true that the novel's nonstop vitriol toward humanities academia, combined with its daunting length, hasn't helped much in getting *Cryptonomicon* on many seminar syllabi.) Still, the novel strides forth with its own undaunted, do-it-yourself, antielitist, university-funded but antiacademic, neocolonial, cybernetic world-making ethos (see Turner 2006).

Consider Avi Halaby, *Cryptonomicon*'s chief executive protagonist, working at the paranoid helm of a budding mid-1990s Silicon Valley start-up called Epiphyte Corp. Avi presents to his staff a map of the world that shows why their upcoming corporate mission to East Asia is so urgent. Pointing to a spot out in the South Pacific, he draws their eyes to the

> "[e]xisting undersea cables. The fatter the line, the bigger the pipe." Avi says. "Now, what is wrong with this picture? [. . .] There is a general paucity of fat lines in a north–south direction, connecting Australia with

---

[1] Other than Hayles's key (2004) early contribution, literary critical assessments of the novel tend rather to appear under the aegis of post-cyberpunk aesthetics (Youngquist 2012; Kilgore 2019), in interdisciplinary forums on humanities and technology (Leonard 2007), or in history of technology journals (Kidwell 2000)—and not within earshot of anything called "world literature" (Beecroft 2008).

Asia. A lot of data packets going from Sydney to Tokyo have to be routed through California. There's a market opportunity." (188)

Passing through those cables at near light speed are human-made, digitally coded multilingual meanings and information, though Avi is indifferent to the particular content any given cable might be conveying. In the swirl of Avi's intense desire for global infrastructural dominium, his attention to these new kinds of shipping containers of networked cheap meaning becomes a totalizing devotion, one that mutes the potential substance of any one message coursing through the cables. Epiphyte Corp.'s singular, stoic, and prohibitive passion is to securitize, through technological innovation, the logistical features of symbolic infrastructure that allow economic globalization to operate the way it had begun to do at millennium's end. This, the mid-1990s, is that boom moment where Cross-Language Information Retrieval and linguistic localization platforms truly began to overtake bilateral, analog forms of translation, and Avi represents for the novel that moment's disinhibited, astringent business and engineering vanguard.

And yet, in a subtle bit of virtue-signaling, Avi is skittish enough about the optics of his own ambitions to commandeer and manage xenos rights over others' meanings globally that he names his corporation "Epiphyte" Corp. The name is a preemptive and self-naturalizing insistence that the group's techno-globalism is symbiotic (i.e., epiphytic), rather than parasitic, in its relationships to the planet and its meaning-making polities, subjects, and languages (Tratner 2008). Through such cloying fig leaves and ambivalent tyrannies, *Cryptonomicon* beta-tests a too-cool-for-school "contempt" for embodied languages and language users that goes beyond mere indifference or language-agnosticism. There is a hunger to dominate and surpass embodied, local practices of meaning, an intense desire to be able to disregard and rise above mere language. But there is also a haunting recognition, throughout the novel, about what is lost in having done so.

As sensitive as most linguistic engineers are personally to the impunities of war, subjugation, predation, and genocide (the Shoah being constant on Avi's mind, for one), *Cryptonomicon* goes to great lengths to depict how presentist and short-termist their work's actual protocols tended to be in the heady 1990s—which was, we had after all been told, the End of History. As the US-based Epiphyte team angle to economically colonize a Pacific Island sultanate at the crossroads of the Pacific's north–south undersea cable routes, *Cryptonomicon*'s narrator hedges:

> In the long run, it may, or may not, be a good idea for the Sultanate of Kinakuta to have a gigantic earthquake-, volcano-, tsunami-, and

thermonuclear-weapon-proof Ministry of Information with a cavernous sub-sub-basement crammed with high-powered computers and data switches. But the sultan has decided that it would be sort of cool. (214)

Holding and housing big-data in these tax-exempt, extraterritorial spaces (fictionalized in the novel as the Sultanate of Kinakuta), Epiphyte Corp. readily awaits language users' willingness around the world to sign over, unawares and in bulk, our everyday spoken and typed utterances to their management and deployment expertise. In their Terms and Conditions, these budding companies alleged, in turn, to use our language and information only for, in Google's subtly menacing words, "the limited purpose of operating, promoting, and improving our Services, and to develop new ones."

Avi's engineers harvest usage data from whichever contemporary sources were presumed to be the most pragmatically relevant to the day's industrial and commercial clients who required, for instance, Cross-Language Information Retrieval services and protocols. *Cryptonomicon* is an early and intense imaginary ethnography into these decision-making spaces, with all of their political and moral hedges, shoot-from-the-hip modellings, and extractive big-data hallucinations. But the novel is also a meditation about the intergenerational memory of those who have peopled these secretive professional spaces, from the Second World War to millennium's end.

On its own, a general mood of precious disdain for human linguistic finitude doesn't make a novel late monolingual—or interesting, for that matter. Nor must an inquiry into literature in late monolingualism draw us to *Cryptonomicon* simply because of the novel's historical themes of military codebreaking and cryptographic translating. Beyond these topics and affects alone, the novel lovingly dramatizes the historical design, financing, appropriation, and construction that made way for a 1990s supply-side culture of dominion over infrastructures for global languages and cultures—of the technological management and subduing of somatocentric language use to comply with economic globalization.[2] The kind of languorous curiosity about global linguistic infrastructure we can read about in *Cryptonomicon* seldom appears in plain sight in novels or even nonfiction—where multilingualism and translation are just as often mystified as they are overlooked.

---

[2] I am grateful here to my UBC colleagues Geoffrey Winthrop-Young and Michael Griffin for clarifying for me the distinction between phonocentrism and somatocentrism as it relates to approaches to human languages, phono referring to the voice but somato referring to the entirety of the enfleshed bodymind that enables the voice. I realize somatocentric may evoke associations with biological determinism, but that is not intended in this usage.

Perhaps a better word for this infrastructural discourse of global linguistic management than *dominion* is, again, "dominium": that is, the asserting of (non-state) political and economic property rights over cultural and linguistic domains of life otherwise usually managed or claimed by national governments, domains which we lay subjects may nonetheless continue to *experience* as more or less "our own" in a limited way (see Slobodian 2018). In *Cryptonomicon*, lay users of language, like Randy Waterhouse's academic girlfriend Charlene, continue to go about their business believing that they maintain relative local control over meaning, information, and language, while that control has—according to the novel—been extracted from them through supranational, technological, extrajurisdictional maneuvers well beyond their fathoming. At least this is the kind of transformation that *Cryptonomicon*'s cast of male programmers strongly presume to be well underway, and they justify this lucrative privatization of information management on the premise that, simply put, governments cannot be trusted to steward or steady civic life in any of its dimensions, from fiat currency and redistributive justice to language and intellectual property.

It is this aggressive departure from lay public belief about the relations of production for meaning-making, among this secretive salvific–technological vanguard, that prepares fertile narrative ground for the novel's radioactive and remorseless overtone of expert contempt, and for its particular *late style*. In this way, it is not so much to war cryptology or cryptography that the novel dedicates its untiring energies of representation. Rather, *Cryptonomicon* bears intense evangelical witness to the bristly expert cultures and technical communities who have doted over this discourse of global linguistic dominium for the last eighty years, a discourse I've previously called "supralingualism" (Gramling 2020).

The novel savors the alienated ecstasies and spiritual abysses of those men who find themselves suddenly, in the 1940s and again in the 1990s, running the supply-side machines of multilingualism for us, so that we lay end users might continue to demand our stable, nationalized monolanguages as they presume we desire them. *Cryptonomicon*'s brand of crypto-economic patriarch is, as Rachel Greenwald Smith suggests in the epigraph above, the likes of economist Paul Volcker, sent to vanquish comparative literature's Harold Bloom (see Tratner 2008 for an extensive discussion of crypto-economics).

Ultimately, though, Stephenson's *Cryptonomicon* is a novel just as obsessed with glorifying meaningful human interiority (and hospicing it for posterity) as it is with engineering the global efficiency of cross-border, cross-language, multilingual, socio-commercial, proprietary data transfer as a value-producing endeavor. The pastoral yearnings for lost meanings are subtle but strong throughout the novel. Therein lies, however, *Cryptonomicon*'s preposterous lateness—its insistence on literature's own autonomous rights and rectitude, despite mounting counterevidence of a worldly infrastructural reality that deems literature's complex *kind* of utterances no longer credible and portable. It lavishes its heroes and antiheros with aesthetic subjectivity and affective interiority, while withholding these dimensions, rights, and faculties from everyone else passing by.

Like one of the disinterested children in Auden's "Musée des Beaux Arts," or like Marx's Englishman in Bedlam in the *Brumaire*, *Cryptonomicon*'s key protagonist Randy Waterhouse is just one of the many belated meaning-makers working away within this mammoth, insuppressibly *extra*, end-of-millennium monolingual novel of excess. Himself an "author" of data-encryption code, Randy asserts his own pathway into and through such authorship by altogether relinquishing any attention to what it is he is typing at the moment, as his operating system Ordo is a code matrix that favors random input as its preferred form of meaningfulness. We will remember this moment from the Introduction:

> [Randy] is not bothering to look at the screen; he is staring out the window at the lights on the trucks and the jeepneys. He is only using one hand, just flailing away loosely at the keyboard. [. . .]
>
> Ordo wants randomness. It only wants the least significant digits. [. . .] It wants a whole lot of random numbers, and it wants them to be very, very random. (1999, 54)

Randy's bodily disattention to language enables the kind of meaning that Ordo requires. He grants his own analog body the privacy it needs to generate these automatic authentication signals, by relinquishing any consciousness toward the endeavor altogether. The random, casuistic disposition of his body is not just the by-product or occupational hazard of a certain kind of writing alienated from itself, but rather the necessary condition for that writing's global salience. Oblivion becomes a means of production. If Randy were to try concentrating on what he was writing—if he had been *intentional* in a literary way—the code would be a failure.

Cryptonomicon's Romantic problem of figuration is thus a problem in the interstices of engineered translational monolingualism and its lost but abject Other: it is not that the world itself has ever been ineffable in any essential way; it's just that one can no longer utter the contemporary world into representation with one's charismatic, beloved, elaborate, bounded "languages." Now that we, and our novels, have conjured into being a particular kind of deterritorialized global economic imaginary that is more effectively Real than the national pastorals it has supplanted, one human language—or even a handful of them—is never enough for the task. The world isn't essentially unrepresentable in the vernacular, but it has indeed been made so—by engineered instantaneous supralingualism. Seeing such an effrontery coming, a novel like *Cryptonomicon* duly swells into endlessness, holding forth one last glorious, defiant, and monolingual filibuster.

Cryptonomicon and other techno-thrillers since 1999 put forth this composite sketch of late monolingualism as a historical emergence—including its prehistory in the 1940s, its enabling preconditions in the 1980s, its discourses and platforms in the 1990s, and its self-disclosed intentions and profit strategies for the future. We can think of the late monolingualism Epiphyte Corp. races to engineer as a global transposability grid, within which various interlocking commercial industries optimize a workable order to ensure low-delta meaning-transfer (i.e., low or diminishing procedural expense and delivery time lag) across 60–170 world languages—often beginning with Japanese, French, Italian, German, Spanish (JFIGS) and continuing to CJKV (Chinese, Japanese, Korean, Vietnamese). Such a delta-minimizing grid has been under active development since 1990, at latest. It aims to obviate the global problem of language learning and language diversity in commercial contexts altogether, aligning with the anti-protectionist metaphysics set in motion by ordoliberal economics in the 1930s.

The 1990s (during which the novel was imagined and composed) was a period in which theories of hybridity and difference became powerful idioms of liberation from hegemonies of nationhood and nativism. We'd learned from Homi K. Bhabha, for instance, that those "caught in the discontinuous time of translation and negotiation" were "now free to negotiate and translate their cultural identities in a discontinuous intertextual temporality of cultural difference" (1994, 38). And yet, in envisioning hybridity in this way as a necessarily liberatory practice, academic cultural studies turns out to have been privileging one angle on the transformative moment of early post-Cold-War political economy. *Cryptonomicon* cannot help itself but suggest that we literary scholars were missing the boat entirely, that this period was likely a race to commandeer unprecedented consolidation and compliance on intercultural, interlingual frontiers.

Love and Hate in Cryptoland

At first glance, and last, Stephenson's *Cryptonomicon* tracks as nerd fiction, military–historical fiction, or as a techno-thriller. Overall, its apparent contributions to the critical discourse about multilingualism, translation, and translingual competence seem cantankerous, insufferable, or blasé, its value to a theory of literary monolingualism opaque and far-fetched. It feels simply too far-off from the traditionally affirmative treatments of multilingualism and translation in academic spheres, which usually want to vindicate those domains against the onslaught of business innovation and financialization. Not so with *Cryptonomicon*. These days, the novel's author appears to hold the office of Chief Futurist for an augmented reality display company in Florida, having worked a while for Jeff Bezos's space launch enterprise previously. Far from a friendly coinvestigator on the project of the multilingual world-literary future, Stephenson hovers out there as a kind of sketchy, prickly, chaotic hermit of those morally noncommittal, antisocial "deep places of the imagination" that the midcentury critic Lionel Trilling saw haunting the rationalist virtues of US America's educated liberal class ([1950] 2008, 98).

Avi and his friends' unapologetic methodological short-termism at Epiphyte Corp. is acute—and, in a sense, rational. Though the data tranches they harvest—and the cross-language translatability synsets that are developed upon them—are always potentially rich in historical dimension, their chronodiversity and heteroglossia were truncated in the 1990s to facilitate the production of effective corpus modeling. This is not to say that thoughtfully designed linguistic corpora aren't capable of registering and cross-referencing for a given year of use or context of utterance, but rather that they tended in the 1990s not to value the kind of historical consciousness that would analytically locate a given usage in its proper ecology of intension and importance. Stephenson's tome is not just an homage to cryptology, but rather to a certain short-termist license to unburden oneself of the need for contextual anchoring, of the cutting-one's-losses that is sanctioned when engineering ambitious linguistic management strategies in a global boom environment. This goldrush mood requires brass neck, selective linguistic indifference (Pipestone Group 2023), a comfort (even ecstasy) around extractivism, and a Darwinistic disinclination to grieve the loss of any meanings that appear unable to traffic globally "at scale"—a readiness for epistemicide (Price 2023).

In its earlier development models in the 1990s, Cross-Language Information Retrieval was achieved primarily through amassing a given linguistic usage's textual collocations and thus forwent the depth of genre, poesis, aesthetics, pragmatics, and polysemy that had enabled the discourse utterance in the first place (particularly in languages other than English). Throughout this period, of course, applied linguists, sociologists of language, and linguistic anthropologists had been developing a wide range of critical frameworks for apprehending the pivotal relationship between utterance and context, between utterance and genre, and between utterance and discursive sequence. These disciplinary methods of analysis were earned through a great deal of thinking and testing since the 1960s, at the latest, in sociology, anthropology, and other interpretive social sciences fields, and are a credit to them. Yet they were as uncompelling for most Cross-Language Information Retrieval engineers' work as they are for Avi and Epiphyte Corp's staff in the gold-rush moment this novel portrays.

Computational engineers in the 1980s and 1990s were not generally party to the discussions about pragmatics, untranslatability, and controlled equivocation (Viveiros de Castro 2004) that burgeon in the humanities and interpretive social sciences; arguably there was a closer relationship between these disciplines in the 1940s (see Halstead's 1949 philosophical reflections on telegraph cables). They tended, at least in the 1990s, to grasp discursive context primarily by large-batching textual proximity and frequency, abstracted from the interactional and illocutionary setting in which all human utterances take place. In the absence of conceptual tools querying the *social* nature of all speech, whether spoken or written, late monolingualism has contracted with a form of engineering that tends to exert a short-term solutionist, decontextualizing effect on the data and language it harnesses.

What has yet to emerge (and certainly hadn't in 1999) is a patient and thoroughgoing conversation between these fields (literary theory, computational engineering, linguistic anthropology, applied linguistics) that would do more than merely slow the pace of technological progress around AI-driven linguistic data management (Future of Life Institute 2023). *Cryptonomicon*, alas, depicts these emerging hard-interdisciplinary conversations in the 1990s as cringeworthy cocktail-party affairs full of false starts among self-satisfied narcissists shouting past each other. But if successful and ongoing, such conversations would ultimately strengthen the technological methods themselves (Dourish et al. 2020), as well as the kind of truth-and-justice claims that frequently crop up as virtuous preambles for the tech innovation write-ups in Institute of Electrical and Electronic Engineers journals.

The contemptuous animus driving li-fi[3] techno-thrillers like *Cryptonomicon* seems particularly poised to taunt the belatedness of literary criticism and the modern-language humanities, as they rounded the corner of the twenty-first century in a messy crisis of self-doubt. One of the novel's techno-innovator protagonists, Randy Waterhouse, is dragooned early in the novel by his liberal arts scholar girlfriend Charlene to help set up a website for the War as Text conference she is organizing, an event which pompously

---

[3] On the conception of a li-fi genre, see Chapter 1 on Tidbeck's *Amatka* (p. 58) and Chapter 4 on Miéville's *Embassytown* (p. 167).

insists on the central relevance of literary critique to international strategic affairs. We are told that

> Charlene is presenting some related work at the War as Text conference: "Unshaveneness as Signifier in World War II Movies." On the strength of her beard work, three different Ivy League schools are fighting over who will get to hire her. (77)

Incredulous toward university lifers and our frenzied, effete "literature" departments, Stephenson's novel delights in punking the 1990s' awkward cleave away from the hubris of elite literary insiderism toward an emerging aspirational antielitist discourse of cultural studies, one that might stand a better chance at countenancing the worldly challenge of popular linguistic diversities in an adequate way. Since 2000, this diversity discourse has emerged powerfully under the aegis of "multilingualism" in various sectors and industries—as an affirmative proposition toward the inclusive social good. But more potently, "multilingualism" has emerged as an ascendant techno-commercial apparatus and global supply-side logic as well, with a political arm that is just as inclined to "disinclude" real human speakers and communities as it is to recognize them (Freire et al. 2017; Katznelson and Bernstein 2017). For those who've found themselves long put out by the kind of high-culture polyglotism and intellectual insiderism that's never had to meet a payroll, this discourse's emergence has seemed like a winning convergence of their vested interests (Bell 1980).

Stephenson's engineers in *Cryptonomicon* indeed revere the same kind of classic virtuosic literary elites that Harold Bloom did (savoring "old" criticism, while scorning deconstructivism and New Historicist cultural studies along the way). They do so even as they are designing the kind of language-configurable financial-technology platforms that economists like Paul Volcker assumed would be the natural and necessary idiom for twenty-first-century global valuation. It is that rugged mix of sentimental paleo-elitism and predatory global antielitist free-marketeering (Davies 2017; Turner 2006) that emboldens *Cryptonomicon*'s mood of hygienic cultural contempt.

(Post)war Political Economy and a New Deal for Meaning

The misanthropy that suffuses *Cryptonomicon*'s storylines frequently comes with a flipside of wistful, adoring affection for a beloved, classic object lost.

Consider this reverent cosmological description of Bletchley Park, home base of the English Codebreakers of the Second World War, which glows here in Stephenson's prose like an oracle:

> This place has been well looked after, but as Waterhouse draws closer, he can see black lianas climbing up the brickwork. The root system that he glimpsed in the Underground has spread beneath forest and pasture even to this place and has begun to throw its neoprene creepers upwards. But this organism is not phototropic—it does not grow towards the light, always questing toward the sun. It is infotropic. And it has spread to this place for the same reason that infotropic humans like Lawrence Pritchard Waterhouse and Dr. Alan Mathison Turing have come here, because Bletchley Park has roughly the same situation in the info world as the sun does in this solar system. Armies, nations, prime ministers, presidents, and geniuses fall around it, not in steady planetlike orbits but in the crazy careening ellipses and hyperbolae of comets and stray asteroids. (143)

The now-ancestral Second World War Codebreakers *Cryptonomicon* honors here are the heralds of a late monolingualism yet to come. In an age of war, they trudged tirelessly back every morning to Bletchley at daybreak, into the menacing disorder of worldly Babelic opacity, with a mandate to save the free world from fascism, and later Stalinism, through translation and cryptology. These devotees become eager to engineer—in an ongoing way and for eventual peacetime contexts, too—efficient, applicable means to dominate opaque differences in language, culture, and meaning, in certain predictable, strategic, and increasingly automated ways. Warren Weaver's foundational 1949 memo about Machine Translation made the irresistible humanistic rationale clear, with the following opening gambit: "There is no need to do more than mention the obvious fact that a multiplicity of language impedes cultural interchange between the peoples of the earth, and is a serious deterrent to international understanding."

In the Weaver Memo, the cryptological endeavor of machine translatability is buoyed by a spirit of postwar humanism, much as the Universal Declaration of Human Rights concurrently announced the need for (and the fait accompli of) global moral translatability in 1948. Within this context, the dual dream of codebreaking and Machine Translation was prized as a boldly interdisciplinary and ecumenical endeavor, and not the purview of one sectoral cabal. Reflecting in the *Proceedings of the American Philosophical Society* in 1949 about the development of Morse code, the Romance literary studies scholar Frank Halstead shared about the difficulty of finding a home in either the arts or sciences for what he called code development: "It is a matter somewhat related to the general art of cryptology, yet it is not wholly divorced from electrical engineering nor from general philology" (Halstead 1949, 456).

In *Cryptonomicon*'s historical conceit, the latter-day inheritors of Bletchley Park's great minds are Epiphyte's Avi, Randy, and the other engineers and coders seeking a perfectly deregulated data shelter in the South Pacific. Their ultimate coup—indeed a coup d'état in the true sense—is co-opting the leadership of a Pacific Island nation whose greatest accidental resource is that it "is ideally situated to act as an electronic crossroads. The perfect place to put big routers" (281). Avi, the CEO, explains the history of this opportunity and the particular postcolonial, postmodern form of sovereignty it offers:

> Kinakuta was run by white sultans for a while. It's a long story. Then it was a German colony. [. . .] The population is Muslim or ethnic Chinese around the edges, animist in the center, and it's always been ruled by a sultan. [. . .] Kinakuta is a member of the United Nations. It is every bit as much an independent country and member of the community of nations as France or England is. [. . .] I have been helping the minister draft a new law that will govern all telecommunications passing through Kinakuta territory. [. . .] The sultan's starting the data haven. I'm proposing to make money off it. (191)

Of course, the enterprise can only be successfully carried off if Avi is able to get the Sultan of Kinakuta to assent, which the latter does gladly during their group visit:

> The sultan has an Oxford English accent with traces of garlic and red pepper still wedged in its teeth. He speaks for about fifteen minutes. [. . .] "Bottlenecks are only one of the structural barriers to the creation of a free, sovereign, location-independent cyberspace," the sultan continues blithely. [. . .] "Another is the heterogeneous patchwork of laws, and indeed of legal systems, that address privacy, free speech, and telecom policy. [. . .] The policy of any given legal system toward privacy issues is typically the result of incremental changes made over centuries by courts and legislative bodies," the sultan says. "With all due respect, very little of it is relevant to modern privacy issues. [. . .] I hereby abdicate all government power over the flow of data across and within my borders. Under no circumstances will any part of this government snoop on information flows, or use its power to in any way restrict such flows.

That is the new law of Kinakuta. I invite you gentlemen to make the most of it. Thank you." (315–19)

While a flat and racist caricature of the sultan's sovereignty, this is also primarily a slam against 1990s governments of all kinds. One of the reasons the early 1990s is such a crucial period for keenly observing global changes in the structural relations among languages, translation teleology, compliance and innovation pathways, and the logistical problem of difference—that is, what I am calling late monolingualism's solutionist disposition—is the phenomenon political scientists of the 1990s then called an international nébuleuse (Cox 1992). Amid the ascendancy of this ideo-logistical nébuleuse of the deregulated "new world order," nations were eagerly ceding cultural power not to a Third Space (Bhabha 1994, 55) of liberatory enunciation, but to a new set of infrastructural principles and motivations for global economistic governance. At the close of the decade, Andrew Baker, a Sheffield-based political economist, described the 1990s retrospectively as a time of the inside-outing of the traditional foreign/domestic affairs of states:

> What were traditionally international functions relating to the exchange rate are now covered by officials with a domestic remit, while the domestic side has been restructured in ways that are favorable to the interests of internationally mobile capital. [. . .] The diversity of opinion between officials within both institutions has lessened considerably on the big macroeconomic questions [and] internationally mobile capital's interests are therefore represented more effectively by officials on both domestic and international sides. (1999, 93)

This 1990s process of reversing how and for whose interests states functioned, that is, the "internationalization of the state," was a matter of great concern among political theorists, observing the rapid transformation of national governments into "transmission belts" (Cox 1992) for international capital and its pet ideas. But their own analyses had predictably little to say about language. If, as the Canadian political theorist Robert Cox wrote as early as 1992, the state has ceased functioning like a state and has begun functioning more like "an agency for adjusting national economic policies and practices to the perceived exigencies of the global economy" (Cox 1992, 30), in what ways would the state's own fiat monolingualism also need to take on precisely those transmission-belt-like features? If Baker was able to speak of an "internationalization of the state" and its ways of working, why would we not also expect to identify a contemporaneous, concerted "internationalization of monolingualism" as well?

An efficient "translatability industry" (Gramling 2020) was the new means by which the global relational consolidation of languages could manifest the spirit and the letter of the so-called "Washington consensus" of the 1990s, a political–economic ideology of globalization that favored sound money, open markets, and pegged monetary exchange over other domestic and social priorities (Baker 1999, 89). In *Cryptonomicon*, Randy's experience of this era bespeaks the nondescriptness often attributed to 1990s-era internationalism:

> The business traveler's world of airports and taxicabs looks the same everywhere. Randy never really believes he's in a different country, until he sees something like Intramuros, and then he has to stand there like an idiot for a long time, ruminating. (50)[4]

Randy's professional life is increasingly also of a similarly placeless, clandestine nature:

> The first line of text, centered on the top of the page, is: NONDISCLOSURE AGREEMENT. More lines follow. Randy has seen them, or ones like them, so many times that his eyes glaze over and he turns away. The only thing that ever changes is the name of the company: in this case EPIPHYTE(2) CORP. (185)

Such are the necessary lives, we're told, of the extractive techno-business traveler, who must dwell endlessly on new multilingual frontiers he does not understand and can never again speak about honestly to anyone anyway, given the NDAs he's always signing. This is the one of the key silences at the core of *Cryptonomicon*'s rambling thousand pages. Randy's silence and nondisclosure are just hard to notice because, simultaneously, he (as a speaker who commands a prestige, colonial idiom) is forging a discursive design for the endless accumulation of capital on ever new data frontiers, one that self-translates incessantly into the languages of subjugated peoples to ensure its global uptake. Few instances of colonial planning, after all, have ever hinged on a sudden linguicide or epistemicide alone, but rather on a decades-and-centuries-long attrition, attenuation, and consolidation of subjugated meanings.

---

[4] Commissioned for construction in the late sixteenth century by the Spanish, Intramuros was and remains the walled interior city of Manila, spanning—in a way that no other such construction does—all of the distinctive and intricate moments of what we call economic "globalization," from early colonial commerce to postindustrial information technology. The Manila–Acapulco trade route circa 1571 solidified for the planet its first truly global commercial infrastructure.

Another term for this often-silent (because proprietary) translingual facilitation of discursive framings for global saturation is diffusionism. Caimotto (2019), for instance, studies Italian environmentally friendly marketing to suss out which marketing campaigns are making ecologically legitimate claims, and which are merely "greenwashing." She evaluates particular uses of Anglicisms and whether Anglicisms are, in each case, part of what Kuppens (2010) views as "the larger marketing strategy of using the same slogan worldwide in order to have a consistent brand image and cut costs" (Caimotto 2019, 208). Warning bells that multilingual greenwashing is afoot include: "the presence of English and Italian together to refer to the same concept, when Italian would suffice, the other one is the use of opaque terminology which does not have a specific semantic equivalent in Italian and is already characterized by opacity in the source language" (Caimotto 2019, 209; see also Piller 2001).

This work of globally diffusionist translation, though hatched in the fifteenth and sixteenth centuries (Hanks 2010; Brickhouse 2014; Butler 2019), bloomed in the neoliberal period of the 1930s–1960s and impacted the way constitutions, educational documents, worker statutes, industrial instructions, economic measures, and procedural justifications were written and conveyed translingually. Meanwhile, the ideology of human dominion over the nonhuman and over Earth's mineral "resources," and other related hierarchies, needed to be translated multilingually with equal emphasis and incessance, since imperial power and capitalist rationality relied in every moment on vernacular languages to house and legitimate these discourses—to "listen" to them, in the Bourdieusian sense. Much of the unpaid work and energy ensuring the endless accumulation of capital has always been linguistic work and energy, activated in the language of women, enslaved people, children, learners, translators, scribes, factory-floor forepersons and—to a lesser extent—capitalists themselves, whose preeminence, historically, has been negatively correlated to the requirement that they use language at all, that they be visible or audible amid the production. Landscapes cannot be transformed, elements cannot be mined, books cannot be kept, and trade routes cannot be maintained without a constant, multilingual supply chain—often with a silent capitalist engineer, like Randy or Avi, at the top.

Diffusionism rhymes politically with the way neoliberals had insisted that nationally embedded liberalism, on the "New Deal for the World" model, leads to isolationism and to the illusion that national economies are indeed sovereign from global systems of value and trade. Instead, Geneva School neoliberals sought supranational institutional means, bridging law and economics, to keep the world safe and open for capitalism. Particularly in the case of South African apartheid and decolonizing Rhodesia, these

Germanophone neoliberal visions were held together by a racialized developmental logic holding that Black majority populations could not be entrusted with decolonial democratic enfranchisement, because they would not grasp the broader anti-protectionist needs of the world economy.

Contemporaneous to the publication of Stephenson's novel, the neoliberal goal of sequestering the political demos into prescribed, defanged exclosures (culture, language, etc.) that would protect unbridled economic value-creation finally ran afoul of Western public opinion in November 1999 in Seattle. World Trade Organization ministers and delegates, faced with so-called rioters (myself included) throughout the central core of the city, had to acknowledge they had simply made their dual-government dominium–imperium approach to world economy—and to the political depoliticization of the economic—too visible and legible. This visibility of neoliberal institutional design had led to widespread public disapproval and umbrage toward its operations. Regrouping, WTO leaders renamed their efforts the "Doha Development Round" and then "The Geneva Consensus," rebranding the WTO through what Ernst-Ulrich Petersmann called the "mainstreaming of human rights into the WTO" (2000). But this "human rights" continued to mean, primarily, a normative world economic order protecting the individual right to trade and move capital. Today, the Geneva School continues to want "market citizenship" to mean connecting individuals economically to the world and, since Seattle, human rights has been one of the primary discourses through which it has garnered a pretext of legitimacy for organs like the WTO.

The revenue-generating neocolonial project of infrastructural dominion through late monolingualism, to which Kinakuta's sultan opens his doors, merits an "-ism" even more aptly perhaps than had high monolingual*ism* or multilingual*ism* before it, in the sense that late monolingualism represents both a structural ideology and an aggressive industrial effort. It is pursued often quite independently of the subjective desires, engagements, and everyday practices of diverse individual language users but, like most neoliberal structures, purports to service their needs and autonomy first. Techno-thrillers like *Cryptonomicon* chronicle the industries and interests actively working—despite all of the translanguaging so plainly in sight (Li Wei 2017)—to retain, fortify, and perfect infrastructural categories like "individual language" in perpetuity, for financial ends. In this industrial landscape, the category "a language" itself becomes an indispensable, load-bearing currency integer of commerce, globalizing the long-held but rarely tested Rooseveltian truism that one common and dominant language is essential for holding together a multicultural society.

Designing for Global Linguistic Dominium

Across the historical sweep of *Cryptonomicon*'s narrative world, it is open season in the novel for disdain toward everything that is socially imperfect and routinely human: political correctness, intellectuals, anti-intellectuals, authenticity, inauthenticity, nationalism, internationalism, hotel mini-bars, inefficiency, sovereignty, feminism, shallowness, depth, credulity, cultural relativity, the humanities, heads of state, democracy, governance, difference, indifference—and embodied mono/multilingualism.

The engineers at the helm of Epiphyte Corp. want to supply a globally authoritative infrastructure for meaning-making that subdues all of these inefficient, sentimental, or myopically un-posthuman dimensions of lifeliness (Chen 2012). I understand their gambit around the financialization of meaning through the heuristic of supply-driven infrastructure, and of monopsony—focusing on what suppliers design and enable for end users' uptake (Dourish et al. 2020). Individual lay language users are no less able, for the time being, to *feel* we maintain our autonomy from these infrastructural norms and supply-side procedures—but the discrepancy and artifice of it all elicit from Avi and Randy, who know better, a default bird's eye contempt.

The critical impacts of this paradigm shift are ones that will appear gradually and over generations, spurred on by ever more minute and well-funded advancements and innovations, which Avi already has in mind in 1999. These are likely to present, in due course, acute and practical implications for language policy, language planning, proficiency assessment, stylistics, and poetics (as Karin Tidbeck suggested in *Amatka* in Chapter 1, for instance). Certainly, the nature and scope of linguistic and cultural diversity is very much at stake. Understanding the work, lines of thought, and sources of funding that drive this form of "applied" language engineering is a first step in developing strategies for proposing and promoting alternatives to late monolingualism, and toward reconsidering institutional priorities accordingly.

Cryptonomicon volunteers such an instructive, though fictionalized, ethnography of this cultural moment of reformation and consolidation. It also shows that late monolingualism cannot be apprehended using just the holistic, subjective vocabulary of embodied multilingualism or translanguaging, widespread as they may be in literary studies and applied linguistics. Both of these bodies of critical thought (multilingualism and translanguaging) are too humanistic in their bearing for the fictional Real World envisioned in *Cryptonomicon*, where a contempt for the local particularities of translanguaging and for the imperfectly enfleshed locus of multilingualism and literary translation pervades. "Late monolingualism" denotes the new industrial and commercial intensifications that have mobilized these already existing rhetorics of language plurality and diversity for scales and purposes that our disciplines could not have foreseen even as recently as the 1980s, scales and purposes for which civic terms like (individual) monolingualism, translation, and multilingualism are now under-equipped.

Like the Central Administration in Tidbeck's *Amatka* (Chapter 1), *Cryptonomicon*'s supply-side protagonists envision for themselves a clandestine yet venerable legacy of language-tech pioneers who courageously persisted in darkness before them. Lawrence Pritchard Waterhouse, one of the novel's ennobled protagonists,

> is as Olympian as anyone right now. Roosevelt and Churchill and the few others on the Ultra Mega list have the same access, but they have other cares and distractions. They can't wander around the data flow capital of the planet, snooping over translators' shoulders and reading the decrypts as they come, *chunkity-chunkity-whirr*, out of the Typex machines. They cannot trace individual threads of the global narrative at their whim, running from hut to hut patching connections together, even as the WRENs in Hut 11 string patch cables from one bombe socket to another, fashioning a web to catch Hitler's messages as they speed through the ether. (162)

This mood of veneration redounds to only a sliver of living people in the novel's world: geniuses, elites, and cybernetic renegades (see Turner 2006). Misanthropic disappointment and embarrassment at lay belief is rather the default characterological feature fueling human figuration in *Cryptonomicon*, and it is ebulliently lathered at the expense of effete, once-were elites and marginalized people alike. Accordingly, the novel's predominant mode of narrative gaze is decidedly colonial and orientalist:

> Upper-class Filipino children brandish cylindrical potato chip canisters like tribal chieftains carrying ceremonial maces. A dignified old bellman carrying a hand-pumped tank circulates around the defensive perimeter and silently sprays insecticide against the baseboard. (49)

Marginalized subjects have a hard time getting a shot at coming across as sensible or just in any of their actions throughout the novel, let alone as heroic; the best attributes most merely human subjects can hope for in it is to be represented as forceful and sincere, even if at something profoundly futile.

Meanwhile, the vaunted history of the technological aspiration dramatized in the novel's thousand pages shows that cryptography and omnilingual translatability have never been opposing sets of principles and purposes, but are rather convergent commercial interests. What these industrial aspirations share, enduringly from the 1940s to the 2020s, is their proprietary, rent-seeking nature—which Avi insists defensively is "epiphytic" rather than parasitic on the world. But only a small expert class gets to own and manage these global means of production.

In the hands of these practitioners, late monolingualism is, among other things, a set of operating principles they can use to embolden and facilitate a hyper-accelerated translatability infrastructure between languages, an infrastructure in which high-dollar commerce enjoys right of way and first refusal over other local forms of semodiversity (Halliday 2007). It is also an age when cross-language information management and MT—in matters as diverse as petroleum extraction, securitarian architecture, global credit–debit relations, immigration control technology, and other means of production—unhinge clients from any individual hegemonic language (say, English) and begin to organize global systems, through synsets and cross-language ontologies, on their behalf.

Late monolingualism succeeds politically to the extent that it forges—like swords are forged—translingually mediated concepts, styles, pseudo-idioms, and control repertoires, which in turn distribute discursive-behavioral procedures, protocols, and norms globally, with varying degrees of uneven but unrelenting performative salience. These varying degrees of success are the working idiom of the engineers of late monolingualism, who ceaselessly innovate ways to close the gaps of optimization, translatability, and logistical supply-chain management. It is no surprise that capitalism discovered this revenue-generating frontier in the 1980s, right about when it began to realize that other natural resources were no longer infinitely extractable.

Cryptonomicon and other contemporary literary artifacts of late monolingualism bear witness to these processes, though they often do so ruefully and vaguely, and are equivocal about their effects for human societies to come. Part ethnography, part geography, part chronicle, part hagiography, *Cryptonomicon* brings an aura of scientific mysticism to the question of how, and why, to manage global languages in the most efficient and exacting ways possible. The novel and its characters themselves exhibit a pungent linguaphobia throughout—a contempt for how people actually speak their various first and additional living languages.

Have Fun Staying Monolingual

It is important to attend to the sectoral ethos that *Cryptonomicon* dramatizes—because that industrial ethos has wrought many of the pernicious social, monetary, medial, and civic outcomes we have been living under, ever more intensively, since the novel's publication. At the end of the 1990s, *Cryptonomicon*'s thoroughly antagonistic protagonists epitomize the alienated affects of the lonely innovator who has left everyone else in the dust—intellectually, practically, politically, and technologically—a sensibility they share with their latter-day fellows in the now borderline defunct cryptocurrency movement. "Crypto bros" circa 2020 were the direct descendants of *Cryptonomicon*'s cocky and aggressive nerds of global xenos dominium.

For those men from whom the cryptocurrency meme "Have Fun Staying Poor" issued in the last decade—for instance, the bitcoin enthusiast Udi Wertheimer—its scornful and contemptuous sentiment isn't just the gruff expression of an otherwise sincere wish that more people could and should succeed at avoiding ongoing, intergenerational poverty. Something else is going on in this gesture of scornful rebuke. The DC-based nonprofit Coin Center's Neeraj Agrawal elaborates, apologetically, that the cryptocurrency meme "Have Fun Staying Poor," far from a social taunt, is meant to convey "that failure to open one's mind will make you miss opportunities."

Even a shallow attempt at circumspection suggests, however, that such men wish primarily for as-yet unpersuaded consumers to not miss out on *their* proprietary opportunities, *their* cryptic alternative to fiat currency. Accordingly, your or my failure to buy in to crypto will *reasonably* merit us their contempt, as well as whatever further disadvantages may befall us from staying (poor) in the old-fashioned fiat system, as we are allegedly insistent on doing. If we "stay poor" even after investing, crypto bros may eventually grant that our poverty has something to do with intergenerational classism; white supremacy; state-sanctioned oppressions; and the crushing, widening aporias of late capitalism. They may grant, further, that these are often insurmountable structures for historically subjugated groups of people, given the "crisis ordinary" (Brickell 2020) today around us—let alone amid the normal workings of modern Liberal political economy.

But they, alongside *Cryptonomicon*'s linguistic engineers, want us to join them in short-circuiting this whole system. What actually animates the meme "Have fun staying poor" is the evangelical conviction that our choice to forgo their cryptocurrency solution reveals how, deep down, we were never all that interested in working to get out of structural poverty in the first place. It is a prosperity gospel. We reveal the truth through our actions and inactions: that we find this—our durable and disempowering lot in life of "staying poor"—fun enough to elect it again and again. We'd rather stay disenfranchised late nationals in the (equally late) fiat system.

In this way, since the 1990s, cryptocurrency and its masculinist culture of ennui and leisure, battle and threat, self-mythologization and opportunistic supremacy have been selling a fortified insider idiom of exceptionalism that tires at the mere sight of a liberal, socialist, or statist virtue. But before it could tire at the trappings of nationalized bourgeois consumerism and the operational inefficiencies of nationism in general (Fishman 1969, 113), this techno-culture needed to self-discover and self-actualize, as it did from the 1970s to the 1990s (Turner 2006).

Set primarily in the 1990s, *Cryptonomicon* is a vivid diorama of that process. It attests to the kind of fortifyingly astringent, elitist (and simultaneously antielitist) ideology about Language that might just as well say: "Have Fun Staying Monolingual." It taunts readers with the menacing suspicion that there is something fundamentally more Real going on above the heads of our practical, Taylorist monolingualisms, and that our credulous investment in the ongoing use of these monolanguages as authoritative repertoires of meaning demonstrates our ultimate unfitness for future action, let alone thought, on the global stage.

Cryptonomicon, like cryptocurrency, evangelizes only for one particular proprietary and technological alternative to high-modern nationalized monolingualism. Conveniently for its protagonists, who own these budding venture-capital-backed technologies, the solution is clearly *not* that people like Randy should become multilingual themselves—by, for instance, learning new languages well and achieving a serious and effective level of symbolic competence within and through them (Kramsch 2009, 2020). The technologists at large in *Cryptonomicon* seek not to be "multilingual persons, but multilingually *empowered* persons, who can harness and harvest multilingual meanings [. . .] in a predictable way" (Gramling 2021, 69), in an existing though volatile economic order, by nearshoring or friendshoring languages in serviceable ways (El-Erian 2023).[5]

Since the 1940s, it has been a working premise of this kind of linguistic dominium that its engineers likely should *not* learn the living languages they are working to manage, as ignorance or indifference to languages and their meanings counts as the best arm's-length test of the effectiveness of their

---

[5] I've previously (in 2020) described this agenda of supralingualism as "a scientific agenda indifferent to conspicuous nationalism and partisanship, both which it treats as irritations to its telos: the global coordination of meaning conveyance across surface languages. Supralingualism is however also a 'client agenda,' in the sense that it is designed to lend, sell, or rent its ongoing innovations to any civil, military, or commercial enterprise that requests its services" (130). "Supralingualism [is a] supply-side industrial conceit and capacity (since around 1990), designed to forge translatabilities-as-commodities and to trade on them, i.e., sell them to clients and end users. Supralingualism is a powerful, innovative means to diffuse meanings reliably and regularly from one language into another, rather than compelling speakers of a language to use loanwords or learn new languages entirely" (13).

cryptanalytical, and later language-managerial, solutions. In 1949, Warren Weaver recalled the then-recent wartime decoding work of a particular

> distinguished mathematician whom we will call P, an ex-German who had spent some time at the University of Istanbul and had learned Turkish there. [...] The most important point, at least for present purposes, is that the decoding was done by someone who did not know Turkish, and did not know that the message was in Turkish. ([1949] 1955, 15–16)

In *Cryptonomicon*'s technological innovators like Avi, we witness this common methodological badge of honor among supralingualism's engineers since the Second World War: to outwit the languages they intend to decipher and manage, rather than to merely learn and use these languages—in a somatocentric, analog fashion.

It is in large part due to *Cryptonomicon*'s gloating, vengeful, antielitist supralingualism that the novel's millennium of pages offers such an extraordinary study in the mood of late monolingualism. The technologist-protagonists of *Cryptonomicon* are ultimately dyed-in-the-wool, elitist, Old-Critical-but-neocolonial culturalists who, with an unreformed paleoethnographic gaze, both scorn and minimize the linguistic practices of the multilingual speakers around them. What motivates their passions and presumptions is not the prospect of insight gained through anyone's living translingual competence, but the pursuit of supralingual data management schemes and a world order that aligns with those schemes.

Despite the urge to dominate the unruly meanings and languages around them on macro and microscales, there is among *Cryptonomicon*'s wayward nerds also a vestigial reverence for erudite, pre-digital multilingualism of the grand-tour cosmopolitan sort, a reverence that is explicitly purchased at the expense of racialized "natives" who are characterized as linguistically deficient and unserious. When, in the novel, the 1990s-era data management company Epiphyte Corp. seeks to relocate from Silicon Valley to the Philippines to secure tax and regulatory advantages, its staff express acute forms of raciolinguistic linguaphobia (Flores and Rosa 2015; on race in *Cryptonomicon*, see also Lewis 2003).

For example, Randy, whom the novel presents as a "tedious, scary, obsessed character" (56) and who "used to be fascinated by software, but now [...] isn't" (53), can only view the multilingual Tagalog speakers around him with a colonizer's suspicion: "Every morning the taxi drivers lined up in front of the hotel, leaning against their cars and smoking, shout 'Taxi? Taxi?' to him. When he turns them down, they say witty things to each other in Tagalog and roar with laughter" (89). People who code-mesh around Randy between

Tagalog, other Pilipinx languages, and English reap from him an even harsher disdain; they are admonished not only for their native cunning but for their inability to insulate themselves from what he regards as the vices of American culture:

> As he goes by the cathedral, children follow him, whining and begging piteously until he puts pesos in their hands. Then they beam and sometimes give him a bright "Thank you!" in perfect American-scented shopping-mall English. The beggars in Manila never seem to take their work very seriously, for even they have been infected by the cultural fungus of irony and always seem to be fighting back a grin, as if they can't believe they're doing anything so corny. (91)

Here Randy takes umbrage at the simulacrum of English—in Bhabha's sense of "a reformed and recognizable Other, as a subject of difference that is almost the same, but not quite" (1984, 86)—that is reflected back upon him in the wake of a century of US American colonialism. It is in such racist and racializing scenes that *Cryptonomicon*'s mood of vitriol, linguamisia ("hatred of languages," Otoo, n.d.), and contempt becomes both turbid and clear at once.

There is a historical throughline to this linguicidal, neocolonial timbre among the novel's personnel. Much of *Cryptonomicon* takes place in the Second World War, where displaced Scottish, Canadian, and US soldiers, like Enoch Root, must make do with the wartime lifestyle that deployment affords them:

> Enoch Root has wedged himself into the back of the fuselage, where it gets narrow, and is perusing two books at once. It strikes Shaftoe as typical—he supposes that the books say completely different things and that the chaplain is deriving great pleasure from pitting them against each other, like those guys who have a chessboard on a turntable so that they can play against themselves. He supposes that when you live in a shack on a mountain with a bunch of natives who don't speak any of your half-dozen or so languages, you have to learn to have arguments with yourself. (175)

The archetypal narcissistic solipsism of playing chess with oneself, because there is sadly no adequate opponent around, translates well to later hallucinatory visions about language innovation that reluctantly assume that no human speaker can live up to what the innovator thinks Language is actually supposed to be. Such encounters fuel what Silke-Maria Weineck has called misolingualism, or what Sharon Dodua Otoo has called linguamisia[6]—the hatred of living languages—in favor of erudite, elite ideal entities that are neatly edited, standardized, and literarily distinguished from one another, ready to be traded from one value-generating market and technological platform to the next.

Before the Late Monolingualism Gold Rush

Through these characters, Stephenson's novel dramatizes how a quiet gold rush has been underway through global language ideologies since 1990, thanks in good part to the development of large-scale corpus-based Machine Translation platforms that replaced old-school, rules-based Machine Translation technologies developed over the previous six decades, primarily in wartime contexts. *Cryptonomicon* depicts in vivid fullness this continuity from high, wartime (nationalized) monolingualism to late (globalized) monolingualism. Up until the 1990s, mechanical translation between languages worked primarily through rules-based—that is, prescriptive—protocols that helped machines make decisions about how to render, for instance, a Mandarin phrase into German. Of course, we human users of languages are bad at following rules, as are our lived languages. Thus machines, even at the advanced stage of rules-based automated translation, made hypercorrect and laughable translations that were sometimes understandable but rarely pragmatically communicative.

Since 1990, Machine Translation had been making exponential progress using large-batch corpus-based algorithm-driven inductions based on real-world, everyday language use by real-world human beings. The ownership and valuation of everyday utterances and usages were thus a brand-new market frontier for capitalization, innovation, and intellectual property. According to the former leader of Google's Machine Translation team, Franz Josef Och, Google Translate "(is) correlating existing translations and learning more or less on its own how to do that with billions and billions of words of text. [. . .] In the end, we compute probabilities of translation" (Schulz 2013, n.p.; see also Van Rensburg et al. 2012 on pedagogical dimensions).

This quantum leap in Machine Translation since 1990 has given us not only the Globalization, Localization, Internationalization, and Translation industry (Cadieux 2002; see also Mazur 2017), but, along with it, a world in

---

[6] I thank Weineck and Otoo both for these concepts, which arose in the course of personal correspondences.

which it is procedurally plausible for content of any kind to be immediately and simultaneously *made* translatable—despite any protests, opacities, or counterevidence. By "made translatable," I mean that translatability can be forced rather than discovered, cutting whatever losses of meaning, culture, or context are not valued for the foreseen commercial exchange (see, for instance, the example of kladd from Chapter 1). This is thus a supply-side translatability matrix that responds to commercial needs primarily (dominium), and only to end user subjectivities to the extent that these demonstrably impact commercial revenue.

Epiphyte Corp. more or less stands in the novel for the energetic but inchoate efforts in the 1990s that would bloom into Google, Meta, and other scrappy, and then too-big-to-fail, multinational information conglomerates by the 2010s. Key to their success has been end users' willingness to part with their linguistic practices for free. Google does not exactly claim ownership over data inputted into its pages, but it finesses the practical ownership of language-in-use in a monopsonic fashion and for an allegedly "limited" yet infinite purpose:

> When you upload, submit, store, send or receive content to or through our Services, you give Google (and those we work with) a worldwide license to use, host, store, reproduce, modify, create derivative works (such as those resulting from translations, adaptations or other changes we make so that your content works better with our Services), communicate, publish, publicly perform, publicly display and distribute such content. (Google, n.d.)

This has been, of course, an extraordinary corner to turn for service industries' communication cultures (Cameron 2000, 2008), as well as for supply-side logistics and global manufacture design planners—and *Cryptonomicon*'s 1990s protagonists are at the cutting edge of it. But this radical industrial transformation and the novel genre are interwoven here: the global industry of literary publishing and acquisition has also been transformed in parallel since the mid-1980s. When companies like Bertelsmann became transnational, they began to seek and secure serial international publishing rights in scores of as-yet-translated versions of the titles they acquired (Rectanus 1987). In the wake of this profound reorientation, authors writing novels today (like Stephenson, Tidbeck, Nors, and Miéville) know that they are compelled systematically and contractually to write for readers in translation, thanks in great part to the global language–infrastructural innovations of the 1990s.

Much of literary writing has always been aspirationally translingual in its address, seeking to reach readers whose idiolects differ from the text by varying subtle or drastic degrees. But in late monolingualism, translatability is an industrial, systemic prerequisite rather than a humanistic, communicative, and hermeneutic ideal. Writing for readers in translation had often been the norm for authors who, like Felipe Guamán Poma de Ayala in 1613 (Pratt 2012), found themselves in complex or precarious geopolitical circumstances of exile, domestic marginalization, diaspora, or ongoing colonization.

But today, the directive of composing for readers always-in-translation (Pennycook 2008) has become generalized. Ruminations have thus ensued among prominent novelists and poets like Kazuo Ishiguro, J. M. Coetzee, Terézia Mora, Junot Díaz, Nils-Aslak Valkeapää, and Ngũgĩ wa Thiong'o for instance, about how literature has itself been changing to meet these global infrastructural expectations of commercial multilingualism, such that authors will themselves feel compelled to decide in the composition stage to avoid using figurations, devices, or terms that are difficult to translate (see Pandey 2016 on such efficiencies of "linguistic exhibitionism" in Anglophone world literature; see also Tidbeck's accounts in Chapter 1).

Monolingualism in the Linguacene

Translational monolingualism, as an accelerant of multilateral cross-border commerce, is not a novelty of the late twentieth century. There is ample evidence that in the seventeenth and eighteenth centuries innovative expertise and entrepreneurial authority in the development of technologies, including fossil-fuel-driven ones, required the intensive consolidation and commensuration of technical discourse in multiple languages. Researching the geography of multiple-language standardization and the industrial revolution in the seventeenth and eighteenth centuries in Northwest Europe, the economist Leonard Dudley notes that "prior to the beginning of the modern period in the West, there were barriers to innovation caused by the difficulty of communicating with those who were neither kin nor neighbours" (2017, 1146).

As Dudley details, very few of the collaborative innovations that succeeded between 1600 and 1800—whether a loom coded with punched cards in Lyon in 1728, a steam-powered wagon in Paris in 1770, a parachute in 1783 in Montpellier, or an iron smelter with coke in Birmingham in 1709 (see also Wrigley 2010; Thomas 1986, and Malanima 2006 on solutions to early modern European energy crises)—would have been possible without standardized or standardizing monolanguages to pave the way for transregional, translocal exchange of practical information among inventors. Literacy, individual genius, and imagination weren't enough on their own, nor were they ultimately as necessary as was translocal communication.

By focusing on cooperative versus noncooperative innovations, Dudley is able to discern how "some three-quarters of the important innovations cited by historians of technology were developed in three narrow bands of territory in England, northern France, and the USA. Other regions in the West with similar institutions and factor prices, or higher levels of literacy, failed to innovate during the century and a half prior to 1850" (2017, 1140). These communicative bands—Manchester–London, Le Havre–Lyon, Connecticut–Potomac—were also bands where national monolanguages were forged, accelerating cooperative innovation in industry (see also Thomas 1993).

As Dudley puts it, intralingual standardization was the key to interlingual commerce in the early Anthropocene: "Had [the Scottish] Watt and [the English] Boulton been born a century earlier, they would have had difficulty communicating with each other" (1139). In this way, standardization is just one, albeit complex, feat of monolingualization; how these standardized or standardizing monolanguages were effectively compelled in early modern, colonial–industrial landscapes to interact with one another in increasingly translatable ways speaks to the systematic spirit of monolingualism as the obviating solution to what Noorani (2013) calls the "hard multilingualism" of pre-national linguistic landscapes. In the late twentieth century, linguistic engineers would inherit and intensify this solutionist spirit.

Dudley argues that, in the context of the eighteenth and nineteenth centuries' Euro-American "Great Acceleration," the standardization of languages—rather than, say, the more charismatic progressive rationales of high literacy rates or advances in education—enabled the hundreds of cooperative carbon-driven innovations that fortified colonial dominance and economic dominion. These translingual inventions came, of course, with an additional price tag: a future global climate emergency two centuries later. So why have languages and their changing translatability regimes—as material means of production, and not merely as representational repertoires—been so entirely overlooked in Anthropocene discourse?[7] If anything, whatever attention is paid to language in this domain has focused either on how language(s) can amplify the message of climate injustice or on addressing how language obscures that message—rather than identifying the ways modernizing language(s) were key, causative dimensions of the industrial matrix in the first instance.

---

[7] As noted elsewhere in this book, I acknowledge the ongoing dissensus around the periodization of the Anthropocene. Whatever periodization readers have decided is most accurate or important to them (whether in eighteenth-century industrialization, fifteenth-century colonization, or earlier moments of urbanization and civil society formation), reintroducing language(s) as a material condition when analyzing anthropogenic planetary effects will be equally revealing.

By describing the Linguacene as a hyperproject, a project of projects,[8] I hold that—in order to get the extractive intensities of Liberal modernity underway—colonial epistemology foresaw and required a slow, uneven, but drastic retrofitting of heretofore relatively endogamous languages into commercially translatable monolanguages. Further, this realignment required very specific kinds of behaviors from languages and language users from the sixteenth century to the twenty-first. Several explicit attempts at commercial supralanguages emerged during the seventeenth century, including Universal Character (1657), Universal Language (1661), Ars Signorum (1661), Philosophical Language (1668), and Logopandecteision (1653). This last was billed as "most fit for such as would with ease attaine to a most expedite facility of expressing themselves [. . .] [concerning] [. . .] mechanick trades" (cited in Crabbe 2017, 24).

A Well-Tempered Supralingualism

As a historical meditation, *Cryptonomicon* portrays the 1990s not just as an unprecedented technological boomtime, but as a recitative of precisely that seventeenth-century supralingual energy which accelerated the Linguacene hyperproject, in a millennial moment when decolonial alternatives were also emerging powerfully (Quijano 1992; Mignolo 2012; Machado de Oliveira 2021).

Cryptonomicon registers its own restlessness with monolingualism in several roundabout ways. In *The Invention of Monolingualism*, I suggested that modern authors who were uneasy about the contractual or coercive monolingualism they were expected to impose on their literary texts sometimes turned to music history to air out some of this claustrophobia, and to commiserate with other nonliterary creative sectors throughout history. It is widespread practice to note how literary authors in the early twentieth century turned to cinema for imaginative compositional innovations for theater and novels, but music theory tends to enter novels in thematic rather than form–critical ways.

But the history of musical temperament since the seventeenth and eighteenth century provides a potent empirical field for literary dissatisfactions around the novel genre's apparent monolingual self-constraints of form

---

[8] I appreciate Timothy Morton's term hyperobject to designate those objects that are so massively distributed in time and space as to transcend spatiotemporal specificity (Morton 2013), and adopt it to describe the Linguacene as the setting for a hyperproject of monolingualization and socio-industrial supralingualism.

and format. Kafka, in his 1914 novel *Amerika: The Missing Person*, devotes a fair amount of his furtive antiliterary dissent around monolingualism to the historical riddle of equal temperament in piano-tuning—that is, the high modern prerequisite that all pianos be tuned in manifest concert with all other pianos, and therefore with all other performance instruments, so they might be played symphonically without any unseemly dissonances. It is a securitarian, future-proofing solution, much like Ordo's interface seeks to transmit meanings safely on global pathways without having to entertain accidence, delay, or theft.

This sense for being hemmed in, and yet enabled, by tonal temperaments innovated long ago, but whose hegemony is almost entirely forgotten in contemporary life, plays a subtle but explicit role in *Cryptonomicon* as well. On one level, this 1999 novel is an extended, ecstatic reflection on codemaking and codebreaking as a potentially mystical experience. On another, it is a novel about the radical acceleration and attenuation of the "traffic in meaning" across various codes and languages in modernity. To situate this contemplation, *Cryptonomicon* avails itself of none other than Johann Sebastian Bach himself—one of Enlightenment modernity's most ardent and virtuosic (though rarely contemptuous) engineers of aesthetic translatability (see also Gramling 2016b, 23).

A Second World War US naval officer and cryptographer, Lawrence Pritchard Waterhouse, distracts himself from the battle wounds to his body with daydreams about Bach, the most ambitious of the Enlightenment-era propagators of universally applicable temperament schemes:

> As soon as he can withstand the pain, Lawrence begins to play Bach's *Art of Fugue* in his lap whenever he is not otherwise occupied. Most of those tunes start out simple: you can easily picture old Johann Sebastian sitting there on a bench on a cold morning in Leipzig, one or two blockflöte stops yanked out, left hand in his lap, a fat choirboy or two over in the corner heaving away on the bellows, faint gasping noises coming from all the leaks to the works, and Johann's right hand wandering aimlessly across the forbidding simplicity of the Great manual, stroking those cracked and yellowed elephant tusks, searching for some melody he hadn't already invented. That is good stuff for Lawrence right now, and so he makes his right hand go through the same motions as Johann's. (66)

In Waterhouse's pain-mitigating reverie, the focus of pleasure and consolation is not the "simplicity" mentioned twice in the passage, but the complex mechanical means by which such simplicity is produced:

not the front-of-house outcome for which Bach's genius is routinely credited among audiences, but the back-of-house means of production and attunement. *Cryptonomicon* is not satisfied with any mystified vision of authoritative repertoires and time-tested registers, insisting rather at every step on an homage to the labored, embodied, hands-on, doubt-ridden means by which those repertoires and registers are produced. Bach's, and monolingualism's, technocratic operations are being prized and caressed here, both in Bach's own yanking movements on the stops and in the choirboy's assistive churnings of air to propel the tone. Colonial trade provides the elephant tusks, laying the basis for ongoing, ever more complex, progressive "invention." It is Waterhouse's grandson Randy who, in the 1990s with Avi and Epiphyte Corp., inherits these harrowed, fragile back-end processes of meaning-making systems through the latter-day *Well-Tempered Clavier* of information technology and computational engineering, called *Ordo*.

One of *Cryptonomicon*'s most generous and poignant contributions to a critical discourse on multilingualism is the kind of contemplation about historical resonances it prompts amid moments like this one—frequently depicted in isolation—of what we might call cryptologic work, across the industrializing eighteenth, wartime twentieth, and emerging twenty-first centuries. The novel wants us to understand the continuing social ancestry of the industrial sectors responsible for these bold and rapturous developments, a continuity that is as frequently sidestepped in Translation Studies and applied linguistics work as it is in Anthropocene discourse. Despite ample evidence that translation has been a "crucial vehicle of diffusion" (Oz-Salzberger 2002, 181) throughout colonial modernity, translation studies scholars have "not engaged much with the study of scientific discourse or of scientific knowledge" (Olohan and Salmara-Carr 2011, 181).

Meanwhile, as Maeve Olohan and Myriam Salmara-Carr put it, natural historians have not been particularly committed to investigating the role of translation for the exchange of scientific knowledge either (2011, 179). And N. Katherine Hayles insists further that

> it is time—indeed, past time—to create a vocabulary and conceptual framework acknowledging the sea change that occurred when computational media permeated the printing industry. Like the slow accretion of chemicals on objects submerged in ocean water, this change took a half a century or more to be fully realized, beginning roughly around 1950 and reaching full penetration with the new millennium. (2021, 2)

Whereas Hayles describes 1950–2000—the transformative period for languages theorized in *Cryptonomicon*—as the era of *postprint*, I have argued for an additional twin set of periodizations: *late monolingualism* (2021) and *the Linguacene* (2016). Each extends beyond the print industry itself, encompassing varying aspects of linguistic–social systematization and their material relationships to extractive planetary commerce and industry— literariness being one such industry.

The term Linguacene shares the -cene suffix with Anthropocene to accentuate how the fortification of monolingualisms for translation–automation purposes accelerates the industrial effects already characteristic of the late Anthropocene: global overheating, climate racism and precarity, ecological destruction, unbridled and secretive extractivism, and human and nonhuman suffering of all sorts. Indeed, translation and multilingual communication could serve as crucial tools in dismantling these disastrous structures and mitigating their effects, but in the Linguacene—and its now accelerated matrix of late monolingualism—client-driven Cross-Language Information Retrieval capacities tend to instead multiply these pernicious effects (see discussion of Caimotto 2019 in Chapters 1 and 2; see Tesseur and Crack 2018 for a more hopeful account of institutional listening across languages).

Translation as Crypto-commodity

Throughout *Cryptonomicon*, Randy and his Epiphyte colleagues' unwillingness to be characterized as anti-intellectual shills for industry (particularly in the company of their academic girlfriends like Charlene, organizer of the "War as Text" conference) is fortified as we've seen through variously ecstatic and mystical venerations of their own encryption work and its culture of secrecy—and through testaments to the rarefied ancestries from which their industrial sector has emerged. Hiddenness and secrecy throughout the novel are thus a presumed practical necessity and a badge of vocational pride. With their sensibility around communication stemming from a need for linguistic meanings to travel undetected, they have developed this one key talismanic tool called Ordo, which is

> a tool for taking [. . .] ideas and converting them into streams of bits that are almost indistinguishable from white noise, so that they can be sent to Avi in privacy. In exchange, it receives noise from Avi and converts it into Avi's thoughts. At the moment, Epiphyte has no assets other than information—it is an idea, with some facts and data to back it up. This

makes it eminently stealable. So encryption is definitely a good idea. The question is: how much paranoia is really appropriate? (53)

In *Cryptonomicon*'s mid-1990s "End of History" moment, Avi's clandestine global operating system Ordo is depicted as an anthropomorphic platform that solicits certain kinds of language as opposed to others. It is characterized as desiring and wanting certain kinds of inputs from users, lay and expert alike, a single-buyer system (monopsony) that sets the terms for the sale: here for unremunerated linguistic input. It is therefore not just the back end of the data platforms themselves that is undergoing drastic changes in late monolingualism when it comes to what kind of language is being made and reproduced for future social use. Rather, *Cryptonomicon* begins to describe the types of everyday literacy and linguistic behavior that is required of social subjects, once "ordering" platforms like Ordo—hiding in plain sight— become central, ubiquitous communicative interfaces in society.

Since 1990, these so-called Cross-Language Information Retrieval platforms, of which Ordo is a forerunner iteration, have been under extraordinarily rapid development and innovation, so as to facilitate the fast, if not immediate transfer of "data" commodities from language to language, serving transnational commercial clients in supply-side manufacture logistics. (The fact that "Cross-Language" in Cross-Language Information Retrieval is an adjective, and that Information is the operative noun, epitomizes the subjugated role that language is made to play in an enterprise where precisely it—and not just "data" and "information"—is at the center of the means of production.)

As Dudley suggested for the eighteenth-century industrial context, this complex multilingual process of Cross-Language Information Retrieval is built on a need for orderly and reliable constituent monolingualisms or monolanguages that will work in concert so as to not diminish revenue, slow down time-to-delivery, or cause expensive optimization errors for developers. Text preprocessing strategies for Cross-Language Information Retrieval include "Lexicon Normalization," "Named Entity Recognition," and "Noisy Entity Removal," procedures that Natural Language Processing technicians may utter earnestly, while applied linguists and philologists will likely have at least a few trenchant questions about them.

This still-new paradigm of global algorithmic language management, which I call supralingualism, seeks not to obviate the diversity of languages entirely, but to manage their threatening plentitude in the most economic and often austere ways possible. One can well imagine what kinds of language and meaning lose out in such a supply-side efficiency model: our treasured local varieties, cryptolects, nuanced and specialized languages, Indigenous knowledges, and counter-languages, which by necessity exacerbate the global just-in-time delivery mandates of commercial multilingualism. So, while Avi and his engineers seek to perfect their own securitarian traffic in language, the platforms they are developing in the 1990s will make it increasingly harder for us lay users of language to secure our own communities' idiolectal repertoires as we are iterated (Dourish et al. 2020) by monopsonic buyers of our utterances.

What is particularly breathtaking about this domain's discourse of research and development (Cross-Language Information Retrieval and NLP) is its bold reliance on philosophically derived concepts like "ontology" to give order to its various closed sets of variables in algorithmic modeling analysis (see Cross and Voss 2000, for instance, for a forerunner). There's certainly nothing wrong with invoking "ontology" for virtual settings such as this, but to flip the concept into a notion of *cross-language* ontology, that is, the prospect of an operationalizable closed set of cognates across multiple languages, fetishizes the securitized synset over any reality or endogamous context to which that synset might intend to refer.

Emily Apter's (2014) wondrous *Dictionary of Untranslatables* and its French-language predecessor (Cassin 2004) help remind us how and why languages cannot reasonably be put in any closed-set ontological relationship to one another—at least not without cleaving off most of the important, emic senses that constitute their meaningfulness for real people. And yet: this kind of virtual, fuzzy ontology-building across languages was the methodological crucible for most Cross-Language Information Retrieval innovations at the start of the 2000s (Cross and Voss 2000), around when the fictional Avi and Epiphyte were staging their data-coup in the Sultanate of Kinakuta. These gambits and methodologies of course didn't stay in the lab: they have quickly made their way onto all our end user devices, and they take up epistemic space in the patent market for language-oriented technologies.

Thanks to this paradigm of Cross-Language Information Retrieval and its commercial implementation platforms, language(s) have—and this is the phrase economists use to describe such a transformation—"crossed the production boundary" in the last two decades from being regarded as "nonproductive" to being "productive" economic activity. They have become value-creating commodities in the way that financial commodities had been made to do in the 1970s (Mazzucato 2018). We are now witnesses to the reckless ruin and violent wealth disparity the recategorization of financial products as "value creating" has yielded between 2008 and 2019 (see Appadurai 2016).

A similarly tumultuous future awaits language(s) too, now that we are no longer just commodifying language, in the pejorative sense we are accustomed to thinking of commodification, but also commodi*tiz*ing it—in the sense of rendering for clients predictably tradeable, switchable, translatable assets for global glossodiversity management. The imprints of this quiet recategorization (and subsequent financialization) of language as "value creating" in a neoclassical economic sense—and the consequent elevation of multilingual engineering to a form of rent-seeking behavior—are made plain in these CLIR methodologies.

But they are expressed also in the legislative language by which bilingualism has been rebranded as "multilingualism" over recent decades. In the United States, Noah Katznelson and Katie Bernstein (2017) have tracked this ascendancy of such reactionary forms of multilingualism in state-level legislative discourse since 1997, in order to show how a rights-and-justice-based bilingualism discourse was rebranded over the course of the 2000s to service commercial needs first, and heritage and community needs only incidentally, if at all. In late monolingualism, language is monetized and securitized in ever more minute commodity units—from voice recognition bytes to sentiment designations in social media utterances (see Zhao and Schütze 2019) to pragmatic disambiguations. All of this expresses a very understandable pursuit of "transcendent" Cross-Language Information Retrieval (Oard 2006)—such that what is at issue is an industrial race for production, the likes and scope of which we have never witnessed globally in matters of language.

In contrast to the bundle of diffuse forms that count under the aegis of "mono-" and "multilingualism" generally over the course of history, late monolingualism is, on its face, a *functionally* unified teleology, if not an internally coordinated agenda. It is a scientistic–financial agenda indifferent to conspicuous nationalism and partisanship, both of which it treats as irritations to its practical purpose of globally coordinating meaning conveyance across surface languages. Late monolingualism is, however, also a "client agenda"—in the sense that it is designed to lend, sell, or rent its ongoing innovations to any civil, military, or commercial enterprise that requests its services. Because late monolingualism is such a profoundly supply-side agenda, it has little room in its discursive imagination for bottom-up notions like "translanguaging."

The Age of Multilingual Coal

Though Stephenson's novel is an ethnographically inclined fiction anchored in the twentieth century, its gold-rush mood about securing dominion over global information infrastructure is heir to the prior four centuries—in which translatability (as an increasingly tradeable commodity unit) was honed as colonial capitalism captured ever-new frontiers of natural resource to exploit. Translatable meanings were thus also closely tied to translatable resources— that is, the moveability of one precious good from one part of the world to another. This is one of the infrastructural dimensions where the linguistic and ecological spheres of colonial modernity meet, and its analytical absence epitomizes what Jason Moore (2016) seeks to expose as the theory of the Anthropocene's "fundamentally bourgeois character" (83). Moore has been one of the more explicit critics of what he understands as the "profound [and] willful misunderstanding of the alternative [to the Anthropocene]: the Capitolocene" (81).

In the ongoing debate as to whether it has been human *industry* in toto that has led to climate crisis in the twentieth and twenty-first centuries, or rather the Global North's Liberal capitalism, Moore indicts a crude simplification of capitalism as something that allegedly burst forth, Athena-like, in the English eighteenth century. He stresses that, between the fourteenth and seventeenth centuries, a symbolic order had to emerge with certain "relations of power and re/production premised on the cash nexus" (81). In Anthropocene historical characterizations, Moore notes, citing Steffen et al. (2011), that "the drivers [of such changes] are typically reduced to very broad 'black box' descriptive categories: industrialization, urbanization, population, and so forth" (2016, 602). For Moore, the change making an Anthropocene possible wasn't economic in a superstructural sense, it was a profoundly local, conceptual, and practical one, involving the ascendancy of Cartesian dualisms of Human versus Nature, Mind versus Body.

"One alternative," continues Moore, "is to think about the rise of capitalism as a new way of organizing nature, and therefore a new way of organizing the relations between work, reproduction, and the conditions of life" (2016, 85). Capitalism, in this sense, is for Moore a world-ecology rather than a world-economy, a form of environment-making in which humans become dependent on the cash nexus for their survival through various processes of proletarianization and alienation, from Poland to Brazil to Peru. And yet, Moore notes:

> It was the alliance of the Iberian crown with Genoese capital that, quite literally, made the space that made capitalism possible. In its early centuries, capitalism was trans-Atlantic or it was nothing. [...] Our third great historical process turned on new ways of knowing the world. These were symbolic, but they were far more than symbolic. The ongoing condition of turning human activity into labor power and land into property was a symbolic-knowledge regime premised on separation—on *alienation*. Let us think of the new knowledge regime as a series of "scientific revolutions" in the broadest sense of the term. This regime made it possible to launch and sustain a process that now threatens

us all today: putting the whole of nature to work for capital. [. . .] The new knowledge regime prized dualism, separation, mathematization, the aggregation of units. Its innovations, clustered into scientific revolutions, were at once producers and products of the previous two transformations—of labor (proletarianization) and land (property). (86)

The mobilization of resources and their translation across spaces and languages created what Barak calls "landscapes of intensification" (2015, 426) that reinforced the effort, as outlined in William Shipley's 1753 proposal for a Society for the Encouragement of Arts, "to render Great-Britain the School of Instruction, as it is already the Centre of Traffic to the greatest part of the known World" (Allan 1968, 7). This *doux commerce* ("gentle commerce") thesis advocated free trade and the civilizing effect of commerce, imagining trade as mutually beneficial. Therefore, Barak suggests,

Rather than trace a narrow and unidirectional market causality driven by either production or demand, [we can focus] on the building of interfacing mobile and fixed infrastructures for the transportation of mineral energy—such as sail- and steamships and coal depots and canals, respectively. (2015, 425)

Intensification and commensuration didn't just facilitate communication and good relations; they produced new beings, entities, languages, and meanings—much like contemporary linguistic engineers like Randy and Avi produce "synsets" as translatability commodities. In the eighteenth century, mechanisms of improvement are epitomized in the horse fair: material from distant places (horses from across the country bred from stallions imported from Arabia) is gathered into a "centre of calculation" (Green 2015, 484). The seventeenth-century Shipley marvels at the powerful potential of this mode of action: the glory not of traditional sovereignty, but of "small means well administered" (ibid.).

Colonial landscapes of intensification and commensuration through "small means well administered" included those trafficked across the Ottoman Empire, which, as Barak characterizes,

fastened together through new carbon fibers Istanbul, the province of Egypt, the coal-producing shores of the Black Sea, and those of the Indian Ocean, animated by Anglo-Indian commercial interests. [. . .] Beginning in the early 1830s, these depots, which had initially serviced only steamers, began providing coal to various interiors, animating riverboats, irrigation pumps, railways, telegraphs, streetlights, and tramways. In light of the scope of this process, "the age of coal" seems like a grounded substitute for the vague designation "modernity," which we implicitly ascribe to the political, social, spatial, and temporal effects of the aforementioned technologies. Modern time/space compression, integration into the global economy, the rise of the interventionist state, and the emergence of industrialized agriculture were all energized by these carbon fibers. (426)

To Barak's term "the age of coal" (instead of "modernity"), we could suggest adding "the age of mass-translated coal" or even "the age of multilingual coal"—so as to redress the long-nurtured invisibility of systems of communication and motility that gave coal its material character and shape as a globally essential hyperobject (Morton 2013).

Inquiry through the lens of the Linguacene is therefore interested, for instance, in highlighting the many domestic, anticolonial attempts to control coal and other colonial resources in India, among Bangladeshi and Marwari entrepreneurs in eastern India after the First World War. Though the managing class of the jute, tea, and coal industries in the early twentieth century were British, multilingual Marwari and Gujarati traders did most of the moving of these resources in the interwar years, from pitheads to consuming centers. Not just focusing on coal itself, we would need to understand the Indian Mining Federation's communicative confrontations with the British-controlled Indian Mining Association up until 1920; British traders had to stabilize the dividends from these production matrices so as to avoid sell-offs while ensuring continuously promising yields (Goswami 1989, 294). A Linguacene approach to global ecology would be interested in these ways in which monolanguages forcibly commensurate international energy markets.

The Conceit of Digital Omnilingualism, circa 2000

> Let's set the existence-of-God issue aside for a later volume, and just stipulate that in *some* way, self-replicating organisms came into existence on this planet and immediately began trying to get rid of each other [. . .] by spamming their environments with rough copies of themselves. (*Cryptonomicon*, 5)

Whether under the aegis of a "new linguistic dispensation" (Aronin and Singleton 2008), a "postmonolingual condition" (Yildiz 2013), a "multilingual turn" (May 2013; Kubota 2016), or an era of "controlled languages" (Cronin 2013) in "late capitalism" (Duchêne and Heller 2012) or "post-humanism" (Pennycook 2017), these labels urge us toward the idea that languages themselves have been subjected to radically new conditions of institutionalization, industrialization, and everyday use, which may indeed be testing the limits of our fields' conceptual imaginations (see also O'Hagan and Ashworth 2002). Perhaps, additionally, these conditions have brought to light how so-called individual languages are not the rugged, sovereign integers that European structuralism believed them to be, or that they may indeed have been empirically, to varying extents, only decades prior.

With good reason, sociopolitically minded research in literature and linguistics over the last two decades has tended to focus on how we can better acknowledge the range of creative practices and positionalities at work in multilingually diverse contemporary cultural landscapes, and on how states, curricula, institutions, and commercial enterprises tend to misrecognize that range of speaker positions. Much of this research has been driven by a bottom-up sensibility that places marginalized, racialized, colonized, and abjected speaker positions in the center of a reconceptualization of the analytic premises of linguistics (see, for instance, Makoni and Pennycook 2006; Makoni and Trudell 2006).

But twenty-first-century thinking about language(s) has not just been a tug-of-war between people and power—that is, between language users' experiences and the elite discourses implemented to marshal them into global employability and (classist) socially adaptive pragmatism. Indeed, since 1990, language industries have been engaged in alleviating supply-side manufactural–commercial challenges in the distribution and monetization of symbolic goods across language borders, and this effort has in some ways surpassed the power and hierarchy wielded by traditional, prescriptivist cultural elites around matters of language.

This is an algorithmic culture that innovates ever more effective ways to shuttle language-bound knowledge from one language to another—simultaneously, instantaneously, and globally. It is the linguistic equivalent to the global credit–debit system, and it is increasingly also an active component to that system (Lezra 2015). Because sociolinguistically minded researchers have been eager to turn our attention to the kind of learner experiences that we feel matter, an entire swath of language-oriented engineering scholarship, innovation, and research in Cross-Language Information Retrieval is going unacknowledged in the literary humanities—even as this branch of research is nonetheless aggressively applying its own version of linguistics in the technologies that we use every day. *Cryptonomicon* goes to great lengths to illustrate the open contempt simmering between late-1990s philologists and language-oriented technology entrepreneurs, whose political worldviews are shown to be aesthetically similar but increasingly inimical in practice.

Cryptonomicon works as a kind of primer for readers at the millennium about what to expect from the literacies and macro-literacy demands of the coming century. Yet the novel's protagonists betray an extraordinary ambivalence toward precisely the changes in hermeneutics that they are proposing to engineer. Randy, for instance, preserves for himself a private privilege to determine what words mean, and this privilege is usually tested out in matters of culture, gender, and race. Ruminating about the "real meaning" of purportedly racist words, he theorizes forth:

> Figur[ing] it all has to do with your state of mind at the time you utter the word. If you're just trying to abbreviate, it's not a slur. But if you are fomenting racist hatreds, as [another character in the novel] occasionally seems to be not above doing, that's different. (212)

Despite being at the cutting edge of how meanings are to be communicated globally in the new technologies Epiphyte Corp. develops, Randy wants to preserve for his own use a deeply Romantic, intentionalist, and sovereign subjectivity around meaning-making. He wants to have his cake and monetize it too.

Under conditions of late monolingualism, it is not just that academic disciplines have critically rethought the usefulness—and the analytic and political costs—of counting and naming individual languages, nor is it just that people's everyday creative and combinatory use of these language(s) in social and digital life has left behind old paradigms. Rather, it is possible that the categorical subject itself—that is, "individual language"—may have undergone, at the hands of romantically and racialistically inclined engineers like Randy, at least functional and heuristic, if not ontological, fortifications and attenuations in this period beginning in 1990. Something can of course be walled off, or walled in, simultaneously as it's being hollowed out.

At the very least, it appears that a new political economy of energetic vested interests, represented by Epiphyte Corp., needs this category "a language" to do and perform different things than it had done in the 1960s. *Cryptonomicon* shows that some of these functional–heuristic changes to the notion of "individual language"—as it is used by experts, researchers, and technicians—have been arising since 1990 from within the technical agenda of commercial multilingualism, which has a deep interest in ascertaining and delimiting what counts as "a language" in current socio-digital contexts.

Both the vernacular use and the everyday value of the concept of "individual language" of course persist among individual speakers and learners in various ways, somewhat independently of how expert technicians have been repurposing it. Language is always a contested, malleable concept—used in utterly different ways in various historical contexts and cultural domains. The phenomena of contempt that emerge in *Cryptonomicon* are in part a result of such emerging differences as they hinge on profound technological paradigm shifts, where computational engineers bring their own, often folk–linguistic notions about meaning into the management and manipulation of large-scale translation. China Miéville's novel *Embassytown* in the next chapter dimensionalizes these paradigm shifts, through the imaginative potency of a science-fiction world in which the notion of monolingualism, and its partner conceit of easy translatability, are long obsolete.

4

An Immerser's Ecstasy

I was willing to be a curio but I disappointed them. [...] The discussion became vague and sociological when they realized that I wouldn't be able to tell them almost anything about Language.

—Avice Benner Cho, in China Miéville, *Embassytown* (2011, 36)

As we round this last corner in *Literature in Late Monolingualism*, China Miéville's 2011 English-language linguistic science-fiction ("li-fi") novel *Embassytown* sets the scene for an axiomatic confrontation that is humanistic and posthumanist at once.[1] Miéville's late monolingual novel asks us: What future value will it ultimately have had, beyond mere market-prospecting and revenue generating aims, for real human speakers in the early twenty-first century to devote time immersing themselves into learning to speak additional languages—by way of their very own voices, affects, musculatures, wits, and minds, rather than just through prosthetic tools of "terre-tech" and "bio-rigging" in their pockets, as Miéville's novel terms them? Such is of course never a stark either/or proposition for us readers and language learners: either choosing unenhanced flesh over augmentive technology, or vice versa. In a vividly agnostic way, Miéville's novel helps us imagine complex competing scenarios for how and why to seek a truly embodied multilingual subjectivity today. And to do so carefully accompanied by the inevitable, even exhilarating utility of added technological assistance (Machine Translation, AI-assisted writing, etc.), without sacralizing or demonizing either pole.

Indeed, despite many zealous and fearsome projections, we know very little about what post-2040 societies will be like on Earth, and about what their sociolinguistic needs will accordingly be. Will embodied multilingual persons—who can indeed speak multiple languages and multilingua francas

---

[1] I have suggested the "li-fi" genre to describe not only Tidbeck's *Amatka* in the first chapter, but also any fiction that attempts to answer a complex conceptual or practical question about languages in their social contexts. Not all li-fi novels are by default "literature in late monolingualism" nor necessarily "novels for the Linguacene," though there will be a newly intensive preponderance of li-fi compositions under the aesthetic and institutional pressures of late monolingual ideology.

very well (Makoni and Pennycook 2012), without the intervention of machine translators and nonhuman intelligence—be civically essential in ways we are not able to foresee right now? Or must we admit that, for any person with a working smart phone and competing demands on their time, human language learning is no longer time prudently spent, and we might just as well all sign up for coding bootcamps instead?

Miéville's intergalactic novel cloaks this question in a puzzlingly enduring conceit that starts back here on Earth. In what seems almost a prank on intellectual history, *Embassytown* chases down the strategic fuzziness around what we do and do not agree to mean when we call something Language/Sprache/dil/langue. What unfolds in the course of the novel is the core fact (hidden from readers throughout the first two-thirds of the story) that the most intensely coveted and yet unknowable object of acquisition and insight in *Embassytown*'s colonial universe is something called "Language" (as mentioned and mystified in Avice's remark in the epigraph above).

But this Language in *Embassytown* is not so easily the mere "essential human faculty" that humans, reared in a Chomskyan or Herderian vein, will expect. Here on Earth, philosophical and even linguistic discourse has for millennia argued back and forth in the name of something it calls "Language"—despite an ongoing agreement to overlook the opportunistic conceptual slippage we permit in English between "Language" and diverse "language(s)," between the alleged cognitive faculty and the particular sociolinguistic expression, between the ideal species-level capacity of Language and the thousands of variously claimed, cherished, and constructed entities called "languages" that provide the practical evidence of such a capital-L Language faculty. Both agnostic and eager to level up on all this fuzziness, Miéville seems to think we're still only in the beginning stages of an adequate usage of these terms, and he poses this challenge as an extended riddle throughout *Embassytown*.

If Karin Tidbeck's novel *Amatka* had been about a world where subjects' performative uttering in language was made to become a totalizing, salvific campaign for frontier survival, prompting cheerful authoritarian engagement from all speakers, Miéville's *Embassytown* flips the critical project around—querying the philosophical concepts as bluntly as it does the praxis in their name. It is not the case in *Embassytown*, for instance, that human speakers need to be hypervigilant about how they speak and how frequently they label objects linguistically. What humans say in the city of Embassytown is, at least in nonemergency moments, much less pivotal than is their own ongoing usefulness as themselves *parts of (an Other's) speech*, as philosophical-linguistic objects for the Host Ariekei population's own enunciative ambitions and designs. In a colonial and decolonial gambit at once, humans in Embassytown agree to serve the Hosts/Ariekei as enfleshed and acquirable spoken Language tokens, helping the Hosts actually think in new ways—that is, as *parts of speech* in and for their Hosts' extended cognition. "Part of speech" is of course an oddly dead metaphor that, when dilated poetically in Miéville's composition to mean something like "speaking subjects integrated syntactically into a new kind of utterance," releases a racy figural repertoire for this novel, in which humans themselves become indelible resources in the otherwise robustly sovereign Language of an alien race.

In *Embassytown*, these willing human similes-in-the-flesh, including Avice Benner Cho from the epigraph above, tend to hang out at a bar in Embassytown called the Cravat, commiserating about the next time the Ariekei will come calling on them to serve some meaning-making purpose for which their human bodies and pragmatic enfleshedness will serve as the now indispensable, singular means. In this way, humans themselves get uttered over and over again by the Ariekei, who stage them in order for certain kinds of cognitive and articulatory achievements to work, particularly for the kind of truth-bending that only human metaphor seems to be able to provide.

Because their thoughts are Language itself, the Ariekei are apparently incapable of lying. Humans are the only living resource through which Ariekei meaning-making can venture untruth, metaphor, simile, hyperbole, exaggeration, poetry, deception, and the like. They do so awkwardly at first, much like monolanguages fumble desirously with tantalizing new loanwords, loangrammars, and loanstyles from without, sometimes for months, sometimes for centuries. The Ariekei appropriate willing humans to become ongoing resources for their growing repertoire of dishonest or propositionally inaccurate "thinking for speaking" (Slobin 1996). Where *Amatka* staged an extreme form of mono- and translingual performativity, *Embassytown* epitomizes what it means for humans to serve as the symbolic figures through which radical others build and convey their own meanings: humans as intermediaries who are iterated and reiterated to serve others' purposes. Of course, this newly robust frontier culture, trafficking readily in "parts of speech," requires of the Hosts that they let down their guard, and that they relinquish any "re-guard" for the linguistic sovereignty they only too late notice they had successfully maintained up until this recent opening toward innovation through the humans they acquire as useable linguistic objects.

For their part, most humans don't feel this function for their Hosts as an oppressive or extractive burden; they have just as many, if not more, problems with other humans as they do with the Ariekei using them to think and language with. The human protagonist of *Embassytown* Avice is a "floaker," a shrewd but debonair experiencer of language, a lay practitioner condescended to by human academic researchers and their networks of expert discourse and abstraction. Her own credibility in Embassytown, which she prizes but does not conspicuously flaunt, derives in part from the fact that she has herself become this kind of indispensable part of the Hosts' Language, encased within it, a rare, painful, and enviable honor among humans. In this sense, she practices a kind of "dirty theory" (Connell 2007; Hardy 2012, 518) in parallel to the academics' zealous discourse about Language—agnostic, rebellious, implicated, embodied, modest, and critical in ways they are unwilling to risk being.

This figural landscape of concepts and linguistic praxis in *Embassytown* is all in service, I wager, of allowing this late-monolingual novel to slow down the expedient ways we in the early twenty-first century make presumptions about what language is, how it works, and whom it serves and services under various conditions. The resulting lessons around aesthetic experience in this alternate conceptual universe—that is, its "bilingual games" (Summer 2003)—are often beautiful, luxurious, and tragic. As the Hosts get better at lying (and making metaphors), they start to love it feverishly, putting on Festivals of Lies, where different Ariekei try out various feats of nontruth, to the ecstatic adulation of their Host peers and the bemused puzzlement of human onlookers. Here is one of the Ariekei's early lyrical attempts to lie, translated from Language into Anglo-Ubic for the humans to understand:

> Before the humans came we [the Ariekei] didn't speak so much of certain things. Before the humans came we didn't speak so much. Before the humans came we didn't speak. We didn't walk on our wings. We didn't walk. We didn't swallow earth. We didn't swallow. There's a Terre who swims with fishes, one who wore no clothes, one who ate what was given her, one who walks backward. There's a rock that was broken and cemented together. I differ with myself then agree, like the rock that was broken and cemented together. I change my opinion. I'm like the rock that was broken and cemented together. I wasn't not like the rock that was broken and cemented together. I do what I always do. I'm like the Terre that swims with the fishes. I'm not unlike that Terre. I'm very like it. I'm not water. I'm not water. I'm water. (140; note that "Terre" means human)

Each of these arresting and moving metaphorical micro-stories from the Ariekei is built of meaning-making resources that they have arduously appropriated, in the form of actual human persons living as settlers in Embassytown, like Avice (above: "the human who wore no clothes," or, sometimes, "the one who ate what was given her"). Here the Ariekei are, among other things, endeavoring to accept Doris Sommer's 2003 invitation to "come play bilingual games with me" (see Chapter 2), but they are also taking the plunge into anti-protectionist "soft multilingualism" (Noorani 2013). They become avid language-learners and undeterred translanguagers, changing themselves and their very cognition through the inventive use of an idiom of experience that is, riskily, not their own. As it turns out, this celebration of lies ends up having mortally addictive qualities for the Ariekei, and it becomes clear that the human governments who run things on a faraway planet have nefariously sent "ambassadors" to infect the Ariekei with this foreign language that would overwhelm, enchant, and debilitate them.

This "Language," the Ariekei's own and incommensurable thought-and-communication medium, has apparently been tough to crack for distant human colonial administrations, because it requires two voices speaking simultaneously to perform a joint utterance (something that, importantly, novels are not typographically equipped to do with any more ease than is a human individual). In this, the Hosts' "Language" is the quintessential exemplar of "hard multilingualism" as Noorani (2013) conceptualized it: indifferent to outsiders' comprehension, arduous to translate, insulated from extraction, intractably contextual, unamenable to even the cleverest scheme to secure "xenos rights" from afar, and yet all this without being deliberately protectionist.

Like the other three novels that drive our explorations of the literary imagination in late monolingualism, Miéville's 2011 *Embassytown* angles to make its own theory on things that literary studies, translation studies, applied linguistics, and second language acquisition research haven't yet abundantly provided. But unlike the other three novels, *Embassytown*'s relationship with late monolingualism is less anxious and constrained than it is hopeful and pugnacious. Like the literary commodities *Amatka* and *Cryptonomicon*, its title is a unique search term that plays the game of algorithmic marketing and telegraphic cross-language messaging in global literary commerce,[2] but the novel's narrative does not set its philosophical sights on universal instantaneous translation or other solutionist tools, as many science-fiction experiments have done since Murray Leinster's 1945 novella *First Contact*.

Embassytown chooses as its conceptual frame for language meditation and mediation not something like Ursula K. Le Guin's ansible (an instantaneous communication device), but instead a form of linguistic subspace, what Miéville calls "the immer," that makes communication across worlds and languages dangerous, unpredictable, rudimentary, and slow (see McKenzie

---

[2] Gemma Rovira's 2013 Spanish translation still carries the English proper noun title *Embassytown*, a unique search term that is therefore also untranslatable (for commercial-algorithmic reasons).

and Punske 2019 on "Language Development During Interstellar Travel"). By staging linguistics on a vastly expanded and arduous intergalactic scale, the novel wants to de-escalate our current Earthly repertoire of conceits and conceptions around language management, language tech, and Machine Translation. The novel is an intense, challenging inventory-taking about the premises that currently shape what constitutes "Language" in globalized late monolingual discourses, from statecraft and diplomacy all the way to literary theory, computational engineering, and Artificial Intelligence. Its figural devotions are generally in the name of the *experience* of languaging in a profoundly multilingual pluriverse, rather than of the dream of removing the problems associated with that experience, as was rather the gold-rush dream in Stephenson's *Cryptonomicon*.

Connecting all of these linguistic communities in *Embassytown* is Avice Benner Cho who, more than anything else, is a middling scrapper disobeying orders and cheerily getting by on skill, luck, laziness, drink, and chutzpah. She has made the questionable choice of marrying an academic linguist—Scile—who, on their first date, tries to pump her about her experiences as a trained Immerser (intergalactic traveler/translator) and as herself an adopted part the Hosts' Language.

Immersing in language doesn't mean mastering a language though, nor having "competence" or "proficiency" in one, as today's Earthly discourses prompt us to have. Rather, as the epigraph to this chapter suggests, Avice experiences and epitomizes what current computational engineering literature tends to call a "language-agnostic" stance (see Ojo et al. 2023 for a standard example)—physically immersed in the Ariekei's Language, as a part of their speech, as well as in the subspace intergalactic translational experience of the "immer," but comfortable with not being able to define these authoritatively. She is an implicated language-agnostic, rather than an indifferent one.[3]

Like linguistic indifference (Pipestone Group 2023), language agnosis has a long history of unintended practical implications, and the term of art is likely as questionable in its methodological bearing as is linguistic prescriptivism (Cameron 1995). As aggrandized last chapter in Stephenson's *Cryptonomicon*, a working premise of some traditions of linguistic engineering has held that its engineers likely should *not* learn the living languages they are working to manage, as such "agnosticism" toward languages and their meanings are themselves the arm's-length scientific guardrail of the effectiveness of

---

[3] A less frequent term of art among today's engineers for language-agnosis is "language-configurability," but I suspect it loses out to "agnostic" in the computational engineering literature because of the alluring mystical timbre of the word *agnostic*.

their codebreaking, counterinsurgency, and business-management-driven solutions. Avice, however, is a different kind of language-agnostic subject, in that she really doesn't know what Language is and doesn't pretend to "master" it, but she has rather become a part of it, and is intuitively dexterous and reverent within it. She does not see in (feigned or actual) agnosis the opportunity to dominate languages from afar or from without—that is, to exert and engineer xenos rights over others' meaning-making practices.

Avice's aesthetic and relational experience poses the vexing contemporary question: what do we really know, or need to know anew, about Language today—after all our millennia of testing and theorizing it? The matter of methodological agnosticism in language engineering as in everyday life is not a simple one unambiguously signaling modesty and reverence toward a complex range of phenomena. "Language-agnostic" was not a term in much circulation in turn-of-the-century computational engineering because agnosticism was not a market value yet when *Cryptonomicon* was published. Back then, engineers were still trying to name and optimize certain bounded entities (or clusters of them) in emerging market-innovations for Machine Translation, like Japanese, French, Italian, German, Spanish (JFIGS) or Chinese, Japanese, Korean (CJK). That era is now over, and has been replaced by a modeling-and-design culture where the emphatic conceit is on resourcing the entire range of "low-resource languages," though not necessarily specific ones. Most models are now operationally "language-agnostic" on the premise that such agnosticism will befit *all* low-resource languages—from Tigrinya to Shona to Tibetan to həṅqəmiṅəṁ.

This shift in the engineering literature toward something like agnosticism or language-configurability retraces an inclination that had been spelled out in the *Varieties of Capitalism* literature (Hall and Soskice 2001) as regards new political economies that favor switchable rather than non-switchable assets—that is, where market suppliers favor dynamic multilateral "switchable" arrangements for supply chains, value chains, and manufacture logistics rather than fixed bilateral ones. Academic disciplines like critical applied linguistics, literary studies, computational linguistics, and supply-side manufacture logistics are each at very different historical junctures regarding their respective investment in the financialized switchable versus non-switchable asset model, and in what the difference means for the overall value of cultural particularity in their respective domains of analysis and practice. That varying investment, in each of these four sectors, is not an expression of belief, ideology, and conceptual adequacy, however. It is a pragmatic investment in what can actually be done—that is, what "value-creation" can be achieved and managed within a particular scale and time. What does the financialized pretext of linguistic agnosticism enable engineers and sellers to purvey as allegedly switchable translatabilities, when the underlying infrastructural innovations purveyed may rest profoundly on extractivist, monolingual, and epistemicidal procedures?

What, after all, does it mean to operate language-agnostically in our time, in and beyond computational engineering? Rarely, in IEEE Machine Translation innovation write-ups, is this term "language-agnostic" defined, and so the figural plain is left open for all sorts of imaginings, which Avice's avowed inability "to tell them almost anything about Language" embodies. Does language-agnosticism mean being:

- agnostic about which named language (i.e., Arabic, Japanese) certain data are assumed to come from, or about whether linguistic data come from any nameable, countable language entity at all?
- agnostic about which linguistic communities, polities, and markets are intended to benefit from a computational linguistic innovation, or which may eventually benefit regardless of intention?
- agnostic about what language is, versus what is paralinguistic or nonlinguistic?
- agnostic about what language is for: information-conveyance, meaning-making, obfuscation, poesis, documentation, conviviality, intellectual activity, political subjectivity, or the facilitation of socio-commercial goods transfer?
- agnostic about whether (in linguistic matters) authority and order exist, or should exist—that is, an agnosticism about the standpoint and relevance of expertise, power, correctness, prescriptivism, or descriptivism?
- agnostic in the sense of who does the knowing, the gnosis, and who doesn't need to know anything at all for a model or practice to be successful?
- agnostic about the difference or distinctiveness among programming languages, artificial languages, and natural human languages?
- agnostic about whether learning a language is necessary in order to manage it or engineer models that service it?
- agnostic about subjectivity and objecthood in language—that is, whether we deploy language(s) or whether languages, or Others' languages, deploy us?

Through Avice and the novel's various floakers and ambassadors, *Embassytown* allows itself to be enchanted by these questions in multidimensional ways, and on a cosmological scale that the current applied computational engineering literature has no practical reason to explore. Making this conceptual landscape sufficiently rich and puzzling is the fact that that Language is for the Ariekei a cognitive state, as well as its simultaneous expression; thought and speech are for them equivalent and coextensive. Because thinking dishonestly is inconceivable for the Ariekei, they can neither lie in Language nor use allegedly basic figural resources like metaphor, hyperbole, and simile. Furthermore, when humans labor to articulate Language to communicate with the Ariekei, they must do so bivocally: that is, by yoking together an intersubjective pair of simultaneous speakers (referred to corporately as "an ambassador"), who collaborate(s) in producing different constitutive phonemic parts of each morpheme simultaneously, like notes in a musical chord.

Being able to carry off these articulations in any socially successful way with the Ariekei is a totalizing and depleting devotion for those humans who undertake it, akin to the kind of exhaustion simultaneous interpreters often describe experiencing when they allow the language of others to fully occupy their body. As such, Miéville appears intent on depicting the aesthetic experience of linguistic hardship and effortful translanguaging, in a far-future setting that has long since surpassed and forgotten anything like our currently powerful solutionist forms of late monolingualism.

Avice, as we have noted, has been adopted as a living simile by the Ariekei as "the one who ate what was given her" and, although she cannot speak Language (as the two-bodied, two-selved, two-voiced Ambassadors can), is recognized as a part of Language nonetheless, rather than a speaker of it. At one point, her husband Scile takes Avice off-world to his profession's Conference of Human Exoterre Linguists (CHEL), where she swaggers around the place scoffing at the pandering panel titles, like "The Healing Power of Story." Aggressively curious about the home world where she was raised and how to extract research insights from it, the thirsty experts at CHEL fish for Avice's views on "life among the Ariekei." She is a hostile informant at best. "That's wrong," corrects Avice tersely. "They're 'Hosts'" (36). Having grown up in the far-off Bremen colonial outpost of Embassytown, which is itself surrounded by an Indigenous Host City atmospherically uninhabitable for humans, Avice is used to people being aggressively wrong about the world where she grew up as a settler.

Punking Langue

Embassytown's universe is, in Noorani's terms, a mix of both soft and hard multilingualisms (2013). In it, a highly advanced translatability industry (Gramling 2021) has made many languages and dialects easy enough to surmount and deploy, even for those who cannot speak them on their own. But there are also species whose languages far exceed the dimensions foreseen in human discourse about language today: meaning-making practices that require interaction between two bodies, simultaneous overlapping articulation, or languages that function without means for comparison, deception, or irony, and the like. These are linguistic formations that, vivid on most pages of the novel, approximate best what Noorani (2013) describes as hard multilingualism, a phenomenon "which requires reckoning with [. . .] radical linguistic difference" (8) and "entails not simply the assimilation of a foreign grammar and lexicon, but the initiation into a system of communication that cannot be abstracted from a foreign way of life and pattern of thought" (9).

Earthly conceptual distinctions for talking about language and speech—like *langue–parole–langage*, *lengua–lenguaje*, *Sprache–Rede*—often lack the enduring social power, even here on Earth, to break through and organize discussions in ways that clarify what dimension is truly at issue in any given moment: whether Language in the idealized singular, or languages in the practical plural, whether language as systemic repertoire or language as what people actually and surprisingly utter. This irresolvable ambiguity in actual conversation about L/language endures because—thanks to yet another caprice of translingual accidence—English has lacked any of the disambiguating terminological options that have long been overt and available in German, Spanish, and French.

Knowing this, Miéville decides in the novel to poke the bear a bit by naming the recalcitrant meaning-making repertoire of the alien Ariekei, on whose world Embassytown is a colonial outpost, with the (translated) endogamous autonym "Language"—rather than, say, "Ariekan" or the like. Meanwhile, other languages in the universe carry ethnonyms like Anglo-Ubic, even though "Earth" and Earthly orders have been forgotten millennia prior. Fearful and desirous empires in this universe engineer extreme mutations of human life so as merely to understand the Ariekei Hosts' "Language." Lives and castes of person are conscripted in brutal ways so as to learn, perfect, and access it.

While it is clear in the world of the novel that a complex political campaign is being intensified upon this one specific Ariekei polity's "Language" sovereignty, there is a strong allegorical overtone that makes this story always also one about the perverse, anxious, and defacing lengths to which we humans have historically gone in the name of penetrating and quickly managing any unknown language, or Language as such. By making this conflation deliberate in his fiction, Miéville dilates this long-standing ambiguity that has typified the urge to master the dyad Language-languages in the history of ideas, short-circuiting the carefully upheld accidence between the two homonyms.

Accordingly, *Embassytown* is a late monolingual novel that dignifies with its figural attentions the slow, arduous, enfleshed experience of transformative language-learning and language-becoming, even in settings jam-packed with the most expedient and accelerated technologies meant to replace these experiences. As such, the novel is a meditation on what gets lost when omnipresent social discourses saturate us with the technological solutions alone, when there is much more in the realm of multilingual subjectivity to attend to than that. Sure, today's "actually existing" somatocentric language proficiency achievements on Earth may no longer feel like the self-evident epic adventures they were for generations of learners before 2000. The sense of possibility and enchantment that accompanies the unique hardships of becoming an additional-language speaker may not have vanished, but the horizon of embodied triumph at speaking or writing a new language well is often not as unalloyed as it once was, when adequate technical assistance was much harder to find or fathom in moments of need.

Consider in this abruptly changing context the fact that, while traditional-classroom modern-language instruction enrollments decline steeply across North America in higher educational settings, one of the clear climbers bucking this trend is American Sign Language (ASL) (MLA 2021). ASL is a language that by its embodied nature offers no other scene of performance than to be fully taken into learners' bodies themselves— that is, to become part of them and their bodies, much as Language must become physically part of Embassytown's ambassadors' flesh. No prosthetic abstraction, phonocentric script, or other representational extension will serve to ease the holistic hardship of articulating ASL well. By the numbers, at least, it seems that this is exactly the kind of challenging arrangement a new generation of language learners is apparently eager to (re)embrace.

Beyond Sign languages though, the horizon for learning a language well feels today less obviously of a sublime kind, character, and resonance than it often did in eras when prosthetic devices did not yet widely exist to translate serviceably for us; when AI platforms of varying quality and price did not exist to write, think, research, and edit for us on demand (in and across many languages); and when being a proficient speaker–listener was still the most obvious rational strategy for understanding, and potentially acting in alignment with, culturally specific knowledges. That is to say: before 2000. For persons making hard choices today about what to do with their time, strategic monolingualism does, alas, seem to be a better and better way to optimize themselves, at least for the moment. China Miéville's novel is, among other things, one complex piece of guidance on these dilemmas, portraying a technologically advanced future in which slow language learning (and the hardship and stamina it entails) becomes more—rather than less—essential to civic well-being and political strategy, not just for an expert class, but for everyone.

In such a moment, we can squarely acknowledge the complex and ongoing potential diminishment in the market value of embodied language proficiency today—without immediately consoling ourselves with the complementary benefits brought forth by multilingual technologies that have been engineered to assist our language-making. In other words, we can grieve the loss of older styles of language learning without ignoring it, covering it up, or wallowing in it in maudlin ways. It is possible indeed that those styles have simply gone underground in a current gold-rush moment, likely to return in new forms a few decades hence, as Miéville's novel helps us imagine they will. Grief and visionary hope can indeed be separate though related matters in the midst of apprehending a broader paradigm change of this sort, and novels like those foregrounded in this book aid generously in that endeavor.

To quote Butler, Guillory, and Thomas's brief book from 2000, *What's Left of Theory?*, we might now ask, circa 2025—without overdramatization, and with earnest interest in the answers and their implications—*What's Left of Language?* What indeed is the broad *will to language(s)* in this currently emerging age, when profound ambivalence about the worthwhileness of embodied language learning, and indeed even about enunciation itself (beyond "data"), has taken the upper hand in a range of powerful discourses and institutional orders? And what vanishing features and disinherited experiences of multilingual being from previous eras must remain grievable and honorable, without indulging in mere nostalgia?

A New Will to Language(s)?

Miéville's *Embassytown* is a humbling, revealing vision about this deeply ambivalent will to language(s) around us in the early twenty-first century—though it is set far from our world and time. Its intergalactic science-fiction scope allows the novel two ostensibly incompatible moves. First, the novel critically refashions current social aspects of global securitarian languages-management discourse and its attendant solutionist technologies. At the same time, it delves deep back into the sometimes painful, sometimes ecstatic experience of "hard translanguaging" (Noorani 2013, sitholé and Gramling 2025), of working toward meaning in a new language incommensurable with one's own dominant one(s), when the tempting opportunity to steal or overwrite that meaning is available nonetheless.

These two arenas—those of linguistic infrastructural supply/modeling and of linguistic subjectivity/desire, respectively—come to the fore in *Embassytown* not primarily through critiques of technological marketing schemes and neoliberal abstractions of "competence," but through the enfleshed, troubled, and transforming subjectivity of language users and language learners. Humans, hybrid "ambassadors," and the alien Hosts— "the Ariekei," who themselves attempt to their peril to acquire humans' "Anglo-Ubic"—all embody and dramatize together the tenuous pretexts of linguistic engineering and modeling and the experiential stakes of language acquisition, that is, of being transformed through its acquisition. This is, importantly for our purposes, a universe that appears to have passed through something like a reductionist epoch of "late monolingualism" already some tens of millennia ago, and that now confronts—in an ongoing and surprising way—how profoundly little it still really knows about Language, despite the industries that have arisen to saturate our lives with expert knowledge about it. The novel brings the cosmological–epistemic stakes of critical multilingualism studies back up into line with the ambitious, humbling high stakes of astrophysics—which is where, I believe, they belong.

Having become a part of speech in Language, Avice's linguistic practice has deeply to do with the body—with her body, and with the body of other nonhuman polities around her—and this is one of the ways the novel critically interrogates today's accelerated externalization of language practice onto prosthetic machines and other forms of algorithmic outsourcing. Avice is a language object, a language subject, a language medium, and a language event; what she is not is an orderly, glossodiverse vehicle for market needs, nor an early and easy adopter of multilingually assistive technologies. This latter inclination to outsource meaning-making to machines beyond the body is less an innovation of late monolingual technologies themselves than it is the legacy of a Cartesian ("3I") linguistics that sees language as "Instrumental, Internal, and Individual" (Steffensen 2015, 106), rather than what a 4E linguistics, akin to Avice's experience and Miéville's figural world, would consider to be true about the "Embodied, Extended, Ecological, and Enacted" essence of language (105).

Mel Chen's 2012 *Animacies* refutes the strange, persistent, almost willful detachment across the interpretive social sciences that hampers the kind of linkages between ideas about language and ideas about materiality that burgeon in Miéville's world-making. In most European conceptual legacies, such detachment has left language "bleached of its quality to be anything but referential, or structural, or performative." Based on their simple observation that "[f]or humans and others, spoken and signed speech can involve the tongue, vocal tract, breath, lips, hands, eyes, and shoulders [and] is a corporeal, sensual, embodied act" (53), Chen's *Animacies* attempts to return to languages their prerogative to be conceived and theorized as both material and alive. Drawing on work by the linguistic anthropologist Michael Silverstein on "animacy hierarchies" (1976), Chen devotes their book's energies to recovering

> the alchemical magic of language, whether benevolent or vicious, by demonstrating explicit ways that it animates humans, animals, and things in between. [They] suggest that this can be done in collusion with existing registers of citizenship, race, sex, ability, and sexuality, depending on the recurrent materializations of iterative power. (2012, 23)

These critical correctives from Chen begin to direct us toward the kind of implicated agnosticism and ecstasy of experience that Avice lives and relives in the novel, and toward a potential consciousness about the predicament of late monolingualism in literature and aesthetic experience more broadly today. Even ambitious linguists though, including her husband Scile, lose patience with Avice when she is less than articulate and instrumentally forthcoming about her experiences with the Ariekei's Language. Much like Sonja in Chapter 2, Avice is a bad local informant, aphasic and useless for experts' fieldwork and extractivist urges, suggesting that Avice's kind of subjectivity will frequently lose out to more confident, evangelical, solutionist takes on language.

Disalienating Language

Li-fi novels like *Embassytown* pose such precocious questions about the swiftly innovating technological sectors that today are thriving adjacent to the compositional spaces in which literature is made. In imagining a subject like Avice—who is both uniquely subjected and even subjugated to Language, while also possessing a unique artisanal prestige as an immersive and conversant translanguager in Embassytown—Miéville re-opens and restages some of these underspecified and shifty terms that fuel the supply-side superstructure of linguistic engineering today, such as "language-configurable" and "language-agnostic" design.

Literature in Late Monolingualism has, thus far, been less about the vital, alchemical power of language and its literary representations than about the existing, enervating registers of extraction and coloniality Chen speaks of above (2012, 23), and the ways those durable registers have found monolingualism (in its translational, ordolingual, and multilingual forms) to be a promising resource and a growth industry. Over the course of this book, we have explored several of the go-to moods and styles for literature in late monolingualism as I conceive it. In Chapter 1, Karin Tidbeck's self-translated *Amatka* (2012) suppresses the potent alternatives deeply but vaguely felt by its protagonists, so as to dramatize a world order in which repressive translingual commensuration and compromise are seen as a primary necessity for species survival. In Chapter 2, Dorthe Nors's 2015 *Mirror, Shoulder, Signal* showed how the presumed commercial order of countable, nameable global languages is only restlessly borne by practitioners of literary translation, and how the embodied experience of this pretext of order makes them agitate (if not clamor) for vivid, if threatening, alternatives. In Chapter 3, Neal Stephenson's 1999 *Cryptonomicon* dilated into a grand conceit of rebuke and revulsion toward lay conceptions and practices of language, amid the high conjunctures of economic globalism, illustrating how that conceit ate away at the engineers of global linguistic dominion pictured in the novel.

Each of these three novels exudes, therefore, a depressive and punitive mood, a disingenuous lashing out about monolanguage's failings—as if to say, as before a breakup, *I never loved you anyway*. But each also comes with an enduring if subtle undertone of true curiosity about the ways out of late monolingualism that remain available to us. They glisten with a furtive, enduring credence toward what Chen calls the "alchemical magic of language." That credence is expressed in Stephenson's, Nors's, and Tidbeck's novels through intense though private moments of ecstasy and, at times, through collective rebellions in search of an effective liberatory conception of linguistic subjectivity and creative credibility. Philosophical fictions like these can help us disalienate our current social and disciplinary imaginations about how and why languages are studied, learned, invented, talked about, and disinvented (Makoni and Pennycook 2006), now and in the future.

In *Embassytown*, Miéville explores the ecstatic rediscovery of language learning and the deep, humble language-agnosticism that is still utterly potential within literary late monolingualism. *Embassytown* redimensionalizes language learning, for instance, by resituating the pursuit among various species who—like the Ariekei—have no metaphors in their home language and, in the process of learning metaphor-laden languages, experience something akin to ecstatic pain:

> Pangs of something finishing, and of birth. Everything changes now: I thought that very explicitly, each word. I thought: Now they're seeing things.
>
> In the beginning was each word of Language, sound isomorphic with some Real: not a thought, not really, only self-expressed worldness, speaking itself through the Ariekei. Language had always been redundant: it had only ever been the world. Now the Ariekei were learning to speak, and to think, and it hurt. [. . .]
>
> The said was now not-as-it-is. What they spoke now weren't things or moments anymore but the thoughts of them, pointings-at; meanings no longer a flat facet of essence; signs ripped from what they signed. It took the lie to do that. With that spiral of assertion–abnegation came quiddities, and the Ariekei became themselves. They were worldsick, as meanings yawed. (312)

At first glance, this gloss of the Ariekei as learners may appear to romanticize or condescend to their experience as subjects of language and language learning. Like Tidbeck's *Amatka*, *Embassytown* is, in the end, an experimental rhetorical meditation upon colonial procedure and sensibility, on an intergalactic scale. While post–Cold War logics of language sovereignty ran on a national rather than imperial model, this novel hearkens back to a nineteenth-century conception of linguistic sovereignty in which dominium and imperium were not coterminous features of state power. Logics of empire, occupation, racialization, othering, xenophobia, and projections of incommensurability are therefore overt and acute throughout the novel, rather than mystically sequestered in the seminar rooms of the Mont Pelerin Society or the Doha Round, as they appear to be in Nors's novel in Chapter 2. The scene of translingual awakening above is an event of dramatic divestment from these structures, after a traumatic near-extinction event that threatened to annihilate the occupied Ariekei.

One can of course read the passage above as a patronizing commiseration around another's learning pains. In such a reading, the Ariekei might be glossed as naïve beings who have failed to tap into the human faculty of intellectual reasoning and abstraction, which is now being introduced to them belatedly and in haste. But this reading of the novel, I think, narrows the conceptual frame too far. It is not that the Ariekei lack intellectual reasoning through language so much as that their language has no apparent need for human metaphor until occupiers begin to require it of them. It is the violent interaction with invaders that required them to translanguage through and with the exotic technology of the lie, the implicature, the simile.

Intergalactic Competencies

One of the serious tasks *Embassytown* sets for itself in the midst of late monolingualism is thus to reject easy frameworks around understanding what language is, in a human age awash with confident, technocratic manipulations of language. The novel puts forth a range of clinical descriptions, lay characterizations, and pragmatic glosses for how languages work in Embassytown. Reflecting on one community of language users, the narrator tells us:

> They were not the only exoterres I'd seen. There were exot inhabitants of Embassytown—a few Kedis, a handful of Shur'asi and others—but with them, while there was strangeness of course there was never that abstraction, that sheer remove one felt from Hosts. One Shur'asi shopkeeper would even joke with us, his accent bizarre but his humor clear.
>
> Later I understood that those immigrants were exclusively from species with which we shared conceptual models, according to various measures. Hosts, the indigenes, in whose city we had been graciously allowed to build Embassytown, were cool, incomprehensible presences. Powers like subaltern gods, which sometimes watched us as if we were interesting, curious dust, which provided our biorigging; and to which the Ambassadors alone spoke. (14)

In this world, incomprehensibility and incommensurability are not philosophical horizons to be pondered post facto so much as institutional and logistical predicaments to be patiently solved in a no-nonsense fashion. The novel imagines incomprehensibilities, untranslatabilities, and incommensurabilities as relatively banal features of everyday interaction, neither precluding nor even subduing social relations between respective speaker groups. There is, further, no unified sense in the novel as to what a "speaker" is and what the linguistic object is that they may be said to speak. In one scene where a former ambassador interacts with one of Embassytown's incomprehensible Hosts, Bren remarks that his own name is unspeakable, because he has been violently split from his partner ambassador counterpart Bren/Dan, a consequence of his dissidence from the social order of the city.

"But then I can't say my name either. *Bren* is as good as any of us can do. It..." He looked at the Host, which nodded gravely. "Now, it can say my name. But that's no good; it and I can't speak anymore." (15)

What is undone here, among other things, is a monolingual vision of language systems and individualistic language users as defined by their ability to say everything in one language, without assistance from other languages or other persons (see Introduction). Bren, a former ambassador partner with "Dan," thus *BrenDan*, cannot any longer say his own name adequately. Though the figures in the novel find this tragic for him, they do not find it conceptually difficult to grasp, nor a fatal flaw for their social order. Divided in half, Bren is now unable to avail himself of the basics of liberal self-representation: the indivisible, identifiable name. The underlying problem—both for Bren and for us Earthly readers and our scripted literatures—is that language for Hosts is polyvocal, not in the metaphorical and analytic way Bakhtin viewed it, but rather in the very vocal activity that produces meaningful vocal sound:[4]

> The Hosts aren't the only polyvocal exots. Apparently there are races who emit two, three or countless sounds simultaneously, to talk. The Hosts, the Ariekei, are comparatively simple. Their speech is an intertwining of two voices only, too complexly various to be pegged as "bass" or "treble." Two sounds—they can't speak either voice singly—inextricable by the chance coevolution of a vocalising ingestion mouth and what was once probably a specialised organ of alarm. (53)

As in *Amatka*, where performativity is imagined as an actual premise of physical chemistry rather than of social theory, polyvocality in *Embassytown* is a brass-tacks everyday phenomenon "theoretical" only to alienated academic conference attendees. Whatever serious theorization about it may take place in the novel is based on the immediately experienced social consequences of polyvocal and univocal species—in their attempts to communicate with one another.

Amid these practical difficulties, the novel's protagonist Avice is a special, talented kind of language user, called an immerser. Here *Embassytown* again enjoys partaking of the range of metaphors, identities, and competencies foreseen without a second thought in various contemporary discourses about language—of intercultural competence, cosmopolitanism, multilingualism,

---

[4] Polyvocal utterances throughout the novel are scripted as fractions, with a nonhierarchical bar between an upper and lower term, while the Audiobook version, read by Susan Duerden, renders the two phonemes simultaneously.

language "immersion" and the like—with all of the imputations of exceptionalism, methodological excellence, and inherent value these attributes often rest upon. Early in her life, Avice had been identified as gifted-and-talented in language, such that she was invited to get tested for suitability as an "immerser." After one successful pre-evaluation, the examiner

> stressed to me, not cruelly but to avoid any later upset, that this concluded nothing and was just stage one of many. But I knew as she explained this that I would become an immerser, and I did. I'd only started to feel the smallness of Embassytown by then, to grumble in claustrophobia, but with her readings came impatience. (29)

With time, Avice succeeds at taking on the status and identity of a naturally talented immerser, and casually mocks the cloying pretensions of those who have to work hard at multilingualism:

> I was drunk in the bar with a bunch of temporary stopover friends, all now thoroughly hazy memories. We were being obnoxious. I went from halfheartedly flirting with a bartender to mocking a table of scholars from CHEL, no less drunk or boisterous than we. We'd eavesdropped on them, then told them with immerser swagger that they didn't know anything about life or even languages in the out, and so on.

> "Go on then, ask me something," I said to Scile. That was the first thing I even said to him. I know exactly how I'd have looked, leaning back in my high chair, turned so resting my back against the bar top, my head back so I could look down at him. I was surely pointing at him with both hands and smiling a bit pinch-mouthed so as to not yet give him any satisfaction. Scile was the least gone at his table, and he was referencing the teasing on both sides. "I know all about weird languages," I told him. "More than any of you buggers. I'm from Embassytown." (35)

These scenes deliberately engage with the discourses of cultural immersion, intercultural competence, translatability, and multilingual subjectivity, albeit set in a remote galaxy setting designed for diplomacy between radically incommensurable species. But the premise of the novel isn't to honor these values uncritically so much as to critique our overhabituation to, and imagine potential divestment from, certain fortified strategies and idealized discourses for dealing with translingual encounter. Bren and his Host comrades are still able to be convivial, but they cannot converse, now that Bren has been severed from his counterpart, Dan. As such, these characters are the traumatic subjects of postmultilingualism (Gramling 2016), a cleaved and ostracized shadow of the empowered, ordering supralingual aspiration they had once been made to fulfill. Most of *Embassytown*'s cast of characters survives somehow in the ruins of these obsolescent and yet insistent late discourses, and of their favored conceptual holy grails. If the commercial landscape of literary late monolingualism prepares the grounds upon which "linguistic exhibitionism and linguistic denigration are both 'created' and sustained in and through 'celebrated,' prize-winning 'flat-world' fiction" (Pandey 2016, 2), it also opens up spaces in which alternatives can be forged, alternatives which return to language the kind of lifeliness and animacy that Chen (2012) sees as proper to it. In the Introduction, I called this creative ground the "scene" of late monolingualism, in the sense that late monolingualism invites and titillates, enchants and promotes certain prescribed kinds of participation and, indeed, pleasure.

Modeling the Language Gold Rush

I suggested in each of these previous chapters that, by necessity and by design, literature in late monolingualism confronts a gap, which the respective novel glimpses in North Atlantic literary theory from a different angle. These are conceptual gaps that have been hollowed out over the course of the nineteenth and twentieth centuries, thanks to the salutary neglect characteristic of monolingualism's implicit and elegant metaformalism, on the one hand, and of national–aesthetic tradition-building on the other. Literary theory from New Criticism through poststructuralism had accordingly even less to say about multilingualism than it did about translation, all the while alleging to hold Language critique and linguistic craft in highest esteem.

Still, now in the twenty-first century, there is no normative school of thought and theory that would assist critics and students of literature in describing these enduring gaps in a theoretically consequential way. With major monographs and collections on the translingual from Steven Kellman (2000), Doris Sommer (2003), Brian Lennon (2010, 2012), Ignacio Infante (2013), Yasemin Yildiz (2012) and others, the effort to reinvigorate literary theory for a multilingual world—and not just for a comparative world—is still in an initial, hortatory, mirative phase.

Certainly, writers of philosophical fiction, from Franz Kafka to Ralph Ellison and Rosario Ferré, have anticipated this need for such transformative theory, particularly as regards the problems that monolingualism and normatively national reading have caused for them. Those authors were forerunners of late monolingual literature, intensively foregrounding the emergence of global, fortified, translational monolingualism in commerce, and the technological order that would only be able to become truly viable after their deaths. Miéville's li-fi, like Stephenson's, devotes some of its attentions to presenting the ecstasies of language–infrastructural dominion, and the boom-town theoreticist logic that fuels it. Consider the energetic research-and-development endeavors propelling what, in the world of *Embassytown*, is called Accelerated Contact Linguistics:

> ACL [. . .] was, Scile told me, a specialty crossbred from pedagogics, receptivity, programming and cryptography. It was used by the scholar–explorers of Bremen's pioneer ships to effect very fast communication with indigenes they encountered or which encountered them.
>
> In the logs of those early journeys, the excitement of the ACLers is moving. On continents, on worlds vivid and drab, they record first moments of understanding with menageries of exots. Tactile languages, bioluminescent words, all varieties of sounds that organisms can make. Dialects comprehensible only as palimpsests of references to everything already said, or in which adjectives are rude and verbs unholy. I've seen the trid diary of an ACLer barricaded in his cabin, whose vessel has been boarded by what we didn't then know as Corscans—it was first contact. He's afraid, as he should be, of the huge things battering at his door, but he's recording his excitement at having just understood the tonal structure of their speech. (51)

Linguists in *Embassytown* are regarded as superhero adventurers, countenancing extraordinarily complex sets of practical differences and solving the predicaments that such differences present:

> "I'm working in Mohash. Do you know it?" said one young woman to me, apropos of nothing. She was very happy when I told her no. "They speak by regurgitation. Pellets embedded with enzymes in different combinations are sentences, which their interlocutors eat." (36)

Avice's subjectivity in the novel is, among other things, a theorization of the experience of untranslatability, but also of the discursive banalization and fetishistic overuse of this term. Embassytown is obviously a setting of matter-of-fact and cosmological untranslatables and other phenomena of hard multilingualism at every step. These suffuse the most basic features of social order, including the very notion of the individual. Once the Ariekei have undergone a true pandemic of addiction to human linguistic input, Avice decides that these axiomatic untranslatables between the two species need to be overcome, if the Ariekei are to survive.

> Did the Ariekei think an Ambassador one person or two? Staff had always told us it was a pointless, untranslatable, impolite question.
>
> "I'm sorry [says Avice] but I need them to understand that you're two people because I need them to understand that I'm one. That these bloody squawks I make are *language*. That I'm *talking to them*." The Ariekei watched one meat-presence emitting noises more quickly and loudly than usual to the others.
>
> After a silence Bren said, "It's never been something Ambassadors have been exactly keen to make clear."
>
> "Make it clear," I said. "Ambassadors don't get to be the only real people anymore." (307)

Here, Miéville's theorizations move right into the territory that Eduardo Viveiros de Castro (2004) identified as "controlled equivocation," the upholding of so-called untranslatables and incommensurables in a relationship that does not resolve into an equivalence. Speaking of the single Cashinahua word *txai*, Viveiros de Castro allows himself an extended explanation of why it cannot adequately be translated into European languages as "brother." It isn't a matter of the word itself, so much as the order of identities and differences into which the Cashinahua and the Portuguese or English words, respectively, are logically positioned:

> The powerful Western metaphors of brotherhood privilege certain (not all) logical properties of this relation. What are siblings, in our culture? They are individuals identically related to a third term, their genitors or their functional analogs. The relation between two siblings derives from their equivalent relation to an origin that encompasses them, and whose identity identifies them. This common identity means that siblings occupy the same point of view onto an exterior world. Deriving their similitude from a similar relation to a same origin, siblings will have "parallel" relations (to use an anthropological image) to everything else. Thus, people who are unrelated, when conceived to be related in a generic sense, are so in terms of a common humanity that makes all of

us kin, that is, siblings, or at least, to continue to use the previous image, parallel cousins, classificatory brothers: children of Adam, of the Church, of the Nation, of the Genome, or of any other figure of transcendence. All men are brothers to some extent, since brotherhood is in itself the general form of the relation. Two partners in any relation are defined as connected in so far as they can be conceived to have something in common, that is, as being in the same relation to a third term. To relate is to assimilate, to unify, and to identify.

The Amazonian model of the relation could not be more different to this. "Different" is the apposite word, since Amazonian ontologies postulate difference rather than identity as the principle of relationality.

Controlled equivocation is a potent antidote to the subjugation of political imperium to commercial dominium, that is, to the predominant depoliticized production of translational equivalence. Given such profound (though suppressed) cosmological differences between European and Indigenous South American languages and symbolic orders, their meanings cannot be made to cohabitate in the way that Avice wants Ariekei's Language and humans' Anglo-Ubic to do.

Yet, once the Ariekei have begun more confidently to "lie" using human similes and metaphors, the drive to commensuration again charismatically takes over. This is the kind of history the Ariekei begin to tell about themselves—of course, in translation from Language into Anglo-Ubic. It is a heart-wrenchingly beautiful but also a desperate leap of faith into translanguaging for them:

> Before the humans came we didn't speak so much of certain things. We were grown into Language. After history we made city and machines and gave them names. We didn't speak so much of certain things. Language spoke us. The words that wanted to be city and machines had us speak them so they could be.
>
> When the humans came they had no names, and we made new words so they would have places in the world. They didn't do as other things do. We spoke them into Language. Language took them in.
>
> We were like hunters. We were like plants eating light. The humans made their town in our town like a star in a circle. They made their place like a filament in a flower. We spoke the name of their place, but we know it had another name, sitting in the city like an organ in a body, like a tongue in a mouth. (332)

As Mel Chen writes in *Animacies*, "Words more than signify; they affect and effect. Whether read or heard, they complexly pulse through bodies (live or dead), rendering their effects in feeling and active response" (54). The Ariekei, speaking this transformed Language, move their listeners and readers with the effortful virtuosity of their story, hewn out of linguistic resources they barely know how to use yet, translated into Anglo-Ubic for the humans straining to listen to them within the novel, and then rendered onward into English for us and further through translation. The theory-making here is painful, ecstatic, hopeful—leaving behind not so much an attachment to monolanguages, but to a belated symbolic order we once enjoyed but can no longer afford to maintain if we intend to survive. The Ariekei sing this late monolingual novel to sleep, hospicing it with truly reverent reminders of what it yet has to offer the meaning-making world.

Afterword

Literacies for the Linguacene

Miéville's novel—like Stephenson's, Nors's, and Tidbeck's before it—is an ambitious opportunity to think about the future in languages beyond monolingualism, and about the infrastructures, concepts, literatures, and epistemes that will characterize languages in 2100 and beyond. How might human beings a hundred years from now conceive of order and disorder in language(s) and linguistic practice? How—if at all—might they speak about the ways we, their ancestors, used language? Will they pluralize language as "languages," like we tend to do without thinking twice, or will such a formulation feel obsolescent and casuistic in the lexicon of their time, like *fishes* does in English usage today? What might people in 2120 make of the industriously innovative theories, policies, technologies, and insights we think we've made about language in the early twentieth century—in part with them, our descendants, all too vaguely in mind?

What, too, will those descendants have to say about discussions in the period 1990–2020, when it rather suddenly became important for so many to discuss, promote, and understand something called "multilingualism"? To whom will this broad turn be attributed, ultimately: to academic disciplines, to industrial and mercantile affordances, to social and cultural evolutions, to powerful institutions of financial globalization, to individual visionaries and creative practitioners, to applied linguists and literary translators, or to a combination of all these? Will the prefix "multi-," for its part, carry the same explanatory power then as it appears to offer in our era? In 2120, will the words *language, idioma,* שפראך*, Tlahtōlli, Sprache, dil, langue,* 語言*, Ngôn ngữ* each favor a similar and shared set of attributes, as they seem to do today?

Linguistic questions, of course, are—and beget—questions of political economy. Will nations, nationalized ethnicities, and nation-states, to the extent that these forms persist in 2120, still claim to rule the roost when it comes to deciding what passes for "a language," or might individuated language status redound by then to functions, rather than to identities and identifications? Either way, which groups of speakers will still be fighting for recognition as credible bearers of "a language," and how will they be doing so? Will the twentieth century's relatively confident ways of distinguishing between the linguistic and the extralinguistic, distinctions that were brutally honed in processes of colonization, persist?

Or will twenty-second-century conceptions find lively ways to re-include within their definitions of language, as Alison Phipps writes in *Decolonising Multilingualism*, "the dress codes, the hair, the patterns on the skin, the gold sewn into the braids, the specific colours of the cloths for specific days; the way of giving thanks for food, the way of kissing a hand and bringing it up to the forehead in greeting; or the three kisses on the cheek in the morning, while bowing in reverence" (Phipps 2019, 59)? Will "language" encompass all or some of these primary socio-symbolic activities, this "whole range of bodily resources that are assembled and coordinated in languaging events, together with external (extrabodily) aspects of situations, environmental affordances, artifacts, technologies, and so on" (Thibault 2011, 7)? The collective venture of imagining linguistic order or disorder decades or millennia hence, as Miéville and Tidbeck have done in their novels, can help sharpen our readiness to forge our own visions of multilingual subjectivity today, out of range from the impositions of big tech and neoliberal education. But also to acknowledge just what prices we've already paid over the course of modernity to establish and maintain the current planetary order of discrete supply-side, switchable monolanguages, and the procedures of exchange that this order presumes and favors.

As they've done since the seventeenth century, monolingual novels will also likely continue to fill out the literary and linguistic future for many of us with their powerful world-making stories. They will be one of the sources that guide us in how best (and worst) to go about engaging with nations, relationships, emotions, lives worth living, communities, liberation, pleasure, dialogue, meaning, violence, erasure, competence, the planet, and the future itself. Published texts of all sorts will quite effectively promote and exclude what counts as a tellable story; how stories ought to be shared from language to language; what counts as vivid, credible articulacy in a language; and in which ways and settings languages are to be cared for or, rather, scrapped and made ungrievable (see Tidbeck in Chapter 1).

Exactly how much of a constitutive and unquestioned role monolingualism, in its various guises, will continue to play in those ongoing literary formations is not a runaway inevitability, but a collective and weighty public decision. In the end, this book may be simply my continued attempt, which began some twenty years ago, to mark monolingualism in civic life as not just an obviously outdated norm, but as an increasingly powerful matrix of production propped up by interests who find it lucrative, efficient, and comforting. It, and they, will make linguistic futures for us as long as we are willing to buy from the monopolies that are supplying us with monolingual forms and formats for us.

While finishing this book, and while continuing to marvel at the literary craft expressed in the novels to which it is devoted, I've found myself yearning to see the (likely impossible) film adaptations of these stories. How, in a visual medium, would we be able to get to know the subjectivity that pulses woozily in Sonja's bouts of vertigo while learning to drive in Nors's *Mirror, Shoulder, Signal*—in these vulnerable moments of translational and vocational contemplation?

In Miéville's *Embassytown*, what would an Ariekes's "fanwing" for hearing and "giftwing" for speaking actually look like, and who would play the charismatic bipartite multilingual ambassador EzRa? Would the film adaptation, and particularly the casting, of Stephenson's *Cryptonomicon* hew toward the sardonic style of *The Office*, the ebullient sincerity of *War Games*, or the hedonic oblivion of *The Social Network*? And how would the filmic medium represent Tidbeck's menacing gloop/kladd? Even the prospect of directing *Amatka*'s hypothetical actors as they "mark" objects aloud over and over, muttering under their breath in private, would make for a complicated and boisterous soundstage. What about Vanja's first moment of transgression—where she, all alone in the storeroom, finds she is physically turning a *pencil* into a *cilpen*, with just her voice?

So many imaginative dimensions of subjectivity and structure, explored in these four novels, call for a courageous leap into the figural unknown. They design a new kind of literacy, meant for a new age—one that is, ironically perhaps, delivered in a quite exquisite form by literary novels—monolingual ones. In speaking about "literacy," I draw specifically on movements within educational and applied linguistics since the 1990s that have thought about multiliteracies as situated practice (Cazden et al. 1996) rather than as an inculcated alphabetic competence. Around the time when our first novel *Cryptonomicon* was being written, multiliteracies scholars were already intent on wresting literacy away from expert prescriptive regimes and deficiency models and reimagining literacy as a co-creative strength that emerges from learners' diverse engagements with the meaning-making world.

We are in such a moment of situated practice—all of us translators, writers, critics, editors, readers, and book promotors—as regards Artificial Intelligence, radically changing political economies and infrastructures of value (Slobodian 2023; Suwandi 2019), and means for translation and multilingual automation, not to mention of literary experience and the very notion of compositional originality. The novels presented in the foregoing chapters are feistily literate and multiliterate about the fact that, as Sonja says in Dorthe Nors's *Mirror, Shoulder, Signal*, "A vast exchange is commencing. [. . .] It's barely visible yet, but it will be, and when it comes, it'll be vast" (2017a, 183). These novels are astute and poised testimonies about this contemporary moment in languages, in the sense that they express surprise and veneration about the linguistic present, while delving critically into its folds, wastelands, and silences.

History could have gone differently, of course. As maintained throughout this book, the design for order that has predominated in shaping economic globalization in the latter half of the twentieth century had been in conscious development in the first half, among a group of economic ordoliberals called the Mont Pelerin Society. From the 1930s to today, these economic designers have been tireless and effective in promoting the rights of property and capital across national borders—despite everything else that might get in their way, including languages, untranslatabilities, and certainly multilingual practice. As the age of empire ceded to movements of national independence across the Global South, MPS members sought recourse not merely to free-market dynamics to ensure stability, but rather to the instrument of law as a guarantor of "xenos rights" in the face of scores of newly sovereign democracies which, in the form of the United Nations General Assembly resolutions, sought to exercise their majority blocs to outstrip Northern dominion over their resources.

Contrary to some characterizations of neoliberal economics, it was not these activists' view that market dynamics would cure everything on their own. Rather, some authoritative roles needed to be reserved, they thought, to supranational law as established by monetary and trade agreements, and certainly not rather to national legislatures that might pursue partisan or redistributive measures detrimental to Global North owners and capitalists. Reining in and quashing new sovereignties in the Global South was a key outcome of this ordoliberal effort. As I have argued in tandem to these more commonly held observations, translational monolanguages were, and remain, an important tool for engineering global anti-protectionism and ensuring the unfettered access of capital to ever-new frontiers and communities of practice.

Rarely did these ordoliberals speak about language, let alone literature, but they were evidently quite scared of multilingualism's power. One of the major players among the so-called Austrian economists, Eugen von Böhm-Bawerk, had written in 1937 about how polities ought to be constituted in the decolonizing twentieth century:

> There is no longer any space for a silent growth, for an orderly formation of things out of the lap of the economy itself, that is, from the bottom up. Social Babels built at such great height and at such an accelerated tempo produce an unholy confusion of languages, unless the idea of order that alone can represent the element of unity illuminates the totality down

to its last details. Unless the idea of order is based on the sentence: Everything at my command. (Cited in Slobodian 2018, 211)

Böhm-Bawerk's fearful heuristic of "social Babels" is indicative of the ordoliberals' hostile views about potential threats to systems-appropriate theorization and implementation of political and economic policy. His views on this point are significantly more authoritarian than those of his colleagues Hayek and Haberler, but they share the same concern about what types of order must guide global economic (and linguistic) life. Polities—democracies and newly decolonized nations—simply could not be permitted to assert, collectively, an "unholy confusion of languages" from the "bottom up." Constant control and adjustment of meaning, policy, and rights of capital needed to be maintained by some reliably anti-protectionist and apparently apolitical mechanism of politics, including orderly monolingual nation-building efforts.

In *The Invention of Monolingualism,* I argued that monolingualism was not a mere miserly combination of linguistic nationalism, linguaphobia, and the complacency of empire, a composite attributable to individual persons who refused to learn more than their own alleged birthright language. If it were this alone—an oblivious refusal to learn or engage—monolingualism would never have been much of a viable global structure for control and management past the 1940s. Early in the century, supranational organizations like the League of Nations, and then the European economic architects of institutional decolonization like Mises and Hayek, designed a globalism in which such forms of individual refusal—linguistic, nationalist, or commercial—would have no place in the planetary order to come. Though individuals and communities have continued to assert various expressions of monolingualism-as-refusal—whether on their own decolonizing grounds or for other isolationist reasons (see Josephson and Einarsdóttir 2016; Domokos 2016)—these expressions steadily became inimical and illegible to the kind of thinking that fueled economic and technological planning and collaboration throughout the latter half of the century.

And yet these thinkers were no Esperantists. Inspired by their experiences in the late Austro-Hungarian Empire—that multilingual, multinational union—Mises and others in the Lippman group envisioned for the coming world a kind of dual government, where each nation could take pride in its local traditions, colors, and languages, but only to the extent that doing so did not impinge on the core, central principle of that governmental dominium: unobstructive economic policy. What was needed to ensure that these two realms (dominium and imperium) did not collide in violent or irritating ways was a set of translational principles that would allow for reliably exogamous relations across borders, which European decolonization planners wished to make efficient, inexpensive, and reliable. One of the ingredients for such a program of stabilization was an apparent or performative monolingualism that would fulfill the needs of both rings of government: the cultural, which would be permitted to continue existing along traditional national lines, and the economic, which needed to follow a newly reliable set of laws and dynamics.

Techno-thrillers like *Cryptonomicon* tell an interwoven story about this infrastructural enterprise: the industries and interests actively working to retain, fortify, and perfect the flexible but integral category "individual language" in perpetuity, despite all of the translanguaging so plainly in sight (Li Wei 2017). In this industrial landscape, the category "a language" itself becomes an indispensable, load-bearing infrastructural component of commerce, doubling down on preexisting Rooseveltian ideas about the civic need for one common language for a multicultural society. Today, this ongoing vision of transcending the tower of Babel by securitizing orderly monolanguages, easily translated with technological assistance, is the kind of near-term fix that is dissuading new generations of potential language learners today from becoming (more) multilingual at all—in their minds, bodies, feelings, relationships, knowledges, contexts, and subjectivities.

Requiring as it does the kind of slow, modest, embodied, relational, and convivial transformation of self that other skills-acquisition- and innovation-driven disciplinary sectors cannot rationally bank on—at least at the timescales of industrial change and personnel onboarding to which they are now habituated—the educational experience of instructed, embodied multilingualism seems now just too high a price to pay "at scale" in many cost-cutting institutional settings. While alleged deficiency in a language is still, and increasingly, used as administrative grounds for excluding petitioners in immigration, residency, and asylum proceedings (Craig and Gramling 2017; Khan 2019), such aggressive scrutiny is applied only to certain vulnerable or civically marked populations. The non-vulnerable are now more or less welcome to dilate in a lavishly and multilingually enhanced monolingualism. At long last, monolingualism has gotten its own elite "gear culture."

Though Premilla Nadasen (2023) has argued that the global care-industrial complex is expressing today the "highest stage of capitalism," I grasp the monolanguage–industrial complex as a strong and related competitor for this distinction. It mobilizes global value chains and encases people in proprietary technologies that ensure fewer and fewer of us who have access to them will ever feel the need to actually learn and use new languages ourselves. Even in traditionally elite-pedigree spaces for cosmopolitan formation, so-called language-immersion programs are shortening and thinning, while state universities are frequently found acting out their globally "inclusive" fiduciary mandate by closing all language programs on campus, and relying instead on the conceit of a universally accessible Anglophone common denominator for all learning and communicating.

If it does turn out that there is an ascertainable and emergent body of literary work that is trying to come to terms with the kind of late monolingualism that economic history has produced for us—of which these four novels may be a small sample—it is a body that accommodates grief and loss for older ways of working with language(s), ways that now feel slightly out of reach, or quaint, or too beholden to the dream of authentic experience and expression. We learn languages in profoundly different ways and rhythms now than we did in 1990—or we don't learn them at all, given all the technologies that are now becoming generally available around us. We find we must frequently cut our losses on beloved connotations or untranslatable meanings in everyday commerce, wagering that global interaction requires cultural compromise at every turn. We acquiesce to autocorrect and autofill, with little time for remorse about the imperfections and uncertainties they overwrite.

Meanwhile, we expect and demand that more and more kinds of texts and messages must necessarily travel well and quickly across language borders, if they deserve to have been conceived and composed at all. These are radically new, and somewhat stoical, habits of being-in-language that are at large in the supply-side-driven world of institutions and industries in which we live and work. Literature in late monolingualism offers a figural space to acknowledge and theorize the shared pain and melancholy—and then also joy and conviviality—that might be allowed to arise, if we let these new forms distill before us, via literary representation, just a bit more slowly than they do in current daily life.

Literature in Late Monolingualism has been about novels trying to insist on a critically sane picture of the abnormal mono/multilingual order that keeps getting engineered for us, over the past four hundred years. In this sense, these novels provide a potentially satisfying moment of realization for many of us multilingual persons, language learners, comparers of literatures, and working translators who have struggled to understand what has been happening around us in languages, particularly in the past several decades. And yet, these novels also move on from old paradigms in other ways. They suggest, for instance, that it is likely time to relinquish the wholesale stereotype in literary criticism that it is always better to read novels in the "original." Rather than insisting on the supremacy of originals, these novels regard their translations as equally originary and critical moments, foreseen and theorized in the compositional processes themselves (see both Tidbeck in Chapter 1 and Nors in Chapter 2).

In a bit of a didactic turn, I've used the subtitle of this book to term these novels by Tidbeck, Nors, Stephenson, and Miéville as themselves *literacies for the Linguacene*. While I remain ecumenical on the question whether late monolingualism in the end needs to be hastened away and superseded by another age in (literary) languages, it is clear that the linguistic acceleration of climate disaster through supralingual discourses (i.e., multilingual greenwashing and AI-mediated industrial extractivism on a planetary scale, including the current second Scramble for Africa and the Indigenous Arctic) is not a phenomenon human societies and policymakers can afford to ignore. At various scales—the subjective (Nors), the civic (Tidbeck), the financialized–postindustrial (Stephenson), and the agnostic–cosmological (Miéville)—these novels play the tape of the Linguacene to the end, intimating its various runaway consequences for people, communities, languages, and meaning-making.

I have claimed that not enough Anthropocene research has engaged questions of translation, multilingualism, and monolingualism, and that a discourse of the Linguacene would help restore some of that analytical rigor. I suspect that Anthropocene research has more or less taken a cue from other language-indifferent discourses and sciences—of economics, manufacture, preservation, commerce, capital, and indeed politics—when they sidestep questions of language in their argumentation and axia. Environmentalism and ecology do not have a strong record on language either since the 1980s, likely for reasons that mirror why Marxian thought has long seen fit to ignore language as well.

In contrast, our four novels are devoted to becoming literate, among other things, in the political and ecocidal workings of monolingualism. They do so through the means of their own monolingual literary artistry, but in a critical way that takes an inventory of this linguistic age, rather than angling merely to escape or rebuke it. They seek not merely to celebrate the transgressions involved in multilingual practice, but to understand the outlandish costs of transgressing the monolingual norm and its mechanisms. A favorite Kafka passage for me, among many that theorize monolingualism as a mechanism, is the scene in the (translingually situated) *Amerika* novel when an unfamiliar tourist guide takes the multilingual protagonist Karl by the hand and helps him to become literate in the logic of the monolingual novel he himself appears in:

> "[C]ome along with me, little fellow," she said; then she said goodbye to her acquaintance, who raised his hat, which seemed like an unbelievably polite gesture in these surroundings, and, taking Karl by the hand, went to the buffet, pushed aside a guest, opened a hinged door in the counter,

and with Karl in tow, crossed the corridor behind the counter, where one had to watch out for the tirelessly circulating waiters, and opened a double door that had been covered with wallpaper, and now they found themselves in large cool pantries. "You simply have to know the mechanism," Karl said to himself. ([1914] 2008, 104)

The novels we have explored here are in a sense this hotel clerk, who takes the literary figure Karl—already suspecting some kind of foul play around him in the novel in which he features—to a standpoint within the commercial establishment where he can effectively learn the monolingual mechanism of the text, to sense its particular lateness, its expansive but delusional finitude. Since the mid-seventeenth century, *mechanismus* (from the Greek mēkhanē) has been an -ism—like monolingualism, feminism, or conservatism—in the sense that we impute to it an enabling, energizing, almost-animate structure that both enlivens and controls otherwise potentially disparate forces of thought, action, and being. Karl's intertitle within the *Amerika* novel glimpses both the triumphal–genial, and the repressive–assimilative senses of what it means to "know the mechanism" of the novel as a monolingualized and monolingualizing proxy for the multilingual world just beyond it.

In *Amerika*, and in any monolingual novel about the multilingual world, we readers are asked to engage in elaborate forms of the "as if" and of "make-believe." We must make ourselves believe that there is some kind of real multilingual, accented, language-becoming subject living and being there, ontologically, in patient spite of the standardized, monolingual novel in which they figure. Kafka's Karl is a multilingual, immigrant cultural laborer who, in order to persist in literary form at all, must depend on such make-believe surrogate proxies of themselves.

In this way, literary monolingualism is a proxy that, in the words of the critical applied linguist Uju Anya, "socializes monolingual bias"—in the sense that it normalizes the suppression of the self-evidently multilingual world, in favor of a monolingual mock-up, such that we indefinitely expect such a version from our peers as well. Socializing monolingual bias, in the way Anya conceives it, is one of the prime hyper-performatives of literature and literary study since the seventeenth century. This is only a problem, though, if we doubt—as many forensic linguists (Filipović 2007) and legal scholars (Solan 2014) do, and I share their view—that single-language text is ultimately the most precise and accurate means to apprehend the world.

Monolingualism is a technology of (mis)recognition, arbitrating how and who gets to speak, write, get translated, get prized, get repeated, and get listened to. It constrains people we might in lay terms call "monolinguals," as well as those we might comfortably wish to call multilinguals. It does this, in part, by pre-constraining the texts—pragmatic, institutional, educational, relational, and aesthetic—that those people produce and reproduce. There has been an alluring sense in the early twenty-first century that these constraints are loosening amid the transnational, transcultural flows and subjectivities that make our world today.

The proposed concept late monolingualism disagrees with this sensibility. In its time, Ernest Mandel's (1972) book on *Late Capitalism* sought to contend with Marxists' and non-Marxists' surprise at how robustly capitalism endured in the postwar *Wirtschaftswunder/Trente Glorieuses* period. Even without adopting the dialectical method Mandel required, we can ponder the ways something like monolingualism is also persisting longer than many scholars, policymakers, and linguistic artisans in the 1970s–1990s wished it would have. It seems that monolingualism has found ways to fortify and dig its heels in through economic, technological, administrative, and civic means, precisely in a moment where its ontological claims to legitimacy are most disputed. That is, right in the historical moment where it is most clear to us that nations, persons, texts, knowledge, aesthetics, friendships, stories, and communities are anything but mono/lingual, monolingualism has assumed a "late" form that powerfully reasserts its stabilizing dominion.

Conceptually, "late" monolingualism does not benefit from a long historicist or dialectic tradition of political economy in the way that Mandel's argument does, nor do I intend the concept to rely on arguments arising from historical linguistics. It does not make any implicit claims, for instance, about the developmental course of individual languages, their lineages and relations, or the relationships among languages, cultures, and people. The reason "late monolingualism" does not speak to these things is because the concept is dedicated rather to understanding the discourses that have been developed in recent decades to stabilize globalized multilingual infrastructures, which indeed resurrect, reinstate, and justify some preexisting substantialist notions about the nature and transformation of individual languages over the course of history.

Meanwhile, monolingualism has served as a kind of fourth "dramatic unity" for literature, not unlike the pseudo-Aristotelian ones that Trissino foisted upon sixteenth-century Italian tragedy and Mairet and Voltaire upon the seventeenth-century French stage. In 1660, the dramatist Corneille's discernment about the unities, sometimes more strictly and sometimes more loosely held than both the ancient dramatists and his contemporaries, was however always grounded in a care for the modern spectator—for their "serene mind" (117), their "pleasant suspense" (118), their "reasonable curiosity" (120)—by avoiding annoyance, awkwardness, and unexpected burdens on their memory. Corneille's is not a discourse venerating the ancients so much as one enumerating the psychological logistics of the contemporary Parisian spectators and their "common sense." For Corneille, demands of extraordinary attention weary the spectator and obstruct real pleasure (121).

Corneille's concern that the mind of the Parisian spectator not become unrelaxed or inconvenienced during his plays reads more like a quality-of-life noise ordinance than literary theory in the twentieth-century critical mode. But his attention to the ergonomics of convenience and spectatorial unburdening in his justification of the unities sheds light on the ways twentieth- and twenty-first-century publishing has, quite gingerly, approached the question of linguistic accessibility among their anticipated readers. In an overabundance of caution, contemporary publishers worry— as did Corneille—about how readers will comfortably handle loan words, passages in other languages, translanguaging practices, code-mixing, and the like. Will they be burdened? Will they not be able to relax? Will it tax their memories unduly? Will it grate upon their quality of life?

This care for the spectator is all the more interesting, though, when we note that Corneille's examples are being drawn from a successful French Crusades play adopted from a Spanish one twenty years older, both of which carry a title adopted translingually from Arabic: *El Cid* from El Sayeed. Moreover, Corneille relies on Aristotle's principles of unified action to claim that the arrival of The Moors will not constitute a disruptive disunity of action (118). Corneille's ideas about spectators' comfort—and thus many of modern literature's ideas—as well as about what unities dramatists needed to provide to ensure that comfort, were forged in scenes of translingual meaning-making, indifferent as Corneille may have ultimately been to this fact. Literature in late monolingualism gives us the chance to reopen this inquiry into the strange unities that quietly govern what is deemed linguistically suitable and unsuitable for an immersive readerly experience, and which broader political trends are shaping those ideas of suitability.

This quality-of-life discourse protecting citizens from the alleged discomfort of languages continues in ever new forms and intensities today. When West Virginia University announced plans in Fall 2023 to shut down all of its instruction in additional languages, this linguistic austerity measure expressed a suspicion that had been brewing since the beginning of the twenty-first century: that North American universities just do not wish to instruct languages anymore to more than a handful of curious, self-selecting students. Already in 2012, US Secretary of the Treasury and former Harvard President Lawrence Summers had sparked stunned consternation among language teaching professionals when, in a *New York Times* editorial dismissively titled "What You (Really) Need To Know," he assured the public that "English's emergence as the global language, along with the rapid progress in Machine Translation and the fragmentation of languages spoken around the world, make it less clear that the substantial investment necessary to speak a foreign tongue is universally worthwhile."

These tendencies and positions are component parts of a broader, powerful set of strategies that guide North American higher education executives and consultants in restricting the university's understanding of "the global" to a certain, linguistically indifferent monolingual sense. Their discourses and practices signal a profound retreat from long-standing traditions acknowledging the centrality of language(s) and language-based multilingual communication in service of global knowledge-transfer, fueling institutional linguaphobia and linguistic indifference in university curricula.

By the end of my career, I would nonetheless like to be able to teach a class called "What was 'The Monolingual Novel'?"—and to have this label come across not as an insufferable tautology, but as a specific and meaningful delineation of one historical format for articulating the world novelistically. By then, I would also like humanities departments that are lucky enough to have "Language" or specific language names in their titles to teach more-than-monolingual novels (and their translations) without fear or caveat, trusting their students to handle these collectively and convivially. For, if a global student body enrolls in your university and brings with them all their heritage languages and adopted languages, why is it the prudent curricular response to socialize them promptly into the Anglophone or monolingual habits of single-language disciplines and discourses?

If those students can handle their own convivial multilingualism without much ado outside of classes for social purposes, why should they not do so just as keenly and deftly in a seminar discussion for scholarly purposes, making a critical home together in linguistic rudimentariness as needed (Rosello 2011)? Equally so, if the justices of the European Court of Justice can interpret law in 24 languages concurrently together (Solan 2009, 2014, 2017), why cannot literary prize committees adjudicate literary works together with their translations as one holistically aesthetic utterance, and not only as separate originals and translations? If universities can hire traveling outreach coordinators to recruit prospective students around the world in those students' preferred languages and idioms, why can't those universities also suit up and organize some actual university-wide learning and intellectual community in those languages? Isn't a full-on Anglogenic curriculum just too high a price for all of us to pay for the commodity economists call "cheap talk" (Farrell and Rabin 1996)?

Closer to the concerns of this book, if publishers can market literary texts globally in an exhaustive sequence of language markets, why shouldn't they also make multilingual interactive hypertext versions of their literary acquisitions available (created either by author-teams themselves or by commissioned translators), so that readers could tap on a phrase or sentence and see how it was rendered in the start-language, or in any other language it has been translated into? Couldn't readers then collaboratively build and share their own translingual iterations of existing novels, highlighting elements from various language versions that bear meaning most tenderly from one passage to the next, crediting the respective translators all the while? Come to think of it, what if the various COPs (Conferences of the Parties to the United Nations Framework Convention on Climate Change) and other policy assemblies around the world made it standard protocol to do the same multilingual work with their deliberations and documents— on the premise that averting climate disaster requires Indigenous and allophone meaning-making repertoires, and not just global–Anglophone ones?

If these sorts of affordances were already widespread in the innovative technological marketplace of 2024, the very matter of the literary overproduction of monolingualism, taken to task by the authors and works explored in this book, might be less alarming. But little of what we might call critical multilingualism studies is happening more than notionally in the universities, publishing houses, decision-making settings, and policy spheres I know of. *Literature in Late Monolingualism* has been dedicated to the literature that is both implicated in and alarmed about this ghostly, austere, monolingual "translating machine" at the heart of "the market system of credit–debt global capital" (Lezra 2015, 175). These are novels that are accordingly anxious about themselves, too, in all of these puzzled and puzzling ways.

This book will not have made much sense for those who feel, in the end, that we all still have control of our language(s), that monolingualism in social and literary life is subsiding or inconsequential, and that any institutional, technological, and political pressure structuring what can be said, where, and how (literarily or otherwise) is overcome with a little courage, grit, and criticality. It will also not have made much sense for those who do not think monolingualism exists, on the grounds that sociolinguistic diversity is the real on-the-ground fact of planetary and local communication, now and forever. What I have tried to present in this book is not a new prisonhouse of language called monolingualism, nor a doom scenario of disempowerment, but rather a range of texts that want to teach us how to think about the complex and elusive challenge of linguistic subjectivity in the twenty-first century, where we (whoever we are) wish to be free, just, peopled, and vigorous users of all the languages that we have labored to learn.

These novels teach us that multilingualism, codeswitching, and translanguaging are not magic talismans that promise to achieve these critical goals for us, nor is monolingualism only a primrose path to epistemic ignorance and aesthetic dullness. They teach us to take monolingualism seriously, to raise our expectations of inquiry into all of the changing forms and expressions it takes around us. They welcome us into seeing the facts of contemporary linguistic life as accurately and as fearlessly as possible, and to finetune the usefulness of multilingual meaning for truth-seeking, for loving our communities, and for forging our cultural politics. Along the way, these novels are not hostile to technological innovation and computational engineering, but befriend them critically and with circumspect appreciation. This literature in late monolingualism is thus a hopeful and ecumenical literature, equipped with stamina, patience, ample imagination, and a wild love for all the ways future literary moments will surprise us, for how they will "affect and effect" us anew, how they'll "complexly pulse through" our bodies and render "their effects in feeling and active response" (Chen 2012, 54).

Works Cited

Adorno, Theodor W. 1993. "Late Style in Beethoven." In *Essays on Music*, edited by Richard D. Leppert, 564–8. Translated by Susan H. Gillespie. Berkeley: University of California Press.

Agamben, Giorgio. 2017. *The Fire and the Tale*. Translated by Lorenzo Chiesa. Stanford: Stanford University Press.

Ahmed, Sara. 2023. *The Feminist Killjoy Handbook*. London: Allen Lane.

Allan, D. G. C. 1968. *William Shipley: A Biography with Documents*. London: Hutchinson.

Anderson, Benedict. (1983) 2006. *Imagined Communities: Reflections on the Origin and Spread of Nationalism*. London: Verso.

Anderson, Susan, and Clorinda Donato. 2015. "The Monolingual International." *ADFL Bulletin* 43, no. 2: 9–10.

Andreotti, Vanessa, Sharon Stein, Cash Ahenakew, and Dallas Hunt. 2015. "Mapping Interpretations of Decolonization in the Context of Higher Education." *Decolonization: Indigeneity, Education & Society* 4, no. 1: 21–40.

Ankler, Elizabeth, and Bernadette Meyler. 2017. *New Directions in Law and Literature*. Oxford: Oxford University Press.

Anya, Uju. 2019. "The Taquito Hot Seat: Socializing Monolingual Bias through Error Correction Practices in a Portuguese Language Classroom." Conference presentation at *Integrationism and Philosophies of Language: Emerging Alternative Epistemologies in the Global North and Global South*, The Pennsylvania State University, September 1, 2019.

Appadurai, Arjun. 2016. *Banking on Words: The Failure of Language in the Age of Derivative Finance*. Chicago: The University of Chicago Press.

Arias, Arturo. 2006. "Constructing Ethnic Bodies and Identities in Miguel Ángel Asturias and Rigoberta Menchú." *Postmodern Culture* 17, no. 1.

Arias, Arturo. 2012. "¿Tradición versus modernidad en las novelas yukatekas contemporáneas? Yuxtaponiendo X-Teya, u puksi'ik'al ko'olel y U yóok'otilo 'ob áak'ab." *Cuadernos de literatura* 32: 208–35.

Aronin, Larissa, and David Singleton. 2008. "Multilingualism as a New Linguistic Dispensation." *International Journal of Multilingualism* 5, no. 1: 1–16.

Baker, Andrew. 1999. "Nebuleuse and the 'Internationalization of the State' in the UK? The Case of HM Treasury and the Bank of England." *Review of International Political Economy* 6, no. 1: 79–100.

Bakhtin, Mikhail M. 1981. *The Dialogic Imagination: Four Essays*. Translated by Caryl Emerson and Michael Holquist. Austin: University of Texas Press.

Bandia, Patrick. 2006. "African Europhone Literature and Writing as Translation: Some Ethical Issues." In *Translating Others, Vol. 2*, edited by Theo Hermans, 349–61. Manchester: St. Jerome.

Barak, On. 2015. "Outsourcing: Energy and Empire in the Age of Coal, 1820–1911." *International Journal of Middle East Studies* 47, no. 3: 425–45.

Barron, Natania. 2012. "Karin Tidbeck's *Jagannath*: Weird in All the Right Ways." *Wired*, November 9, 2012.

Baur, Aaron. 2017. "Harnessing the Social Web to Enhance Insights into People's Opinions in Business, Government, and Public Administration." *Information Systems Frontiers* 19: 231–51.

Beecroft, Alexander. 2008. "World Literature without a Hyphen: Towards a Typology of Literary Systems." *New Left Review* 54: 87–100.

Bell, Derrick A., Jr. 1980. "*Brown v. Board of Education* and the Interest-Convergence Dilemma." *Harvard Law Review* 93, no. 3: 518–33.

Bernofsky, Susan. 2014. "Schleiermacher's Translation Theory and Varieties of Foreignization: August Wilhelm Schlegel vs. Johann Heinrich Voss." *The Translator* 3, no. 2: 175–92.

Bhabha, Homi. 1984. "Of Mimicry and Man: The Ambivalence of Colonial Discourse." *October* 28: 125–33.

Bhabha, Homi. 1994. *The Location of Culture*. London: Routledge.

Bhagat, Chetan. 2007. *One Night at the Call Centre*. Windsor: Bath.

Bhattacharya, Kakali. 2018. "Nonsense, Play, and Liminality: Putting Postintentionality in Dialogue With De/colonizing Ontoepistemologies." *Qualitative Inquiry* 26, no. 5: 1–5.

Bigelow, Allison Margaret. 2020. *Mining Language: Racial Thinking, Indigenous Knowledge, and Colonial Metallurgy in the Early Modern Iberian World*. Chapel Hill: University of North Carolina Press.

Bodin, Jean. (1606) 1962. *The Six Books of a Commonweale: A Facsimile Reprint of the English Translation of 1606, Corrected and Supplemented in the Light of* a *New Comparison with the French and Latin Texts*, edited by Kenneth Douglas McRae. Cambridge, MA: Harvard University Press.

Bourdieu, Pierre. 1993. *The Field of Cultural Production*. edited by Randal Johnson. 1st ed. New York: Columbia University Press.

Boyden, Michael, and Eugenia Kelbert. 2018. "The Theory Deficit in Translingual Studies." *Journal of World Literature* 3: 127–35.

Boyer, Henri. 2012. "Idéologie sociolinguistique et politiques linguistiques 'intérieures' de la France." *Synergies Pays germanophones* 5: 93–105.

Braun, Juliane. 2019. "Bioprospecting Breadfruit: Imperial Botany, Transoceanic Relations, and the Politics of Translation." *Early American Literature* 54, no. 3: 643–71.

Brechin, Grey. 2000. *Imperial San Francisco: Urban Power, Earthly Ruin*. Berkeley: University of California Press.

Brickell, Katherine. 2020. *Home SOS: Gender, Violence, and Survival in Crisis Ordinary Cambodia*. Oxford: Royal Geographical Society (with the Institute of British Geographers) and John Wiley and Sons, Ltd.

Brickhouse, Anna. 2014. *The Unsettlement of America: Translation, Interpretation, and the Story of Don Luis de Velasco, 1560–1945*. Oxford: Oxford University Press.

Brossard, Nicole. (1987) 2006. *Mauve Desert*. Toronto: Coach House Books.
Bryant, Sherwin K. 2014. *Rivers of Gold, Lives of Bondage: Governing through Slavery in Colonial Quito*. Durham: University of North Carolina Press.
Bull, Hedley. (1977) 1995. *The Anarchical Society – A Study of Order in World Politics*. 2nd ed. London: Macmillan.
Butler, Judith. 2004. *Undoing Gender*. New York: Routledge.
Butler, Judith. 2019. "Gender in Translation: Beyond Monolingualism." *philoSOPHIA: A Journal of Continental Feminism* 9, no. 1: 1–25.
Butler, Judith, John Guillory, and Kendall Thomas, eds. 2000. *What's Left of Theory?* New York: Routledge.
Cadieux, Pierre. 2002. "Feeling GILTy: Defining the Terms Globalization, Internationalization, Localization, and Translation." *Language International: The Business Resource for a Multilingual Age* 14, no. 3: 22–25.
Caimotto, Maria Cristina. 2019. "Anglicisms in Italian Environmentally Friendly Marketing: English as the Global Language of Capitalism or Sustainability?" In *Translating and Communicating Environmental Cultures,* edited by Meng Ji, 202–17. London: Routledge.
Cameron, Deborah. 1995. *Verbal Hygiene*. London: Routledge.
Cameron, Deborah. 2000. Good to Talk? Living and Working in a Communication Culture. New York: Sage.
Cameron, Deborah. 2008. "Talk from the Top Down." *Language & Communication* 28, no. 2: 143–55.
Cameron, Deborah. 2013. "'The One, the Many and the Other': Representing Multi- and Mono-lingualism in Post-9/11 Verbal Hygiene." *Critical Multilingualism Studies* 1, no. 2: 59–77.
Canavan, Gerry, and Andy Hageman. 2016. "Introduction: Global Weirding." *Paradoxa* 28: 7–14.
Çandar, Başak. 2018. "Art that Scars: Literary Re-enactments and Self-Conscious Representations in Si te dicen que caí and Kar." *MLN* 133, no. 5: 1337–61.
Çandar, Başak. 2019. "World Literature's Outsides: Transnational Turkish(es) in Murat Uyurkulak's *Tol*." *Critical Multilingualism Studies* 7, no. 3: 7–31.
Çandar, Başak. 2021. "Framing the World: Texts that Circulate and People Who Cannot." In *Trauma and Literature in an Age of Globalization*, edited by Jennifer Ballengee and David Kelman, 141–154. London: Routledge.
Cassin, Barbara, ed. 2004. *Vocabulaire européen des philosophes: Dictionnaire des intraduisibles*. Paris: Le Seuil/Le Robert.
Cassin, Barbara, Emily Apter, Jacques Lezra, and Michael Wood. ed. 2014. *Dictionary of Untranslatables: A Philosophical Lexicon*, Princeton, NJ: Princeton University Press.
Cazden, Courtney, Bill Cope, Norman Fairclough, Jim Gee, Mary Kalantzis, Gunther Kress, Allan Luke, Carmen Luke, Sarah Michaels, and Marin Nakata. 1996. "A Pedagogy of Multiliteracies: Designing Social Futures." *Harvard Educational Review* 66, no. 1: 60–93.

Cerny, Philip. 1997. "Paradoxes of the Competition State: The Dynamics of Political Globalization." *Government and Opposition* 32, no. 2: 251–74.
Cheah, Pheng. 2014. "World against Globe: Toward a Normative Conception of World Literature." *New Literary History* 45: 303–29.
Chen, Mel. 2012. *Animacies: Biopolitics, Racial Mattering, and Queer Affect*. Durham: Duke University Press.
Coetzee, J. M. 1986. "Into the Dark Chamber: The Novelist and South Africa." *The New York Times*, January 12, 1986.
Cole, Stewart. 2020. "Sex in a Warming World: Lady Chatterley's Lover as Fossil Fuel Fiction." *Studies in the Novel* 52, no. 3, 288–304.
Colón, Cristóbal, Valeria Añon, and Vanina Teglia. (1493–1504) 2012. *Diario, cartas y relaciones: Antología esencial*, edited by Valeria Añón y Vanina Teglia. Buenos Aires: Corregidor.
Connell, Raewyn. 2007. *Southern Theory: Social Science and the Global Dynamics of Knowledge*. London: Routledge.
Cortés, Hernán and Valeria Añón. (1519-) 2010. *Segunda carta de relación y otros textos*, edited by Valeria Añón. Buenos Aires: Corregidor.
Cox, Robert. 1992. "Global Perestroika." In *The New World Order? The Socialist Register 1992*, edited by Ralph Miliband and Leo Panitch, 26–43. London: Merlin Press.
Crabbe, Stephen. 2017. *Controlling Language in Industry: Controlled Languages for Technical Documents*. New York: Palgrave Macmillan.
Craig, Sarah, and David Gramling. 2017. "Is there a Right to Untranslatability? Asylum, Evidence, and the Listening State." *Tilburg Law Review* 22, no. 1–2: 77–98.
Cronin, Michael. 2013. *Translation in the Digital Age*. London: Routledge.
Cross, Valerie V., and Clare R. Voss. 2000. "Fuzzy Queries and Cross-Language Ontologies in Multilingual Document Exploitation." *Proceedings of the Ninth IEEE International Conference on Fuzzy Systems* 2: 641–6.
Dáte, Shirish V. 2023. "Four Months After Ukraine Stumble, DeSantis Offers Tucker Carlson Word Salad Instead." *Yahoo News*, July 14, 2023.
Davies, William. 2017. "Elite Power under Advanced Neoliberalism." *Theory, Culture and Society* 34, no. 5–6: 227–50.
De Swaan, Abram. 2002. *Words of the World: The Global Language System*. Cambridge: Polity.
Didion, Joan. 1967. "The Howard Hughes Underground." *The Saturday Evening Post*, September 23, 1967.
Di Muzio, Tim, and Matthew Dow. 2016. "Uneven and Combined Confusion: On the Geopolitical Origins of Capitalism and the Rise of the West." *Working Papers on Capital as Power*, no. 2016/03, Forum on Capital as Power—Toward a New Cosmology of Capitalism, York University, June 2016.
Domokos, Johanna. 2016. "Prohibiting Translations: Nils-Aslak Valkeapää and the Question of Text-, Process-, and Agent-driven Untranslatability." *Critical Multilingualism Studies* 4, no. 1: 44–56.

Donald, Dwayne T. 2009. "Forts, Curriculum, and Indigenous Métissage: Imagining Decolonisation of Aboriginal–Canadian Relations in Educational Contexts." *First Nations Perspectives* 2, no. 1: 1–24.

Dourish, Paul, Christopher Lawrence, Tuck Wah Leong, and Greg Wadley. 2020. "On Being Iterated: The Affective Demands of Design Participation." In *Proceedings of the 2020 CHI Conference on Human Factors in Computing Systems*, 1–11. Honolulu: ACM.

Dowling, Sarah. 2018. *Translingual Poetics: Writing Personhood Under Settler Colonialism*. Iowa City: University of Iowa Press.

Down, Mickey and Konrad Kay, dir. 2020. *Industry*. Home Box Office.

Duchêne, Alexandre and Monica Heller, eds. 2012. *Language in Late Capitalism: Pride and Profit*. London: Routledge.

Dudley, Leonard. 2017. "Language Standardization and the Industrial Revolution." *Oxford Economic Papers* 69, no. 4: 1138–61.

Eldridge, Hannah. 2023. "When are Research Journals Linguistically Indifferent?" *The German Quarterly* 96, no. 3: 378–82.

El-Erian, Mohamed. 2023. "From Near-shoring to Friend-shoring: The Changing Face of Globalisation." *The Guardian*, March 9, 2023.

El Shakry, Hoda. 2024. "*Adab*: Literary Form and Social Praxis." *PMLA* 139, no. 1.

Fals Borda, Orlando. (1979) 2009. "Cómo investigar la realidad para transformarla." In *Una sociología sentipensante para América Latina*, edited by Victor Manuel Moncayo. Siglo del Hombre Editores y Clacso.

Farrell, Joseph, and Matthew Rabin. 1996. "Cheap Talk." *Journal of Economic Perspectives* 10, no. 3: 103–18.

Felski, Rita. 2015. *The Limits of Critique*. Chicago: The University of Chicago Press.

Filipović, Luna. 2007. "Language as a Witness: Insights from Cognitive Linguistics." *International Journal of Speech, Language and the Law* 14, no. 2: 245–67.

Fishman, Joshua. 1968. "Nationality-Nationalism and Nation-Nationism." In *Language Problems of Developing Nations*, edited by Joshua A. Fishman, Charles A. Ferguson, and Jyotirindra Das Gupta, 39–51. New York: John Wiley and Sons.

Fishman, Joshua. 1969. "National Languages and Languages of Wider Communication in the Developing Nations." In *Language in Sociocultural Change*, edited by Anwar S. Dil. Stanford: Stanford University Press.

Flores, Nelson. 2016. "A Tale of Two Visions: Hegemonic Whiteness and Bilingual Education." *Educational Policy* 30, no. 1: 13–38.

Flores, Nelson and Jonathan Rosa. 2015. "Undoing Appropriateness: Raciolinguistic Ideologies and Language Diversity in Education." *Harvard Educational Review* 85, no. 2: 149–72.

Freire, Juan A., Verónica E. Valdez, and M. Garrett Delavan. 2017. "The (Dis) Inclusion of Latina/o Interests from Utah's Dual Language Education Boom." *Journal of Latinos and Education* 16, no. 4: 276–89.

Future of Life Institute. 2023. "Pause Giant AI Experiments: An Open Letter." March 22, 2023. https://futureoflife.org/open-letter/pause-giant-ai-experiments.

García, Ofelia. 2019. "Education, Multilingualism and Translanguaging in the 21st Century." In *Multilingual Education for Social Justice: Globalising the Local*, edited by Ajit Mohanty, Minati Panda, Robert Phillipson, and Tove Skutnabb-Kangas, 128–45. New Delhi: Orient Blackswan.

Garrido, Maria Rosa, and Eva Codó. 2017. "Deskilling and Delanguaging African Migrants in Barcelona: Pathways of Labour Market Incorporation and the Value of 'Global' English." *Globalisation, Societies and Education* 15, no. 1: 29–49.

Gibeau, Mark. 2013. "Indigenization and Opacity: Self-Translation in the Okinawan/ Ryūkyūan writings of Takara Ben and Medoruma Shun." In *Self-Translation: Brokering Originality in Hybrid Culture*, edited by Anthony Cordingley, 141–56. London: Bloomsbury.

Gifford, Terry. 1999. *Pastoral: The New Critical Idiom*. London: Routledge.

Goatly, Andrew. 1996. "Green Grammar and Grammatical Metaphor." *Journal of Pragmatics* 25: 537–60.

Google. n.d. Privacy & Terms. Available at: https://policies.google.com/terms?hl=en-US#toc-content.

Gordin, Michael D. 2015. *Scientific Babel: How Science Was Done Before and After Global English*. Chicago: University of Chicago Press.

Goswami, Omkar. 1989. "Sahibs, Babus, and Banias: Changes in Industrial Control in Eastern India, 1918-50." *The Journal of Asian Studies* 48, no. 2: 289–309.

Gramling, David. 2007. "Pamuk's Dis-Orient: Reassembling Kafka's *Castle* in *Snow*." *TRANSIT* 3, no. 1: 1–20.

Gramling, David. 2008. "Where Here Begins: Monolingualism and the Spatial Imagination." PhD diss., University of California Berkeley.

Gramling. David. 2009. "The New Cosmopolitan Monolingualism: Linguistic Citizenship in Twenty-First Century Germany." *Die Unterrichtspraxis/ Teaching German* 42, no. 2: 130–40.

Gramling, David. 2012. "An Other Unspeakability: Levi and Lagerszpracha." *New German Critique* 39, no. 3: 165–87.

Gramling, David. 2014. "Losing Multilingual Literature." *American Book Review* 35, no. 5: 8.

Gramling, David. 2015. "Interculturality and Multilingualism on the Threshold of the Third Reich." In *The Multilingual Challenge*, edited by Ulrike Jessner and Claire Kramsch, 159–81. Berlin: Mouton De Gruyter.

Gramling 2016a. "Translanguagers and the Concentrationary Universe." In *Interpreting in Nazi Concentration Camps: Challenging the "Order of Terror,"* edited by Michaela Wolf, 43–58. London: Bloomsbury.

Gramling, David. 2016b. *The Invention of Monolingualism*. London: Bloomsbury.

Gramling, David. 2019. "On Reelecting Monolingualism: Fortification, Fragility, and Stamina." *Applied Linguistics Review* 13, no. 1: 1–18.
Gramling, David. 2020. "Supralingualism and the Translatability Industry." *Applied Linguistics* 41, no. 1: 129–47.
Gramling, David. 2021. *The Invention of Multilingualism*. Cambridge: Cambridge University Press.
Gramling, David, and Chantelle Warner. 2012. "Critical Multilingualism Studies: An Invitation." *Critical Multilingualism Studies* 1, no. 1: 1–11.
Grandner, Michael, and Franz Traxler. 1984. "Sozialpartnerschaft als Option der Zwischenkriegszeit? Liberalkorporatistisches Krisenmanagement am Beispiel der Wirtschaftskonferenz von 1930." In *February 1934*, edited by E. Fröschl and H. Zoitl, 75–117. Vienna: Wiener Volksbuchhandlung.
Green, Georgina. 2015. "Translating Hemp into a Transatlantic 'Band of Reciprocal Interest': The Society for the Encouragement of Arts, Manufactures and Commerce as a 1760s' Actor Network." *Journal for Eighteenth-Century Studies* 38, no. 4: 483–95.
Grice, H. Paul. 1975. "Logic and Conversation." *Syntax and Semantics* 3: 41–58.
Guillory, John. 2022. *Professing Criticism: Essays on the Organization of Literary Study*. Chicago: The University of Chicago Press.
Gumperz, John, and Stephen Levinson. 1996. *Rethinking Linguistic Relativity*. Cambridge: Cambridge University Press.
Haff, Peter K. 2012. "Technology and Human Purpose: The Problem of Solids Transport on the Earth's Surface." *Earth System Dynamics* 3, no. 2: 149–56.
Hageman, Andrew. 2019. "Bringing Infrastructural Criticism to Speculative Fiction: China Miéville's 'Covehithe.'" *C21 Literature: Yearbook of 21st-century Writings* 7, no. 1: 1–10.
Hale, Charles R. 2006. *Más que un Indio: Racial Ambivalence and Neoliberal Multiculturalism in Guatemala*. Santa Fe: School for Advanced Research Press.
Hale, Charles R. 2007. "Rethinking Indigenous Politics in the Era of the 'Indio Permitido.'" *NACLA Report*, September 25, 2007.
Halliday, M. A. K. 2007. *Collected Works. Language and Education, Vol. 9*, edited by J. Webster. London: Continuum.
Hall, Peter and David Soskice. 2001. *Varieties of Capitalism*: London: Oxford University Press.
Halstead, Frank. 1949. "The Genesis and Speed of the Telegraph Codes." *Proceedings of the American Philosophical Society* 93, no. 3: 448–58.
Hanks, William. 2010. *Converting Words: Maya in the Age of the Cross*. Berkeley: University of California Press.
Haraway, Donna. 2016. *Staying with the Trouble: Making Kin in the Chthulucene*. Durham: Duke University Press.
Hardy, Ian. 2012. "Researching Professional Educational Practice: The Case for 'Dirty Theory.'" *Educational Theory* 62, no. 5: 516–33.
Hayles, N. Katherine. 2021. *Postprint: Books and Becoming Computational*. New York: Columbia University Press.

Heidegren, Carl-Göran, and Henrik Lundberg. 2010. "Towards a Sociology of Philosophy." *Acta Sociologica* 53, no. 1: 3–18.
Heller-Roazen, Daniel. 2017. *No One's Ways: An Essay on Infinite Naming*. Princeton: Zone Books.
Henríquez Ureña, Pedro. (1928) 2020. *Seis ensayos en busca de nuestra expressión: Piezas escogidas*, edited by Bruno Rosario Candelier. Madrid: Asociación de academías de lengua Española.
Hiss, Florian. 2017. "Workplace Multilingualism in Shifting Contexts: A Historical Case." *Language in Society* 46, no. 5: 697–718.
Hochschild, Arlie Russell. 1979. "Emotion Work, Feeling Rules, and Social Structure." *American Journal of Sociology* 85, no. 3: 551–75.
Hogan-Brun, Gabrielle. 2017. *Linguanomics: What is the Market Potential of Multilingualism?* London: Bloomsbury.
Holquist, Michael. 2014. "What Would Bakhtin Do?" *Critical Multilingualism Studies* 2, no. 1: 6–19.
Huakang Li, Zheng Xu, Tao Li, Guozi Sun, and Kim-Kwang Raymond Choo. 2017. "An Optimized Approach for Massive Web Page Classification Using Entity Similarity Based on Semantic Network." *Future Generation Computer Systems* 76: 510–18.
Hutchins, John W. 2000. *Early Years in Machine Translation: Memoirs and Biographies of Pioneers*. Philadelphia: John Benjamins.
Ichikawa, Jonathan. 2024. *Epistemic Courage*. London: Oxford University Press.
Infante, Ignacio. 2013. *After Translation: The Transfer and Circulation of Modern Poetics across the Atlantic*. New York: Fordham University Press.
Iwata, Tomuharu, and Katsuhiko Ishiguro. 2016. "Robust Unsupervised Cluster Matching for Network Data." *Data Mining for Knowledge Discovery* 31: 1132–54.
Josephson, Jyl, and Þorgerður Einarsdóttir. 2016. "Language Purism and Gender: Icelandic Trans* Activists and the Icelandic Linguistic Gender Binary." *Transgender Studies Quarterly* 3, no. 3–4: 376–87.
Kadir, Djelal. 2004. "To World, To Globalize—Comparative Literature's Crossroads." *Comparative Literature Studies* 41, no. 1: 1–9.
Kafka, Franz. 1982. *Das Schloß*. Frankfurt am Main: Fischer.
Kafka, Franz. (1924) 1998. *The Castle: A New Translation, Based on the Restored Text*. Translated by Mark Harman. New York: Schocken Books.
Kafka, Franz. (1914) 2008. *Amerika: The Missing Person*. Translated by Mark Harman. New York: Schocken Books.
Katznelson, Noah, and Katie Bernstein. 2017. "Rebranding Bilingualism: The Shifting Discourses of Language Education Policy in California's 2016 Election." *Linguistics and Education* 40: 11–26.
Kellman, Stephen. 2000. *The Translingual Imagination*. Lincoln: University of Nebraska Press.
Kellman, Stephen. 2016. "Omnilingual Aspirations: The Case of the Universal Declaration of Human Rights." *Critical Multilingualism Studies* 4, no. 1: 5–24.

Kelly-Holmes, Helen. 2010. "Raising Language Awareness or Reinforcing Monolingual Norms? A Study of International Marketing Textbooks." In *Language and the Market*, edited by H. Kelly-Holmes and G. Mautner, 185–200. Basingstoke: Palgrave Macmillan.

Kelman, James. 2002. *Translated Accounts*. New York: Anchor Books.

Keohane, Oisín. 2015. "Bodin on Sovereignty: Taking Exception to Translation?" *Paragraph* 38, no. 2: 245–60.

Khan, Kamran. 2019. *Becoming a Citizen: Linguistic Trials and Negotiations in the UK*. London: Bloomsbury.

Khider, Abbas. 2019. *A Slap in the Face*. Translated by Simon Pare. Kolkata: Seagull Books.

Kidwell, P. A. 2000. "Cryptonomicon [Reviews]." *IEEE Annals of the History of Computing* 22, no. 2: 79.

Kilgore, Christopher D. 2019. "Post-Cyberpunk." In *The Routledge Companion to Cyberpunk Culture*, edited by Anna McFarlane, Lars Schmeink, and Graham Murphy. London: Routledge.

Kitsikopoulos, Harry. 2013. *Agrarian Change and Crisis in Europe, 1200–1500*. London: Routledge.

Komska, Yuliya. 2018. "Why Curious George Did Not Speak: The Conspicuous Multilingualism of Margret and H. A. Rey." *The German Studies Review* 41, no. 3: 505–28.

Komska, Yuliya, Michelle Moyd, and David Gramling. 2019. *Linguistic Disobedience: Restoring Power to Civic Language*. London: Palgrave.

Kong, Shuyu. 2004. *Consuming Literature: Best Sellers and the Commercialization of Literary Production in Contemporary China*. Stanford: Stanford University Press.

Köni, René. 1979. "Gesellschaftliches Bewusstsein und Soziologie. Eine spekulative Überlegung." In *Deutsche Soziologie seit 1945. Entwicklungsrichtungen und Praxisbezug*, edited by Günther Lüschen. Oplade: Westdeutscher Verlag.

Kramsch, Claire. 2006. "From Communicative Competence to Symbolic Competence." *The Modern Language Journal* 90, no. 2: 249–52.

Kramsch, Claire. 2009. *The Multilingual Subject: What Foreign Language Learners say about their Experience and Why it Matters*. Oxford: Oxford University Press.

Kramsch, Claire. 2020. *Language as Symbolic Power*. Cambridge: Cambridge University Press.

Kristeva, Julia. 2000 "Humanity is Rediscovering Existential Solitude, the Meaning of Limits, and Mortality." Interview by Stefano Montefiori. Translated by Mariya Chokova. *Corriere della* Sera, March 29, 2020.

Krystallis, Ilias, Giorgio Locatelli, and Niamh Murtagh. 2020. "Futureproofing Complex Infrastructure Projects Using Real Options." *IEEE Engineering Management Review* 49, no. 1: 127–32.

Kubota, Ryuko. 2016. "The Multi/Plural Turn, Postcolonial Theory, and Neoliberal Multiculturalism: Complicities and Implications for Applied Linguistics." *Applied Linguistics* 37, no. 4: 474–94.

Kumar, Prakash. 2013. *Indigo Plantations and Science in Colonial India*. Cambridge: Cambridge University Press.

Kumar, Prakash. 2014. "Planters and Naturalists: Transnational Knowledge on Colonial Indigo Plantations in South Asia." *Modern Asian Studies* 48, no. 3: 720–53.

Kuppens, An H. 2010. "English in Advertising: Generic Intertextuality in a Globalizing Media Environment." *Applied Linguistics* 31, no. 1: 115–35.

Lawrence, David H. (1928) 2015. *Lady Chatterley's Lover*. London: Alma Classics.

Leinster, Murray. 1945. *First Contact*. In *Astounding Science Fiction*, edited by John. W. Campbell, Jr., 7–34. New York: Street and Smith Publications, Inc.

Lennon, Brian. 2010. *In Babel's Shadow: Multilingual Literatures, Monolingual States*. Minneapolis: University of Minnesota Press.

Lennon, Brian. 2012. "Can Multilingualism Be Simulated?" *Critical Multilingualism Studies* 1, no. 1: 94–106.

Leonard, Philip. 2007. "'Secure, Anonymous, Unregulated': 'Cryptonomicon' and the Transnational Data Haven." *Humanities and Technology Review* 26: 65–86. https://irep.ntu.ac.uk/id/eprint/4632/.

Lewis, Gwyn, Bryn Jones, and Colin Baker. 2012. "Translanguaging: Origins and Development from School to Street and Beyond." *Educational Research and Evaluation* 18, no. 7: 641–54.

Lewis, Jonathan Peter. 2003. "Transformations of Contents: Race, Power, and Technology in 'Mason & Dixon,' 'V.,' 'Gravity's Rainbow,' 'Mumbo Jumbo,' and 'Cryptonomicon.'" PhD diss., University of California Riverside.

Lezra, Jacques. 2015. "This Untranslatability Which Is Not One." *Paragraph* 38, no. 2: 174–88.

Li Wei. 2017. "Translanguaging as a Practical Theory of Language." *Applied Linguistics* 39, no. 2: 1–23.

Machado de Oliveira, Vanessa. 2021. *Hospicing Modernity: Facing Humanity's Wrongs and the Implications for Social Activism*. Berkeley: North Atlantic Books.

Macaulay, Thomas. 2001. "Minute on Education in India [1835]." In *Politics and Empire in Victorian Britain: A Reader*, edited by Antoinette Burton, 18–20. New York: Palgrave.

Makoni, Sinfree and Alastair Pennycook. 2006. *Disinventing and Reconstituting Languages*. Bristol: Multilingual Matters.

Makoni, Sinfree and Alastair Pennycook. 2012. "Disinventing Multilingualism: From Monological Multilingualism to Multilingua Francas." In *The Routledge Handbook of Multilingualism*, edited by Marilyn Martin-Jones, Adrian Blackledge, and Angela Creese, 439–53. London: Routledge.

Makoni, Sinfree and Barbara Trudell. 2006. "Complementary and Conflicting Discourses of Linguistic Diversity: Implications for Language Planning." *Per Linguam* 22, no. 2: 14–28.

Malanima, Paolo. 2006. "Energy Crisis and Growth 1650–1850: The European Deviation in a Comparative Perspective." *Journal of Global History* 1, no. 1: 101–21.

Malm, Andreas. 2017. "'This is the Hell that I have Heard of': Some Dialectical Images in Fossil Fuel Fiction." *Forum for Modern Language Studies* 53, no. 2: 121–41.

Mandel, Ernest. 1972. *Der Spätkapitalismus: Versuch einer marxistischen Erklärung*. Frankfurt: Suhrkamp Verlag.

Mandel, Ernest. 1975. *Late Capitalism*. Translated by Joris Des Bres. London: New Left Books.

Ma, Ning. 2017. *The Age of Silver: The Rise of the Novel East and West*. Oxford: Oxford University Press.

Marx, Karl. (1867) 1976. *Capital: A Critique of Political Economy, Vol. 1*. Translated by Ben Fowkes. London: Penguin.

Matsuda, Paul K. 2014. "The Lure of Translingual Writing." *PMLA* 129, no. 3: 478–83.

May, Stephen, ed. 2013. *The Multilingual Turn: Implications for SLA, TESOL, and Bilingual Education*. London: Routledge.

Mazur, Iwona. 2017. "The Metalanguage of Localization: Theory and Practice." *Target: International Journal of Translation Studies* 19, no. 2: 337–57.

Mazzucato, Mariana. 2018. *The Value of Everything: Making and Taking in the Global Economy*. New York: PublicAffairs.

McKenzie, Andrew, and Jeffrey Punske. 2019. "Language Development During Interstellar Travel." *Acta Futura* 12: 123–32.

Melamed, Jodi. 2011. *Represent and Destroy: Rationalizing Violence in the New Racial Capitalism*. Minneapolis: University of Minnesota Press.

Menasse, Robert. 2017. *Die Hauptstadt*. Frankfurt: Suhrkamp.

Menasse, Robert. 2019. *The Capital*. Translated by Jamie Bulloch. New York: Livelight.

Mentz, Steve. 2019. *Break Up the Anthropocene*. Minneapolis: University of Minnesota Press.

Miéville, China. 2011. *Embassytown*. London: Pan Macmillan.

Miéville, China. 2013. *Embassytown: La ciudad embajada*. Translated by Gemma Rovira. Barcelona: Fantascy.

Mignolo, Walter. 2012. *Local Histories/Global Designs: Coloniality, Subaltern Knowledges, and Border Thinking*. Princeton: Princeton University Press.

Miller, Jacques-Alain. 1968. "Action de la structure." Translated by Andrew Goffey. *Cahiers pour l'analyse* 9: 93–103.

Modern Language Association (MLA). 2021. "Enrollments in Languages Other Than English in United States Institutions of Higher Education." https://www.mla.org/content/download/191324/file/Enrollments-in-Languages-Other-Than-English-in-US-Institutions-of-Higher-Education-Fall-2021.pdf. Accessed January 20, 2024.

Moksnes, Heidi. 2012. *Maya Exodus: Indigenous Struggle for Citizenship in Chiapas*. Norman: University of Oklahoma Press.

Mora, Terézia. 2009. *Der einzige Mann auf dem Kontinent*. Munich: Luchterhand Literaturverlag.

Moore, Jason W. 2016. "The Rise of Cheap Nature." In *Anthropocene or Capitalocene? Nature, History, and the Crisis of Capitalism*, edited by Jason W. Moore, 78–115. Oakland, CA: PM Press.

Moore, Robert. 2015. "From Revolutionary Monolingualism to Reactionary Multilingualism: Top-down Discourses of Linguistic Diversity in Europe, 1794–present." *Language and Communication* 44: 19–30.

Morrison, Irene. 2017. "Dystopian Surrealism for Our Times: Karin Tidbeck's 'Amatka.'" *LA Review of Books*, October 14, 2017.

Morton, Timothy. 2013. *Hyperobjects: Philosophy and Ecology after the End of the World*. 1st ed. Minneapolis: University of Minnesota Press.

Myers-Scotton, Carol. 1993. "Elite Closure as a Powerful Language Strategy: The African Case." *International Journal of the Sociology of Language* 103: 149–63.

Nadasen, Premilla. 2023. *Care: The Highest Stage of Capitalism*. Chicago: Haymarket Books.

Nielsen, Jens Petter. 1996. *A Miniature Empire: The Copper Works at Kåfjord and the Community that Grew Up Around It*. Alta: Alta Museum.

Noorani, Yaseen. 2013. "Hard and Soft Multilingualism." *Critical Multilingualism Studies* 1, no. 2: 7–28.

Nors, Dorthe. 2016. *Spejl, skulder, blink*. Copenhagen: Gyldendal.

Nors, Dorthe. 2017a. *Mirror, Shoulder, Signal*. Translated by Misha Hoesktra. London: Pushkin Press.

Nors, Dorthe. 2017b. "Man Booker International Prize Q&A—Dorthe Nors." Interview by Eric M. B. Becker. *Words Without Borders*, April 20, 2017.

Nors, Dorthe. 2019. "A Certain Way of Singing: Talking with Dorthe Nors." An interview with Nina Moog. *The Rumpus*, March 27, 2019.

Oard, Douglas. 2006. "Transcending the Tower of Babel: Supporting Access to Multilingual Information with Cross-Language Information Retrieval." In *Emergent Information Technologies and Enabling Policies for Counter-Terrorism*, edited by Robert Popp and John Yen, 299–314. IEEE Press Series on Computational Intelligence. Hoboken: John Wiley and Sons.

Obioma, Chigozie. 2019. *An Orchestra of Minorities*. New York: Little, Brown and Company.

O'Hagan, Minako and David Ashworth. 2002. *Translation-mediated Communication in a Digital World: Facing the Challenges of Globalization and Localization*. Clevedon: Multilingual Matters.

Ojo, Olumide E., Olaronke O. Adebanji, Hiram Calvo, Damian O. Dieke, Olumuyiwa E. Ojo, Seye E. Akinsanya, Tolulope O. Abiola, and Anna Feldman. 2023. "Legend at ArAIEval Shared Task: Persuasion Technique Detection using a Language-Agnostic Text Representation Model." In *Proceedings of ArabicNLP 2023, Singapore (Hybrid)*, 594–99. Association for Computational Linguistics. https://arxiv.org/pdf/2310.09661v1.pdf.

Oller, John. W. 1997. "Monoglottosis: What's Wrong with the Idea of the IQ Meritocracy and its Racy Cousins?" *Applied Linguistics* 18, no. 4: 467–507.

Olohan, Maeve, and Myriam Salmara-Carr. 2011. "Translating Science." *The Translator* 17, no. 2: 179–88.

O'Neill, Patrick. 2005. *Polyglot Joyce: Fictions of Translation.* Toronto: University of Toronto Press.

Orelus, Pierre W. 2017. "Accentism Exposed: An Anticolonial Analysis of Accent Discrimination with Some Implications for Minority Languages." In *Language, Race, and Power in Schools: A Critical Discourse Analysis,* edited by Pierre W. Orelus, 127–37. New York: Routledge.

Otoo, Sharon Dodua. 2023. *Ada's Realm.* Translated by Jon Cho-Polizzi. London: Hachette.

Oz-Salzberger, Fania. 2002. "Translation." *Encyclopedia of the Enlightenment.* Vol. 4, edited by Alan C. Kors, 181–88. Oxford, UK: Oxford University Press.

Pamuk, Orhan. 2002. *Kar.* Istanbul: Iletişim.

Pandey, Anjali. 2016. *Monolingualism and Linguistic Exhibitionism in Fiction.* London: Palgrave.

Parks, Tim. 2010. "The Dull New Global Novel." *The New York Review of Books,* February 9, 2010.

Parvulescu, Anca, and Manuela Boatcă. 2022. *Creolizing the Modern: Transylvania across Empires.* Ithaca: Cornell University Press.

Patel, Raj Charles, and Jason W. Moore. 2018. *A History of the World in Seven Cheap Things: A Guide to Capitalism, Nature, and the Future of the Planet.* 1st Ed. Berkeley, CA: University of California Press.

Peel, Quentin. 2001. "The Monotony of Monoglots." *Language Learning Journal* 23: 13–14.

Pennycook, Alastair. 2008. "English as a Language Always in Translation." *European Journal of English Studies* 12, no 1: 33–47.

Pennycook, Alastair. 2017. *Posthumanist Applied Linguistics.* London: Routledge.

Petersmann, Ernst-Ulrich. 2000. "From 'Negative' to 'Positive' Integration in the WTO: Time for 'Mainstreaming Human Rights' into WTO Law?" *Common Market Law Review* 37, no. 6: 1363–82.

Phipps, Alison. 2019. *Decolonising Multilingualism: Struggles to Decreate.* Clevedon: Multilingual Matters.

Piller, Ingrid. 2001. "Identity Constructions in Multilingual Advertising." *Language in Society* 30, no. 2: 153–86.

Pipestone Group. 2023. "On Linguistic Indifference." *The German Quarterly* 96, no. 3: 378–82.

Pratt, Mary Louise. 1991. "Arts of the Contact Zone." *Profession,* 33–40.

Pratt, Mary Louise. 2002. "The Traffic in Meaning: Translation, Contagion, Infiltration." *Profession,* 25–36.

Pratt, Mary Louise. 2012. "'If English Was Good Enough for Jesus . . .' Monolinguismo y Mala Fe." *Critical Multilingualism Studies* 1, no. 1: 12–30.

Price, Joshua Martin. 2023. *Translation and Epistemicide: Racialization of Languages in the Americas.* Tucson: University of Arizona Press.

Quijano, Anibal. 1992. "Colonialidad y modernidad/racionalidad." In *Los conquistados. 1492 y la población indígena de las Américas,* edited by Heraclio Bonilla. Quito: Tercer Mundo-Libri Mundi.

Ramanathan, Vaihedi. 2005. *The English–Vernacular Divide: Postcolonial Language Policies and Practice*. Clevedon: Multilingual Matters.

Ramjattan, Vijay A. 2019. "Racializing the Problem of and Solution to Foreign Accent in Business." *Applied Linguistics Review* 13, no. 4: 527–44.

Rectanus, Mark W. 1987. "Literary Publishing in the Federal Republic of Germany: Redefining the Enterprise." *German Studies Review* 10, no. 1: 95–123.

Rich, Adrienne. 1997. "Arts of the Possible." *The Massachusetts Review* 38: 319–37.

Riley, Denise. (1979) 1983. *War and the Nursery: Theories of the Child and Mother*. London: Virago.

Robbins, Bruce. 2007. "The Smell of Infrastructure: Notes Toward an Archive." *boundary 2* 34: 125–33.

Robinson, Kim Stanley. 2020. *The Ministry for the Future*. New York: Orbit.

Rosello, Mireille. 2011. "Rudimentariness as Home." In *A Companion to Comparative Literature*, edited by A. Behdad and D. Thomas, 312–31. London: Wiley-Blackwell.

Rubenstein, Michael. 2010. *Public Works: Infrastructure, Irish Modernism, and the Postcolonial*. South Bend: University of Notre Dame Press.

Ryan, Marie-Laure. 1994. "Immersion vs. Interactivity: Virtual Reality and Literary Theory." *Postmodern Culture* 5, no. 1.

Ryan, Marie-Laure. 2001. *Narrative as Virtual Reality: Immersion and Interactivity in Literature and Electronic Media*. Baltimore: Johns Hopkins University Press.

Sabino, Robin. 2018. *Languaging Without Languages*. Amsterdam: Brill.

Said, Edward. 2004. "The Rage of the Old." *The Guardian*, August 1, 2004.

Saif, Abdulgabbar, Mohd Juzaiddin ab Aziz, and Nazlia Omar. 2015. "Mapping Arabic WordNet Synsets to Wikipedia Articles Using Monolingual and Bilingual Features." *Natural Language Engineering* 23, no. 1: 53–91.

Saktanber, Ayşe. 2002. "'We Pray Like You Have Fun': New Islamic Youth in Turkey between Intellectualism and Pop Culture." In *Fragments of Culture: The Everyday of Modern Turkey*, edited by Deniz Kandiyoti and Ayşe Saktanber, 254–76. Camden, NJ: Rutgers University Press.

Salas-Zarate, Maria del Pilar, Rafael Valencia-García, Antonio Ruiz-Martínez, and Ricardo Colomo-Palacios. 2017. "Feature-Based Opinion Mining in Financial News: An Ontology-Driven Approach." *Journal of Information Sciences* 43, no. 4: 458–79.

Sanchez Prado, Ignacio M. 2023. "Cultural Capital: Reflections from a Latin Americanist." *Genre* 56, no. 1: 49–7.

Sasaki, Yu. 2017. "Publishing Nations: Technology Acquisition and Language Standardization for European Ethnic Groups." *The Journal of Economic History* 77, no. 4: 1007–47.

Schenstead-Harris, Leif. 2017. "Dystopic Nordic Weird: Review of 'Amatka' by Karin Tidbeck." *Weird Fiction Review*, July 31, 2017.

Schieffelin, Bambi, and Elinor Ochs. 1986. *Language Socialization across Cultures*. Cambridge: Cambridge University Press.

Schleiermacher, Friedrich. (1813) 1838. "Ueber die verschiedenen Methoden des Uebersetzens." *Sämtliche Werke III, Vol. 2*. Berlin: de Gruyter.
Schulz, Thomas. 2013. "Translate This: Google's Quest to End the Language Barrier." *Der Spiegel*, September 9, 2013.
Shankar, Shalini. 2008. "Speaking like a Model Minority: 'FOB' Styles, Gender, and Racial Meanings among Desi Teens in Silicon Valley." *Journal of Linguistic Anthropology* 18, no. 2: 268–89.
Shih, Shu-Mei. 2004. "Global Literature and the Technologies of Recognition." *PMLA* 119, no. 1: 16–30.
sitholé, ganyamatopé dzapasi tawona t., 2024. "kuwanda huuya: mutuality as intercultural abun-dance in a teaching practice of listening." PhD diss., University of Glasgow School of Education.
sitholé, ganyamatopé dzapasi tawona t. and David Gramling. 2025. "Hard Translanguaging: A Mutualizing Practice of Abun-dance." In *Handbook of Translanguaging,* edited by Jerry Won Lee, Li Wei, Ofelia García, and Prem Phyak. London: Wiley-Blackwell.
Slobin, Dan. I. 1996. "From 'Thought and Language' to 'Thinking for Speaking.'" In *Rethinking Linguistic Relativity*, edited by J. Gumperz and S. Levinson, 17–70. Cambridge, UK: Cambridge University Press.
Slobodian, Quinn. 2018. *The Globalists: The End of Empire and the Birth of Neoliberalism*. Cambridge: Harvard University Press.
Slobodian, Quinn. 2023. *Crack-Up Capitalism: Market Radicals and the Dream of a World Without Democracy*. New York: Macmillan.
Silverstein, Michael. 1976. "Hierarchy of Features and Ergativity." In *Grammatical Categories in Australian Languages*, edited by R. M. W. Dixon, 112–71. Canberra: Australian Institute of Aboriginal Studies.
Smith, Jordan A. Y. 2017. "Translationscape: On the Legibility of Transnational Ideologies in World Literary Systems." *Comparative Literature Studies* 54, no. 4: 749–70.
Smith, Rachel Greenwald. 2014. "Six Propositions on Compromise Aesthetics." *The Account*, Fall.
Smith, Rachel Greenwald. 2015. *Affect and American Literature in the Age of Neoliberalism*. London: Cambridge University Press.
Smith, Rachel Greenwald. 2021. *On Compromise: Art, Politics, and the Fate of an American Ideal*. New York: Graywolf Press.
Solan, Lawrence. 2009. "The Interpretation of Multilingual Statutes by the European Court of Justice." *Brooklyn Journal of International Law* 34, no. 2: 277–301.
Solan, Lawrence. 2014. "Multilingualism and Morality in Statutory Interpretation." *Language and Law / Linguagem e Direito* 1, no. 1: 5–21.
Solan, Lawrence 2017. "Some Risks and Rewards of Europe's Multilingual Legal Order." *Contemporary Readings in Law and Social Justice* 9, no. 2: 388–399.
Sommer, Doris. 2003. *Bilingual Games: Some Literary Investigations*. New York: Palgrave Macmillan.
Steffen, Will, Åsa Persson, Lisa Deutsch, Jan Zalasiewicz, Mark Williams, Katherine Richardson, Carole Crumley, Paul Crutzen, Carl Folke, Line

Gordon, Mario Molina, Veerabhadran Ramanathan, Johan Rockström, Marten Scheffer, Hans Joachim Schellnhuber, and Uno Svedin. 2011. "The Anthropocene: From Global Change to Planetary Stewardship." *Ambio* 40, no. 7: 739–61.

Steffensen, Sune Vork. 2015. "Distributed Language and Dialogism: Notes on Non-locality, Sense-Making and Interactivity." *Language Sciences* 50: 105–19.

Stephenson, Neal. 1999. *Cryptonomicon*. New York: Avon Books.

Stephenson, Neal. 2005. *Cryptonomicon I: El código Enigma*. Translated by Pedro Jorge Romero. Madrid, Spain: Ediciones B.

Stephenson, Neal. 2022. *Cryptonomicon*. Translated by Wojciech M. Próchniewicz. Warsaw: Wydawnictwo MAG.

Sternberg, Meir. 1981. "Polylingualism as Reality and Translation as Mimesis." *Poetics Today* 2, no. 4: 221–39.

Stetkevych, Jaroslav. 1970. *The Modern Arabic Literary Language: Lexical and Stylistic Developments*. Chicago: University of Chicago Press.

Steuer, Jonathan. 1992. "Defining Virtual Reality: Dimensions Determining Telepresence." *Journal of Communication* 42, no. 4: 73–93.

Stibbe, Arran. 2015. *Ecolinguistics: Language, Ecology, and the Stories We Live By*. London: Routledge.

Stockhammer, Robert. 2017. "Converting Lingualism into Linguality (Langagification des Langues) in Goethe's Wilhelm Meister Novels." Translated by Judith Menzl. *Critical Multilingualism Studies* 5, no. 3: 32–51.

Summers, Lawrence. 2012. "What You (Really) Need to Know." *The New York Times*, January 20, 2012.

Suwandi, Intan. 2019. *Value Chains: The New Economic Imperialism*. New York: Monthly Review Press.

Szurek, Emmanuel. 2015. "The Linguist and the Politician: The Türk Dil Kurumu and the Field of Power in the 1930s–40s." In *Order and Compromise: Government Practices in Turkey from the Late Ottoman Empire to the Early 21st Century*, edited by Marc Aymes, Benjamin Gourisse, and Élise Massicard, 68–96. Leiden: Brill.

Tankosić, Ana, and Sender Dovchin. 2021. "(C)overt Linguistic Racism: Eastern-European Background Immigrant Women in the Australian Workplace." *Ethnicities* 23, no. 51–32.

Tannen, Deborah. 1981. "New York Jewish Conversational Style." *International Journal of the Sociology of Language* 30: 133–49.

Táíwò, Olúfẹ́mi O. 2022. *Elite Capture: How the Powerful Took Over Identity Politics (And Everything Else)*. Chicago: Haymarket Books.

Taylor, Analisa. 2009. *Indigeneity in the Mexican Cultural Imagination: Thresholds of Belonging*. Tucson: University of Arizona Press.

Taylor-Batty, Juliette. 2013. *Multilingualism in Modernist Fiction*. London: Palgrave.

Tekgül, Duygu. 2019. "Book Club Meetings as Micro-Public Spheres: Translated Literature and Cosmopolitanism." *Language and Intercultural Communication* 19, no. 5: 380–92.

Tesseur, Wine, and Angela M. Crack. 2018. *Respecting Communities in International Development: Languages and Cultural Understanding*. Intrac.org.

Thibault, Paul J. 2011. "First-Order Languaging Dynamics and Second-Order Language: The Distributed Language View." *Ecological Psychology* 23: 1–36.
Tholpadi, Goutham, Chiranjib Bhattacharyya, and Shirish Shevade. 2017. "Corpus-Based Translation Induction in Indian Languages: Using Auxiliary Language Corpora from Wikipedia." *ACM Transactions on Asian and Low-Resource Language Information Processing* 16, no. 3: 1–25.
Thomas, Brinley. 1986. "Was There an Energy Crisis in Great Britain in the 17th Century?" *Explorations in Economic History* 23, no. 2: 124–52.
Thomas, Brinley. 1993. *The Industrial Revolution and the Atlantic Economy*. London: Routledge.
Thompson, John. 2010. *Merchants of Culture: The Publishing Business in the Twenty-First Century*. New York: Plume.
Tidbeck, Karin. 2012. *Amatka*. Uppsala, Sweden: Mix.
Tidbeck, Karin. 2017a. *Amatka*. Translated by Karin Tidbeck. New York: Vintage Books.
Tidbeck, Karin. 2017b. "SDCC '17: Interview: Author Karin Tidbeck Uncovers the Dreamlike Storyline of 'Amatka.'" By Nicholas Eskey. *The Beat*, July 28, 2017.
Tidbeck, Karin. 2017c. "Language Matters." Interview. *Locus*, September 10, 2017.
Tratner, Michael. 2008. "Crypto-Economics: Neal Stephenson, Milton Friedman, and Post-Postmodernism." In *Tomorrow through the Past: Neal Stephenson and the Project of Global Modernization*, edited by Jon Lewis, 98–113. Newcastle: Cambridge Scholars Publishing.
Trilling, Lionel. (1950) 2008. *The Liberal Imagination: Essays on Literature and Society*, edited by Louis Menand. New York: New York Review of Books.
Turner, Fred. 2006. *From Counterculture to Cyberculture*. Chicago: University of Chicago Press.
Tuck, Eve. 2011. "Rematriating Curriculum Studies." *Journal of Curriculum and Pedagogy* 9, no. 1: 34–7.
Urciuoli, Bonnie. 2000. "Strategically Deployable Shifters in College Marketing, Or Just What Do They Mean by 'Skills' and 'Leadership' and 'Multiculturalism'?" *Language and Culture* 6.
Valkeapää, Nils-Aslak. 1988. *The Sun, My Father*. Translated by Lars Nordstrom, Harald Gaski, and Ralph Salisbury. Seattle: University of Washington Press.
Valkeapää, Nils-Aslak. 1991. *Beaivi, áhčážan*. Guovdageaidnu/Kautokeino, Sápmi: DAT.
Van Parijs, Philippe. 2011. *Linguistic Justice for Europe and Beyond*. Oxford: Oxford University Press.
Viveiros de Castro, Eduardo. 2004. "Perspectival Anthropology and the Method of Controlled Equivocation." *Tipití: Journal of the Society for the Anthropology of Lowland South America* 2, no. 1: 3–22.
Vizenor, Gerald. 2008. *Survivance: Narratives of Native Presence*. Lincoln: University of Nebraska Press.
Walkowitz, Rebecca. 2007. "Unimaginable Largeness: Kazuo Ishiguro, Translation, and the New World Literature." *NOVEL: A Forum on Fiction* 40, no. 3: 216–39.

Walkowitz, Rebecca. 2017. *Born Translated: The Contemporary Novel in an Age of World Literature*. New York: Columbia University Press.
Warner, Chantelle. 2024. *Multiliteracy Play: Designs and Desires in the Second Language Classroom*. London: Bloomsbury.
Waterhouse, Peter. 2011. "Übersetzung wird interessant, wenn sie außer Kontrolle gerät." Uni Wien Medienportal.
Weaver, Warren. (1949) 1955. "Translation." Reprinted in *Machine Translation of Languages: Fourteen Essays*, edited by W. N. Locke, and A. D. Booth, 15–23. Cambridge: Technology Press of the Massachusetts Institute of Technology.
Webster, Jamieson. 2020. "The Real Real." Interview with Alison M. Gingeras. *Artforum*, May 5, 2020.
Wennerlind, Carl. 2011. *Casualties of Credit: The English Financial Revolution, 1620–1720*. Cambridge: Harvard University Press.
Williams, Bernard. 2002. *Truth and Truthfulness: An Essay in Genealogy*. Princeton: Princeton University Press.
Williams, Cen. 1994. "Arfarniad o Ddulliau Dysgu ac Addysgu yng Nghyd-destun Addysg Uwchradd Ddwyieithog." PhD diss., University of Wales Bangor.
Worley, Paul M. 2017. "Máseual excluido/indio permitido: neoliberal translation in Waldemar Noh Tzec." *Latin American and Caribbean Ethnic Studies* 12, no. 3: 290–314.
Wrigley, Edward A. 2010. *Energy and the English Industrial Revolution*. Cambridge: Cambridge University Press.
Wu, Shellen Xiao. 2015. *Lost and Found in Translation: Geology, Mining, and the Search for Wealth and Power*. Stanford: Stanford University Press.
Yeager, Patricia. 2007. "Introduction: Dreaming of Infrastructure." *PMLA* 122: 19–26.
Yildiz, Yasemin. 2013. *Beyond the Mother Tongue: The Postmonolingual Condition*. New York: Fordham University Press.
Youngquist, Paul. 2012. "Cyberpunk, War, and Money: Neal Stephenson's Cryptonomicon." *Contemporary Literature* 53, no. 2: 319–47.
Zaghir, Jamil, Mina Bjelogrlic, Jean-Philippe Goldman, Soukaïna Aananou, Christophe Gaudet-Blavignac, and Christian Lovis. 2023. "FRASIMED: a Clinical French Annotated Resource Produced through Crosslingual BERT-Based Annotation Projection." *arXiv preprint*, arXiv:2309.10770. https://arxiv.org/pdf/2309.10770.pdf.
Zhao, Mengjie and Hinrich Schütze. 2019. "A Multilingual BPE Embedding Space for Universal Sentiment Lexicon Induction." In *Proceedings of the 57th Annual Meeting of the Association for Computational Linguistics*, edited by Anna Korhonen, David Traum, and Lluís Màrquez, 3506–17. Florence, Italy: Association for Computational Linguistics. https://doi.org/10.18653/v1/P19-1341.
Zhu Hua and Li Wei. 2019. "Translanguaging and Diasporic Imagination." In *Routledge Handbook of Diaspora Studies*, edited by Robin Cohen and Carolin Fischer, 106–12. London: Routledge.

Index

Ada's Realm (Sharon Dodua Otto) 12
affect 4, 26, 38, 46, 54, 59–61, 69, 95, 100, 102, 109, 118
Agrawal, Neeraj 146
Ahmed, Sara 87
algorithm 37, 71, 150, 158–9, 164, 171, 179. *See also* CLIR
Alten Copper Works 72
American Sign Language (ASL) 177
Amerika: The Missing Person (Franz Kafka) 155, 198–9
Animacies (Mel Chen) 179–80, 186, 190, 204
Anthropocene 58, 61–2, 70–5, 121, 153, 156–7, 161, 198
antipastoral 97, 99, 121–4
anti-protectionism 2, 26, 31, 89, 96, 99, 125. *See also* ordoliberalism; protectionism; xenos rights
Anya, Uju 199
Appadurai, Arjun 74, 159
Apter, Emily 159
artificial intelligence (AI) xii, 7, 15, 18, 41 n.14, 54, 113, 135, 167, 172, 193
austerity, linguistic xviii, 48, 201
authoritarianism 4, 12, 56, 69, 79–80, 105, 168, 192

Baker, Andrew 139–40
Bakhtin, Mikhail xiii, 184
Barak, On 162–3
Bernstein, Katie 6, 160
Bhabha, Homi 113, 133, 139
Bigelow, Allison 67
bilingual
 "bilingual games" 64, 87, 91–2, 171
 bilingualism 6, 160
 speech xviii, 37
Bloom, Harold 127, 131, 136
Bodin, Jean 84
body, the. *See* embodiment; late style
Böhm-Bawerk, Eugen von 194
Bourdieu, Pierre 4, 10, 18 n.10, 61, 120, 141
Braun, Juliane 70, 84
breadfruit 63, 70, 84
Break Up the Anthropocene (Steve Mentz) 74
Brown v. Board of Education 111
Bryant, Sherwin K. 67
Buckley, Bill 111
Bulloch, Jamie 12
Butler, Judith 28, 61, 141, 178

Çandar, Başak 38, 105, 108
Capital, The (Robert Menasse) 12–13
capitalism. *See also* neoliberalism; ordoliberalism
 colonial 68, 160–2
 global 9, 21, 31, 72, 141–2
 late 6, 10, 19, 39, 146, 164, 196
 Liberal 61, 161
Capitalocene 74, 121
care for language xiv, 45–8, 192
cheap meaning 21, 31, 58, 60, 97–8, 105, 108, 110, 129
cheap talk 30, 202
Chen, Mel 179–80, 186, 190, 204
Chthulucene 61, 74
cilpen 80–2, 193

citizenship 26, 38, 108, 180
  application 6 n.4
  linguistic 5, 59
  market 142
climate, change and emergency 8, 50–1, 72, 121–2, 153, 157, 161, 198, 203. *See also* Anthropocene; Capitalocene; Chthulucene; Linguacene; Plantationocene
climate fiction (cli-fi) 58
coal 63, 71, 72, 162–3
codebreaking 130, 137, 155, 172. *See also* cryptography
Coetzee, J. M. 105, 108, 152
colonial modernity 3, 27–8, 38, 62, 154, 156. *See also* capitalism; commensuration; monolingualism
coloniality 2, 179
  in *Amatka* 47–9, 75
  in *Embassytown* 168–76
commensuration 9, 49–51, 57, 65, 69–70
  and colonial modernity 52, 63–4, 67, 70, 162–3
  and compromise aesthetics 2–3, 59, 79, 181
  and xenos rights 83
compromise aesthetics 2–3, 49, 59–61, 99, 127, 131
computational engineering. *See also* CLIR; IEEE; MT
  and commensuration 70
  and commerce 31, 36, 131–3, 138–41, 145, 147–8, 159–60
  corpora development 134–5
  feminist and Indigenous critique of methods 69
  and humanities and social sciences 37, 134–6, 164–6, 172
  and "individual language" 165–6

and infrastructure 8, 39, 127–31, 143
and language agnosticism (configurability) 29, 31, 47, 147–8, 172–4, 180–1
  reliance on user testing 6 n.5, 7, 46, 48, 69
and supralingualism 132–3, 158
text preprocessing strategies 158 (*see also* Named Entity Recognition; Natural Language Processing)
configurability. *See* language agnosticism
Connell, Raewyn 170
contact zones 117
contempt xvii, 2–3, 14, 127, 129–31, 136, 143–5, 149, 164, 166
controlled equivocation 135, 188–9
COP (Conference of the Parties, United Nations Framework Convention on Climate Change) 50, 203
copper 67, 72–3
Corneille, Pierre 200–1
corpus 9, 35, 40, 48, 58, 62, 73, 134, 150
Cox, Robert 33, 139
crisis 57–8, 74–5, 81, 135, 161
  "crisis ordinary" 56, 146
Cronin, Michael 13, 17 n.9, 20, 163
Cross-Language Information Retrieval (CLIR) 7, 17, 30, 40, 70, 73, 82, 113, 129–30, 134–5, 157–60, 164
cryptocurrency 146–7
cryptography 126, 130–1, 144, 187. *See also* codebreaking
cultural sovereignty 31–2, 40. *See also* protectionism

data 41 n.14, 70, 130–2, 134–5, 148, 158–9, 174 *See also* data mining; Google

data mining 37, 69
decoloniality 7 n.6, 40–1, 107–8, 114, 142, 154
decolonization 31, 99, 110–12, 141–2, 195–6
depoliticization 80, 111–12, 142, 189. *See also* dominium
Díaz, Junot 25, 152
Dictionary of Untranslatables (Emily Apter) 159
Didion, Joan 4, 22
diffusionism 103, 141, 156
dirty theory 27, 170
discursive holdings 83
disorientation. *See* vertigo
dithering 121, 123
Doha Round 111, 142, 180
Dollimore, Jonathan 34
dominium, definition of 83. *See also* imperium; xenos rights
   and depoliticization 111–12, 142, 189
   and Geneva School ordoliberals 111–14
   global linguistic management 123, 129, 147–8, 151
   in literary themes 123, 182
   neoliberal 142
   and translatability 115
Dourish, Paul 7, 46, 48, 69, 135, 143, 159
Dowling, Sarah 5, 10, 19
Dudley, Leonard 152–3, 158

ecstasy 3, 14, 180–1
Ellis, John 84
embodiment. *See* multilingualism
   of experience 89–90, 95, 181
   of knowledge 103
   of language xii, 46, 48, 127–9, 176–8
enslaved labor 63, 67, 70, 141

epistemicide 134, 140, 174
   epistemic theft 67
Ericcson English (EE) 51–2
exclosure 123–5, 142
exhibitionism, linguistic xvii, 11, 105, 107, 152, 186
extractivism 58, 67, 75, 154, 157, 173, 198
   linguistic and cultural 7, 12, 42, 69, 134

femicide 90–2, 94, 100, 104, 113, 117
feminism 27, 69, 87, 143
Filipović, Luna 14, 122, 199
First Contact (Murray Leinster) 171
fossil fuel fiction 74
Franzen, Jonathan 59–60

Gaski, Harald 41
gender 2, 27, 146, 165
Geneva School 110–12, 142
Gingeras, Alison M. 52
globalization 23–4, 38, 56, 62, 99–100, 115–16, 129–30, 140, 164, 194. *See also* xenos rights
Globalization, Localization, Internationalization, and Translation industry 150
gloop 45, 47, 53–4, 58, 63, 65–6, 76, 79, 193
glossodiversity 57, 159, 179
Google 98, 130, 150–1
Grand, George Francois, First Collector of Tirhut 69
greenwashing 12, 83, 141, 198
Guamán Poma de Ayala, Felipe 152

Haberler, Gottfried von 110, 117, 195
habitus 4, 89, 117–18
Haff, Peter 63
Hageman, Andy 23, 56

Hale, Charles 107–8
Halstead, Frank 135, 137–8
Hanks, William 63, 70, 141
Haraway, Donna 74, 121
Harman, Mark 1
"Have Fun Staying Poor"
  (meme) 146
Hayek, Friedrich 16 n.8, 30, 83, 195
Hayles, N. Katherine 20, 74, 128
  n.1, 156–7
heteroglossia xiii, 5, 134
heteronormativity 2
History of the World in Seven Cheap Things (Raj Patel and Jason Moore) 31
Hochschild, Arlie Russell 91
Hoekstra, Misha 87, 93, 94 n.8, 114
hospice (Vanessa Machado de Oliveira) xi, 24, 131, 190
human rights 142. *See also* Universal Declaration of Human Rights
Human-Computer Interaction (HCI) 46, 69
hygge 97
hyperobject 154 n.8, 163

Ichikawa, Jonathan 121–2
illusio 18, 120
immer 172
immerser 172
immersion 1, 32–3, 98, 172, 185, 194, 201
imperium, definition of 83. *See also* dominium; xenos rights
  and Geneva School ordoliberals 111–14
  in literary themes 123, 182
  neoliberal 142
  and translation 115
indigo 63, 69
individual languages, so-called 28, 62, 93, 142, 164–5, 196, 200
Infante, Ignacio 17 n.9, 186

infraperformativity 61–3
infrastructure 23, 35, 37, 103, 115, 124–5, 193
  economic 7, 20, 30, 140 n.4
  of language 8, 20, 21, 63, 80, 89, 128–30, 196, 200
  of late monolingualism 39–40, 113, 145
  of supply chain 1, 15, 21, 26, 56
Institute of Electrical and Electronic Engineers (IEEE) 8, 31, 135, 174
interdisciplinarity xv, 17, 28, 29, 128 n.1, 135, 137
Intramuros 140
Invention of Monolingualism, The (David Gramling) 3–4, 66, 154, 194
Invention of Multilingualism, The (David Gramling) 7 n.6
Ishiguro, Kazuo 52, 152
iteration
  hidden costs of 7
  "iterative power" (Chen) 180
  and language-tech engineering 7, 46, 69
  as marking (*Amatka*) 45–9, 75, 79–82, 85
  and monopsony 41
  and supply-side production 93

Kafka, Franz 1, 15, 24, 124, 154–5, 198–9
Kars (Orhan Pamuk) 12
Katznelson, Noah 6, 160
Kellman, Steven 16, 38, 40, 50, 54, 103, 186
Keohane, Oisín 84–6
killjoy 87, 91, 93, 97
Kitsikopoulos, Harry 72
kladd 45, 53, 58, 63, 65–6, 82, 151, 193
Komska, Yuliya xvii, 5, 36

Kristeva, Julia 53
Kumar, Prakash 68–9

Language (distinct from language) 58, 68, 147, 149, 168, 175, 184, 200
  for Ariekei 169–80, 187–8
language agnosticism 47, 129, 136, 147–8, 171–4, 180–1, 198
language standardization 12, 34, 150, 152–3, 199
"a language" 28, 62, 93, 142, 164–6, 191, 195
Large Language Models (LLMs) xii, 7, 29–31
late capitalism 6, 10, 19, 39, 146, 196, 200
late monolingualism
  concept of 6, 9, 12, 26, 39–40, 145, 201
  vs. high 7, 31, 34, 41, 69–70
  moods of 3, 181
  periodization 16–19, 57
  ways out of 181
late style xi–xii, 4, 18–19, 41, 90, 119–20, 131
lateness xi–xii, 1, 6, 39, 132, 135, 199
lawfare 5
Le Guin, Ursula 171
Lennon, Brian 184
Lezra, Jacques 8–9, 82–3, 164, 203
Linguacene 62, 70–5, 154, 157, 163, 198
lingualism 34, 42
linguamisia 149–50
linguaphobia 145, 148, 195, 200
linguistic accidence 49, 54, 154, 157, 163, 177
linguistic austerity xviii, 48, 201
linguistic exhibitionism xvii, 11, 105, 107, 152, 186
linguistic fiction (Li-fi) 58, 135, 167, 180, 187

linguistic indifference 29, 38, 95, 134, 202
linguistic purism 35, 67, 82
linguistic relativity 63
linguistic sovereignty 33, 40, 41, 84, 100, 114, 180
literacies 87, 152–3, 158, 165, 193, 198
literary criticism/critique xv–xvi, 23, 29, 37
literary theory 36–7, 186, 201
low-resourced languages 173

machine translation (MT) xii, 7, 9, 17, 30, 35, 57, 62, 64–5, 137, 145, 150, 167, 172–4, 202. See also CLIR; LLMs
macrotext 45 n.1, 61, 65–6, 79–82
Malm, Andreas 75
Mandel, Ernest 6, 39, 200
marking 50, 53, 57, 62, 75, 77, 79–82, 85, 90. See also iteration
Marx, Karl 39, 58, 62, 132, 198
Marx, Leo 123
Matsuda, Paul Kae xvii
Menasse, Robert (Die Haupstadt) 12–13
mining. See also data mining
  colonial 67, 72–3, 75, 112, 163
  opinion 46
Ministry for the Future, The (Kim Stanley Robinson) 12
misolingualism 150
monolanguage 58, 63, 68, 88, 91–5, 121, 147, 163, 194
  definition of 28
mono/lingual 34
monolingual international xiv, 98
monolingualism. See also late monolingualism
  colonial 26, 69
  definition of 27
  high 6, 26, 30, 32–4, 41, 142
  literary 11, 40, 134, 198

political   xii, 4, 5
racialized   4
securitarian   58
settler   19
translational   132, 152, 187
monopsony   41, 48, 54, 143, 151, 158–9
Mont Pelerin Society (MPS)   112, 182, 194
Moore, Jason   21, 23, 31, 161
Mora, Terézia   12, 152
Morrison, Irene   54, 56, 68
multilingualism. *See also* CLIR; MT
 and authorship   13–14, 25, 36, 89, 94–5
 commercial   63–4, 71, 152, 165 (*see also* supply side)
 conspicuous   xvii, 36
 embodied   143, 167, 196
 hard   40, 53, 170, 174, 186
 and late monolingualism   6, 8–9, 18–19, 35, 142
 social   xix, 5, 202
 soft   9, 175
 and subjectivity   2, 20, 22, 24, 185
 and translanguaging   28–9

Nadasen, Premilla   196
named entity recognition   47, 78, 80, 82, 158. *See also* CLIR
NARPy   4
nationalism   4–6, 17, 33, 40, 90, 147 n.5, 160, 195
nationism   79, 90, 101, 104, 120, 147
Natural Language Processing   47–8, 158
neocolonialism   71, 84, 112, 128, 142, 148, 149
neoliberal translation   42, 107–8
neoliberalism   8, 35, 59–61, 74, 110–11, 141–2, 194
Ngũgĩ wa Thiong'o   152
Noorani, Yaseen   9, 33–4, 40, 108, 153, 170, 176

Nordstrom, Lars   41
Nors, Dorthe, excerpts of interviews   96, 97, 103–4, 113–14

Olohan, Maeve   156
omnilingual
 aspirations   16, 37–8, 40, 54, 93 n.7, 103, 163–6
 and cryptography   144–5
 and Universal Declaration of Human Rights   40, 50
One Night at the Call Center (Chetan Bhagat)   12
Only Man on the Continent, The (Terézia Mora)   12
ontology, cross-language   159
Orchestra of Minorities, An (Chigozie Obioma)   12
Ordo   21–3, 132, 155–8
ordoliberalism   2, 7 n.6, 40, 83, 99–116, 124–5, 133, 194
ordolingualism   7–8, 20, 89–90, 96, 100, 102–3, 114–20, 181
 definition of   7 n.6
Otoo, Sharon Dodua   12, 149–50
Oviedo y Valdés, Gonzalo Fernández de   67

Pamuk, Orhan   12, 33
Pandey, Anjali   10, 24–5, 125
Parks, Tim   xvii, 10, 52, 106
pastoral   22–3, 41, 131–3
periodization   16–17, 31, 71–2, 121, 153 n.7, 157
Phipps, Alison   82, 189–90
plain language
 in *Amatka*   47, 49–50, 56, 58, 75, 84
 and translation   54, 64–5, 79, 81–2, 88
Plantationocene   74
plantations   63–4, 67–9, 74, 112

political economy   6, 12, 23, 36–9, 68, 73, 75, 88, 94, 110, 165, 191, 200. *See also* neoliberalism; ordoliberalism; supply side
postcolonial   19 n.11, 111, 113–14, 138. *See also* coloniality; decolonization
posthumanism   56, 143, 164, 167
postimperial   83 n.16, 99, 110–11
post/modernism   34
postmonolingual   17 n.9, 163
postmultilingual   65, 186
postprint   20, 73–4, 157
Pratt, Mary Louise   98, 102, 117, 152
Próchniewicz, Wojciech   22
protectionism   7 n.6, 28, 32, 40–1, 110–12, 114, 123, 171. *See also* anti-protectionism; cultural sovereignty
publishing industry   10, 19, 24–5, 89, 94–5, 97–9, 151
purism (linguistic)   35, 67, 82

raciolinguistic ideology   19, 148
racism   4–5, 12, 149, 157, 165. *See also* white supremacy
Real, the   5, 52–3
reiteration. *See* iteration
rematriation   8, 42
Rich, Adrienne   56
Robinson, Kim Stanley   12, 121
Romero, Pedro Jorge   22
Rovira, Gemma   171 n.2
Rumpus   103, 114
Ryan, Marie-Laure   1 n.2, 32–3, 98. *See also* immersion

Sabino, Robin   29
Said, Edward   xi–xii, 4, 18–19, 41, 90, 119–20, 131
Salisbury, Ralph   41
Salmara-Carr, Myriam   156

Schenstead-Harris, Lief   68
Schleiermacher, Friedrich   37, 98, 99
Schmitt, Carl   83 n.16, 84, 111
securitarianism   13, 58, 63, 117, 145, 155, 159, 178
securitized (language)
    definition of   9 n.7, 9, 35–7, 66, 91, 103, 115, 159–60
Seis ensayos in busca de nuestra expresión (Pedro Henríquez Ureña)   32
semodiversity   9, 145
Shih, Shu-mei   101–2, 106
Shipley, William   162
short-termism   129, 134–5
silencing   50, 55. *See also* epistemicide
    and diffusionism   141
    and global colonial capitalism   72–3, 140
Silverstein, Michael   180
skavank   94, 109, 118, 122
Slap in the Face, A (Abbas Khider)   12
Slobodian, Quinn   31, 110–12
Smith, J. A. Y.   93
Smith, Rachel Greenwald   2, 49, 59–60, 99, 127, 131
solutionism   50–2, 135, 153, 178, 180
    definition of   139
Sombart, Werner   6
Sommer, Doris   87, 91, 104, 170, 186
sovereignty   30–2, 111–12, 138–9, 162, 176. *See also* linguistic sovereignty
standardization, of language   12, 34, 150, 152–3, 199
Stephenson, Neal   134
Stetkevych, Jaroslav   33
Summers, Lawrence   201
supply chain   20–1, 56, 81, 98, 115, 141, 173

supply side 7, 17, 26, 63, 68–70, 74, 93, 147 n.5, 151, 192
supralanguages 17th century 154
supralingualism 54, 131–3, 148, 154, 158, 186, 198
 definition of 147 n.5
sustainability 50, 113
Suwandi, Intan 21, 25, 193
switchable assets 159, 173
synset, cross-language 62, 70, 80, 145, 159, 162

Tannen, Deborah xix, 42
Taylor, Analisa 42
temperament (piano tuning) 66, 154–6
theory deficit 11, 36, 88 n.1
Tidbeck, Karin (*Amatka*)
 authorial intent 65–6, 82
 interview excerpt 80
 as self-translator 2, 45, 47, 54, 61, 64, 79, 82–6 (*see also* macrotext)
traffic in meaning xviii, 2, 80, 102–3, 108, 115–17, 120, 124, 155, 159
translanguaging 28–9, 40, 143, 160, 189, 196, 204
translatability 1–2, 7–9, 37, 65, 66, 68, 74–5, 137, 144–5, 147, 151, 160
 the industry 95, 118, 140, 175
 securitized 9
Translated Accounts (James Kelman) 12
translationscape 93
transplantation 69–70, 79
Tuck, Eve 42

Universal Declaration of Human Rights 6, 40, 50, 137

untranslatability 9, 24, 40, 84–6, 97, 135, 159, 187

Valdes, Guadalupe xviii
Valkepää, Nils-Aslak 40–1, 152
verbal hygiene 51, 55, 67
vertigo 89–90, 96, 100, 109, 117–18, 193
Viveiros de Castro, Eduardo 135, 188
Volcker, Paul 127, 131, 136

Walkowitz, Rebecca 17 n.9
Washington Consensus 140
Weaver Memo 137
Weaver, Warren 57, 137, 148
Webster, Jamieson 52, 54
Weineck, Silke-Maria 149–50
Well-Tempered Clavier 66, 156
West Virginia University 201
white supremacy 4, 26, 111, 146. *See also* racism
Wilkins, John 72
world language system 2, 10, 74, 80, 105
World Trade Organization (WTO) 111, 142
Worley, Paul 42, 107–8

xenos rights 4, 16, 92, 95, 107, 112–13, 129, 146, 171, 173, 195. *See also* dominium; imperium
 definition of 83
 linguistic, definition of 92

Yanti 41
Yildiz, Yasemin 17 n.9, 163

Zaimoglu, Feridun 25
Zhang, Jenny 41